IMAGES
*of America*

# UPSHUR COUNTY

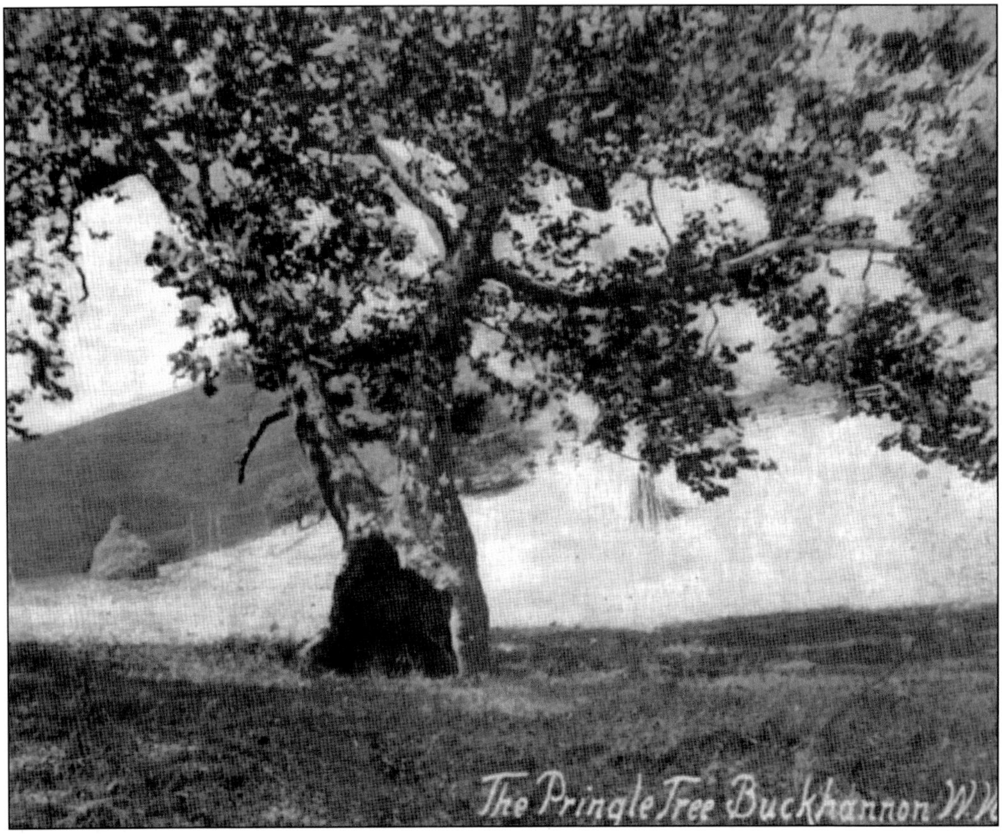


**Pringle Tree.** Between 1765 and 1768, brothers John and Samuel Pringle, deserters from the British army at Fort Pitt, lived in a hollow sycamore tree along the Buckhannon River at the mouth of Turkey Run. In 1769 they persuaded other pioneers to create a permanent settlement in the Buckhannon Valley. The third generation of the tree still stands and is located in a historic park area maintained by the Upshur County Commission. Pictured in this postcard image is the second generation tree, which fell around 1900. (Photo courtesy of UCHS, Phyllis Miller Collection.)

*On the Cover:* **Lorentz Community.** G.A. Barry, photographer, took this view of the early village of Lorentz between 1905 and 1910, showing a typical Upshur County rural community village. This was one of the first communities established in the Buckhannon Valley. The last Indian foray in Upshur County resulted in the massacre of an entire family in this community. (Photo courtesy of UCHS, Clara Jett Lawson Collection.)

IMAGES
*of America*

# UPSHUR COUNTY

The Upshur County Historical Society

ARCADIA
PUBLISHING

ISBN 978-0-7385-1352-2

Published by Arcadia Publishing
Charleston, South Carolina

Printed in the United States of America

Library of Congress Catalog Card Number: 2001088737

For all general information contact Arcadia Publishing:
Telephone 843-853-2070
Fax 843-853-0044
E-Mail sales@arcadiapublishing.com
For customer service and orders:
Toll-Free 1-888-313-2665

Visit us on the Internet at www.arcadiapublishing.com

*This book is dedicated to all Upshur County photographers who have, over the decades of time, preserved these minute "windows of the past."*

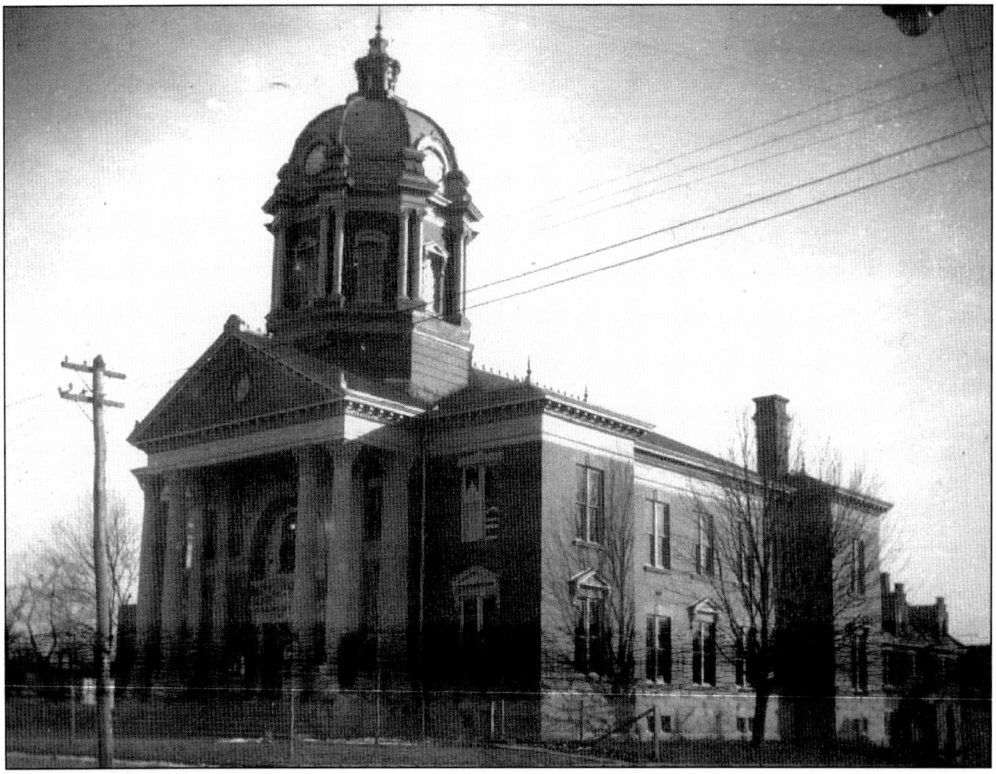

**UPSHUR COUNTY COURTHOUSE.** Pictured here is the present Upshur County courthouse shortly after its construction in 1899. The sheriff's house and jail is shown at the far right. (Photo courtesy of UCHS, WV Wesleyan Collection.)

# Contents

# Acknowledgments

Even with the preparation of a "picture" book like this one, a great deal of time and resources must be used to compile a "readable" record of local history. The Upshur County Historical Society is fortunate to have a large collection of photographs and resources in its Repository and Research Center. Through the cooperative efforts of the society and the West Virginia Department of Culture and History, Archives and History Unit, and most importantly, citizens of Upshur County, hundreds of local historic photographs have been copied and made available for various publication, exhibition, and distribution purposes. We especially want to thank Fredrick H. Armstrong, director of Archives and History, and his department for their ongoing efforts on behalf of the citizens of Upshur County and for supplying more than half of the images used in this book.

Collecting historical memorabilia and compiling pertinent data are ongoing activities of this society. However, preparing specific collections for publication requires a great amount of special attention and effort to research, design, and complete. Two individuals specifically have worked on this project and special thanks is given to Amy Williams Tenney and Noel W. Tenney. We also want to thank Lemoyne Wentz Wolfe for her assistance as well as Beth Almond, Mary Ann Spears, Brent Scott, Amy Rohr, and Zachary Orsburn. Ron Williams of Mountain State Print is also to be thanked for scanning many of our original images used in this publication. Last, but by no means least, we want to thank all of the people who have shared their treasured photographic images with the society over the years. We are the county-level caretakers of historical material culture and appreciate the continuing trust and support of our membership and friends.

We welcome comments and input to what is contained in this publication. Photographs have been identified as accurately as possible with available researched information. We trust you will enjoy these images of Upshur County, West Virginia.

The Upshur County Historical Society
P.O. Box 2082
Buckhannon, WV 26201

# INTRODUCTION

Upshur County, West Virginia was formed on March 26, 1851 from parts of Randolph, Lewis, and Barbour Counties. Buckhannon, the county seat, is the only incorporated city therein. The county is located in the north central section of the state in the rolling foothills of the Allegheny Mountains, reaching an altitude of over 3,000 feet in the southeastern section. It contains 354.86 square miles and was divided into six magisterial districts in 1863 when West Virginia became the 35th state. These districts are Banks, Buckhannon, Meade, Union, Washington, and Warren. The Buckhannon River is the major waterway flowing north nearly the entire length of the county.

Evidence indicates early Native American habitation. Indian Camp Rock, Ash Camp, and indications of village sites on Hacker's Creek support this evidence. The Buckhannon Valley was one of the earliest settled regions in the Upper Monongalia Valley. The Pringle brothers arrived in 1765, and by 1770 a permanent settlement had been established, complete with "Bush's Fort." This pioneer defense fort was located where the new section of Heavner Cemetery is today. It was destroyed in an Indian foray in 1782. Early family names in the area included Pringle, Hacker, Cutright, Hughes, White, Jackson, Westfall, Brake, Bozarth, Strader, Post, Bush, Lorentz, Carper, Rohrbough, and others.

By 1795 the Native American conflict era had ended, and in 1801 the first of a large number of New Englanders settled in Upshur County, mostly in the French Creek area. Family names from this migration included Gould, Young, Phillips, Burr, Tenney, Brooks, Bunten, Thayer, Leonard, and others. The effect of this population can still be felt today with its influence on education, politics, and religion.

Throughout the Civil War, Upshur County was a firm Union supporter. The only major events of that era to take place in the county were the capture of the Upshur Militia at Centerville (now Rock Cave), and the "Battle of Water Tank Hill" near the intersection of Marion and Kanawha Streets in Buckhannon.

After the coming of the railroads in the 1880s, Upshur County followed the rest of the state in developing various natural resources and industry. Timbering was heavy in the southern end of the county in the late 1880s, and mining began at Lorentz in 1901. Adrian developed as a major mining center, and in modern times extremely large (deep and strip mining) operations were created by Island Creek and Badger Coals here in the county. There have been many other industries to develop here, now mostly gone. These included a tannery, a chemical plant, glass and glass sand plants, as well as more contemporary operations such as Moore Business Forms, Corhart Refractories, Uponor ETI, Trus Joist MacMillan, and Coastal Lumber.

In 1936, the Central West Virginia Strawberry Festival was organized to encourage agricultural production. The West Virginia Farm Bureau state headquarters is housed in Buckhannon, as well as the West Virginia Department of Highways' state headquarters for equipment repair and distribution (located in the 1940s large cut stone building on the Weston Road). The United Methodist Annual Conference is held on the campus of West Virginia Wesleyan College. The West Virginia Wildlife Center is located at French Creek where it was established in 1923.

This book contains over 200 historical photographs representing life in Upshur County from the time it was formed until more recent days. In 2001, Upshur County is celebrating its sesquicentennial. For 150 years, her citizens have lived "the good life" here, and we invite you to open these "windows" to our past and get to know more of our rich historical context. Enjoy.

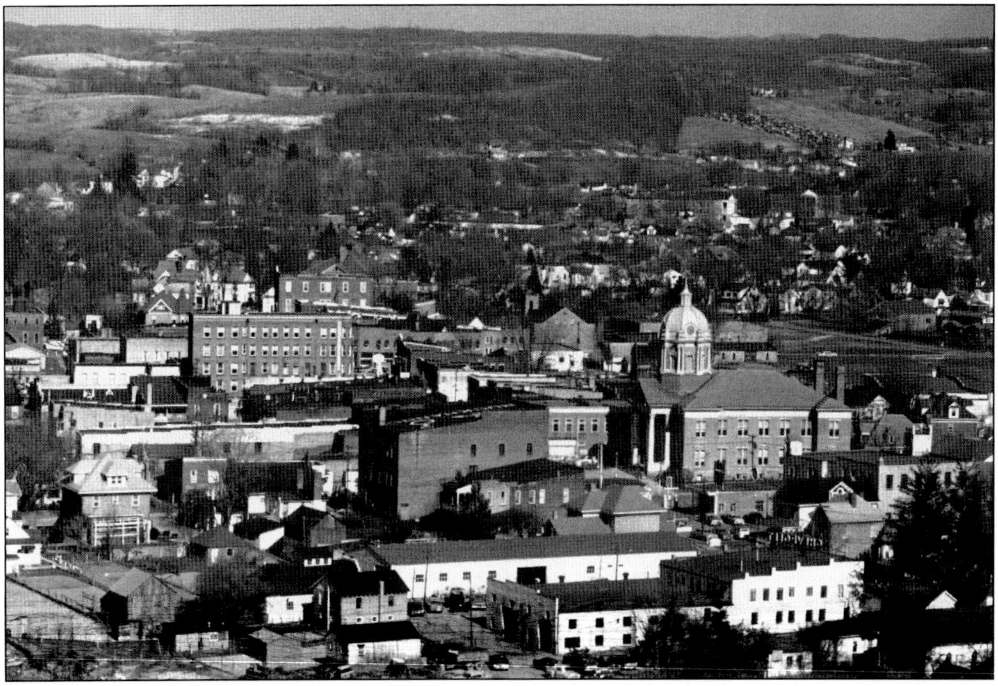

**Bird's-Eye View of Buckhannon.** This c. 1950 photograph by the late Delf A. Narona shows a view looking southeast at Buckhannon, the county seat of Upshur County, West Virginia. Pictured are the rolling foothills of the Allegheny Mountains. The courthouse is located center right with the WV Wesleyan College campus on the upper right. (Photo courtesy of UCHS, Delf A. Narona Collection.)

# *One*

# Early Buckhannon Street Scenes

*Buckhannon, the central focus of Upshur County because of its location and government centers, contains about a mile-long business Main Street. The county courthouse and its governing body of commissioners are located on the west end; Buckhannon City Hall and the mayor and council's offices are located on the east end of Main Street. Streets leading from Main contain the college, small businesses, and residences. These photographs show the change that has taken place over the years as well as that which has remained the same.*

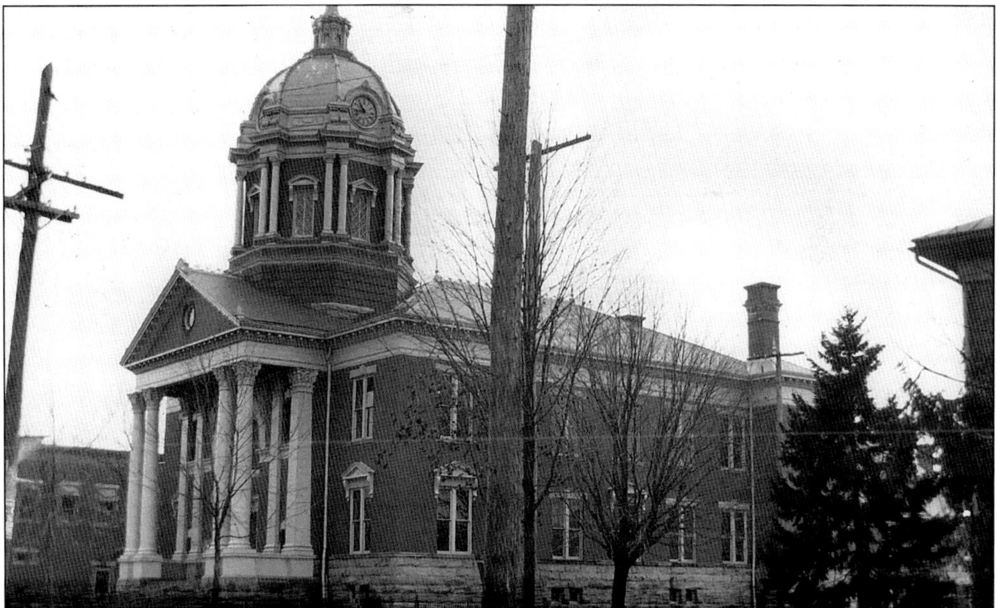

**Present Upshur County Courthouse.** Upshur County's present courthouse was built in 1899 at a cost of $37,650 and was designed by Harrison Albright of Charleston. Within the cornerstone of this building lies a time capsule containing many artifacts from the turn-of-the-century era. This early 20th-century image was made by the late Hode Clark, one of Buckhannon's most prolific photographers. (Photo courtesy of UCHS, Alan Sturm Collection.)

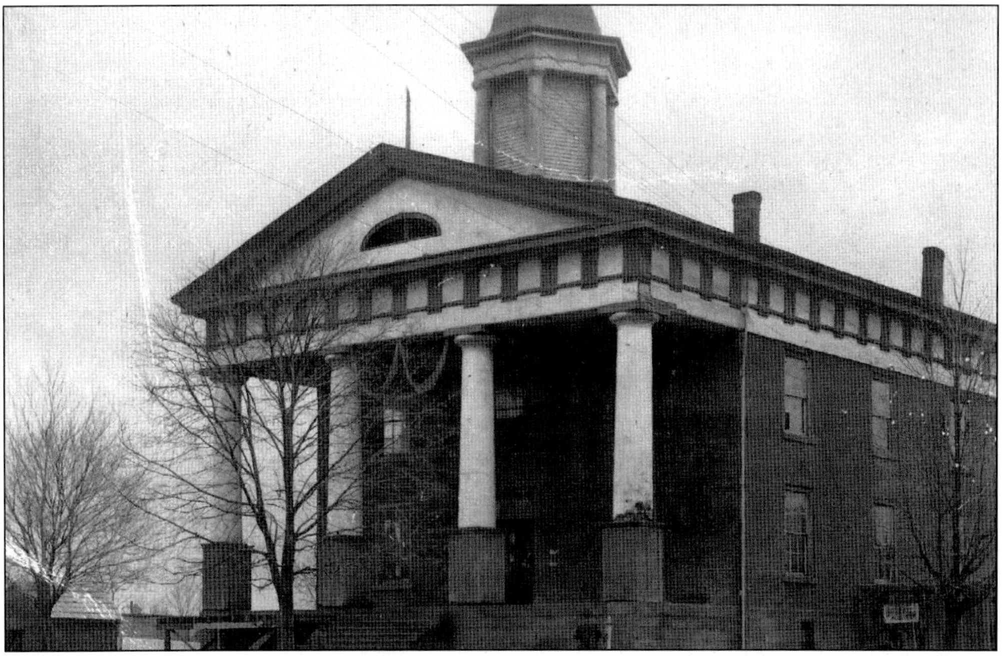

**Original Upshur County Courthouse.** Located on the corner of Locust and Main Streets facing the Staunton Parkersburg Turnpike, Upshur County's first courthouse was completed in 1854. The price of the lot was $750 and the building cost $7,300. Robert Maxwell was the architect. The building was damaged three times in the first six months by fire and saw heavy abuse during the Civil War. It was demolished in 1898 and replaced with the current building. (Photo courtesy of UCHS, permanent collection.)

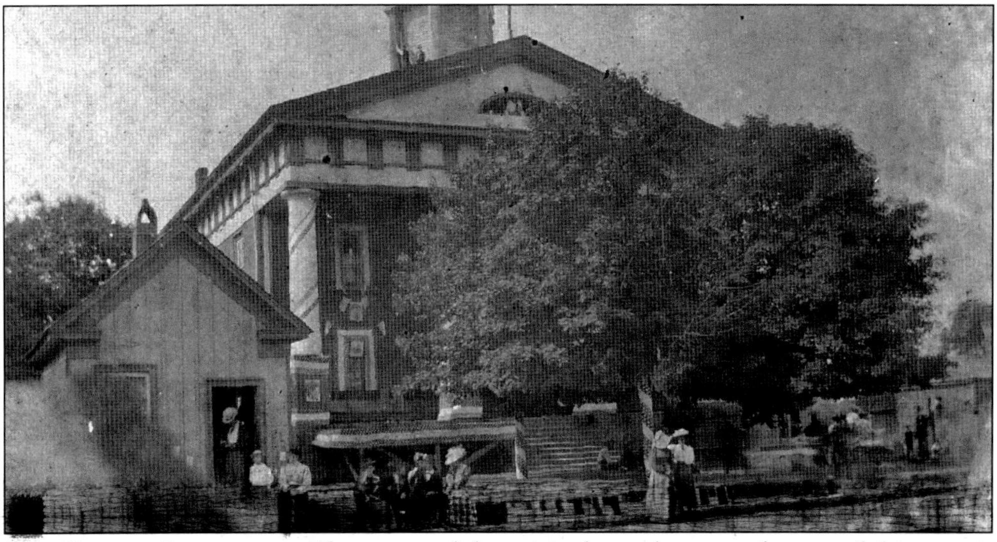

**Old County Courthouse.** The image of the original courthouse at the top of this page is considered the official portrait of the building taken just before its destruction, while this second photograph from the early 1890s is the only other known image of the structure. This building housed the opera hall and/or town hall, the only meeting place in town. Electricity was installed in 1891 to replace oil lamps. The small building to the left housed the sheriff's office. (Photo courtesy of UCHS, permanent collection.)

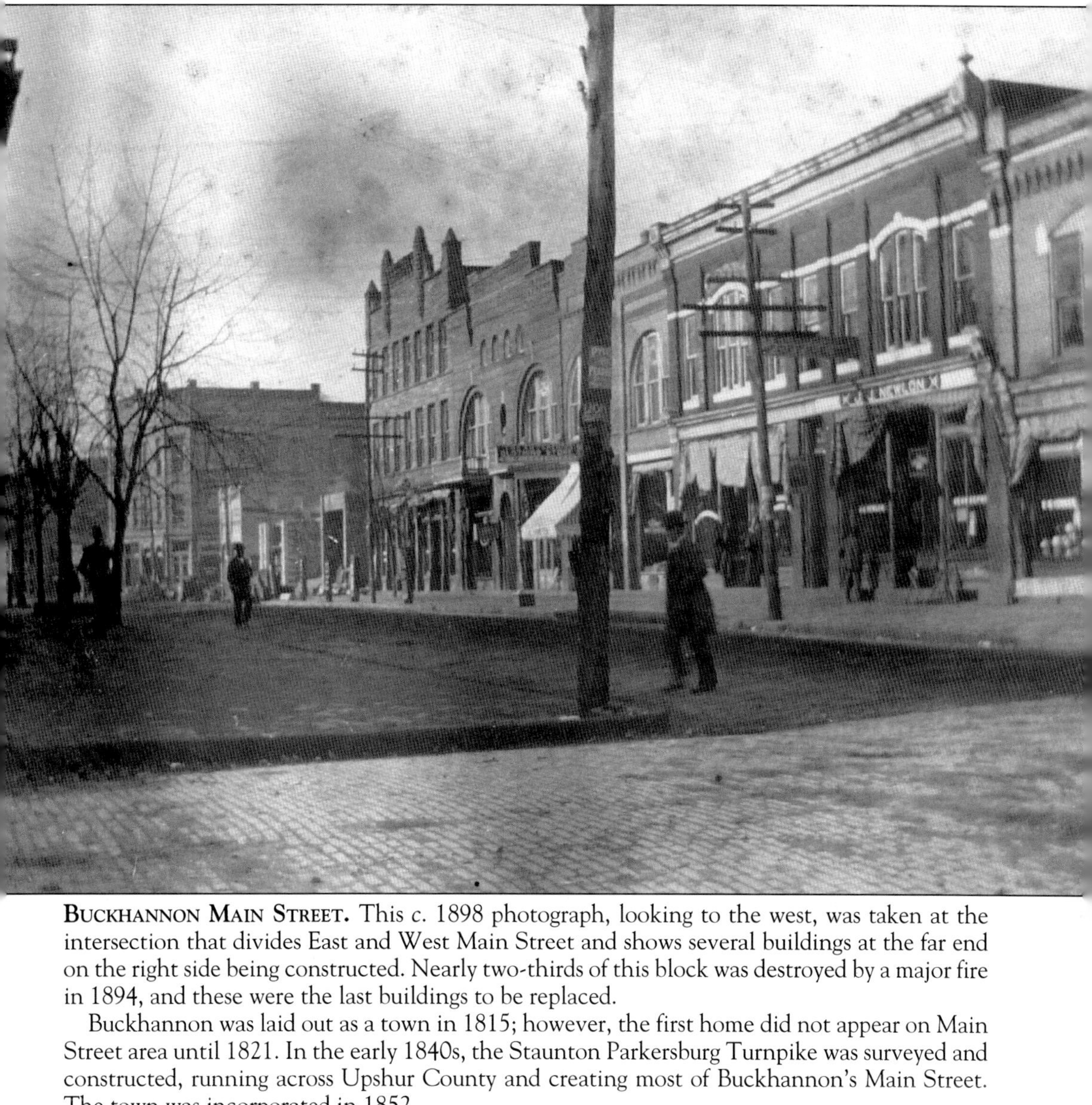

**BUCKHANNON MAIN STREET.** This *c.* 1898 photograph, looking to the west, was taken at the intersection that divides East and West Main Street and shows several buildings at the far end on the right side being constructed. Nearly two-thirds of this block was destroyed by a major fire in 1894, and these were the last buildings to be replaced.

Buckhannon was laid out as a town in 1815; however, the first home did not appear on Main Street area until 1821. In the early 1840s, the Staunton Parkersburg Turnpike was surveyed and constructed, running across Upshur County and creating most of Buckhannon's Main Street. The town was incorporated in 1852.

The origin of Buckhannon's name has many explanations. It is most likely that the river was named first, in the 1760s; the post office next in 1804 with John Jackson as its first postmaster; and the village last. The controversy over the name's origin centers around the legendary story of Delaware Chief Buckongohanon or Buckongahelas, as well the name's attribution to Colonel John Buchanan, a Mr. Buck Hannon, buck deer on the river, and Buckwheat. The Buckhannon Valley settlement was the earliest in the Upper Monongalia Region. (Photo courtesy of UCHS, Nellie Drummond Collection.)

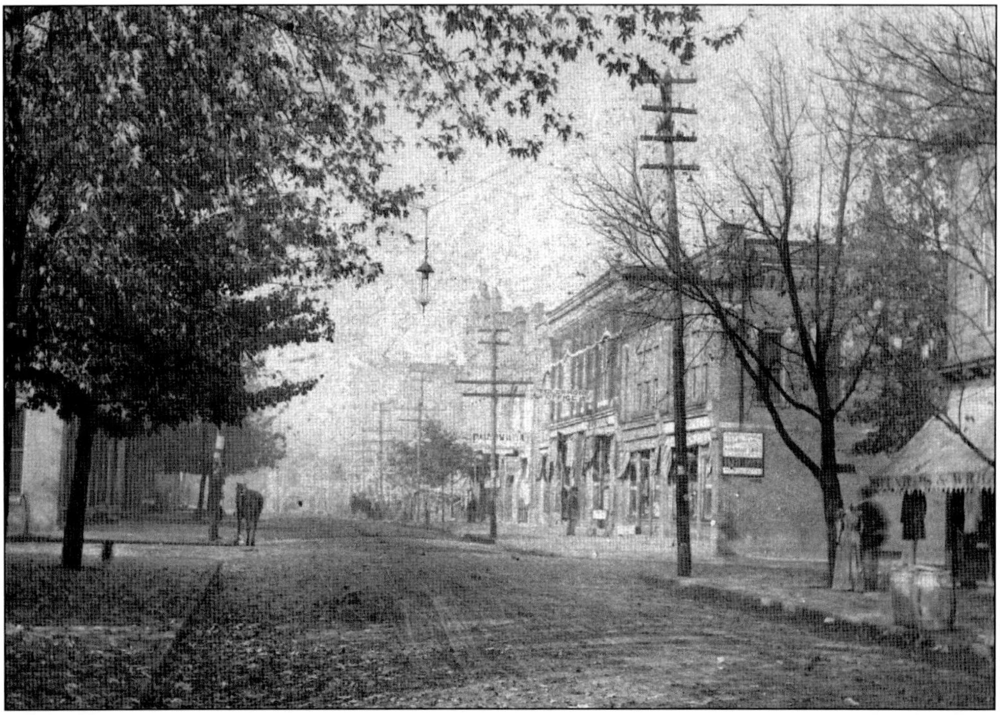

**MAIN STREET.** This view of Buckhannon's Main Street looking west from the Kanawha Street intersection was taken in the early 1890s. The original cyanatype image pictures the Sharps & Wright store on the right and the telephone company in the next block. Note the unpaved street with the horse and buggy tracks. Main Street was first brick-paved road in 1893. (Photo courtesy of UCHS, Richard Anderson Collection.)

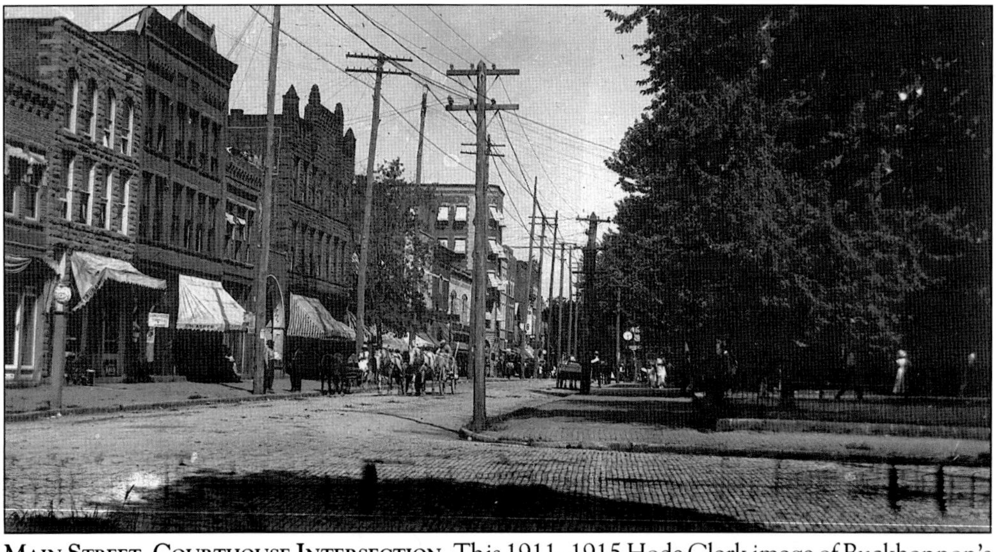

**MAIN STREET, COURTHOUSE INTERSECTION.** This 1911–1915 Hode Clark image of Buckhannon's Main Street looks to the east with the courthouse within the fenced area to the right. The row of buildings to the left, built between 1888 and 1898, represent the oldest intact block on Main Street. Utility poles were not removed from Main Street until 1928. (Photo courtesy of UCHS, Alan Sturm Collection.)

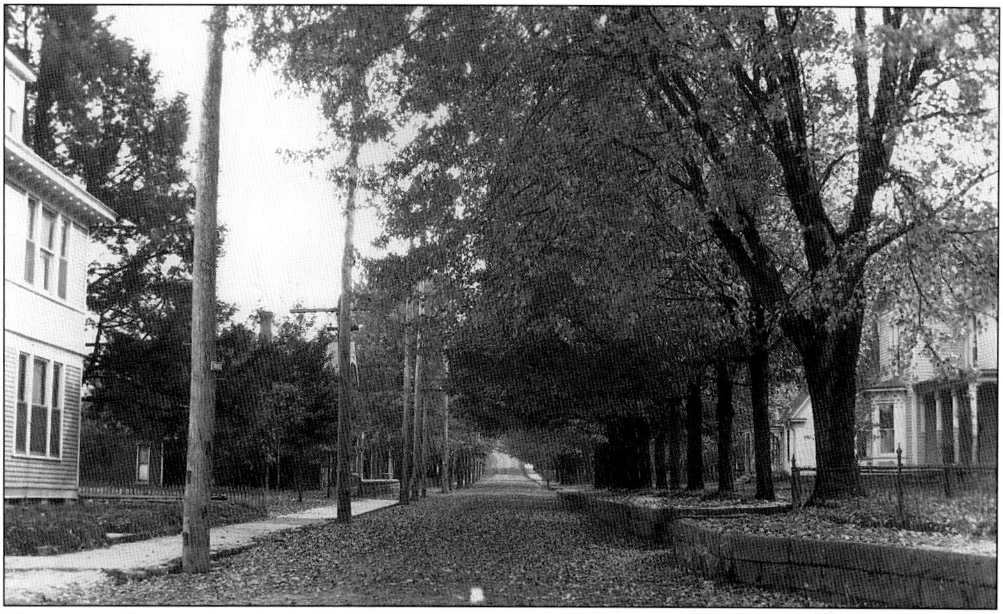

**Kanawha Street, Looking South.** This Hode Clark photograph was made in the very early 20th century by the look of the buggy tracks on the dirt street. By the time this image was made, Kanawha Street had become known as "Quality Hill" because of the fine homes that had been established all along the tree-lined avenue. (Photo courtesy of UCHS, Alan Sturm Collection.)

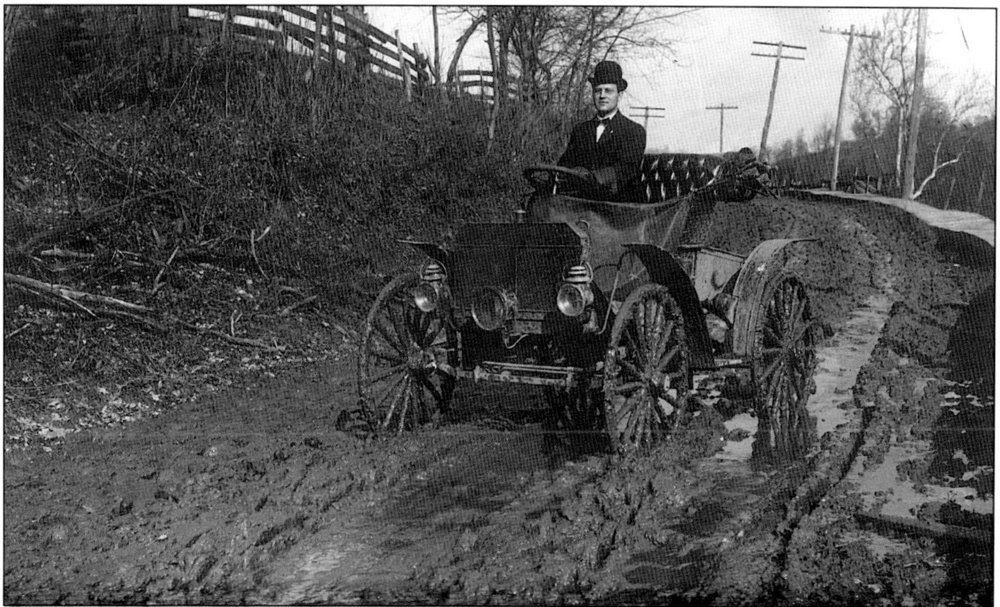

**Dr. Beer's Auto.** Pictured here is Dr. O.B. Beer coming down a muddy hill on the old Weston road in one of the first autos in Upshur County, *c.* 1905. Dr. Beer and Dr. P.D. Barlow opened the first hospital in Buckhannon in 1902 on the southwest corner of College and Meade Streets. Dr. Beer later purchased the Shinn property on West Main Street and opened the Beer Electro Therapeutic Sanitorium. This building was later purchased by the Rusmisell family and was operated for many years as the Leonard Memorial Hospital. (Photo courtesy of UCHS, Howard Hiner Collection.)

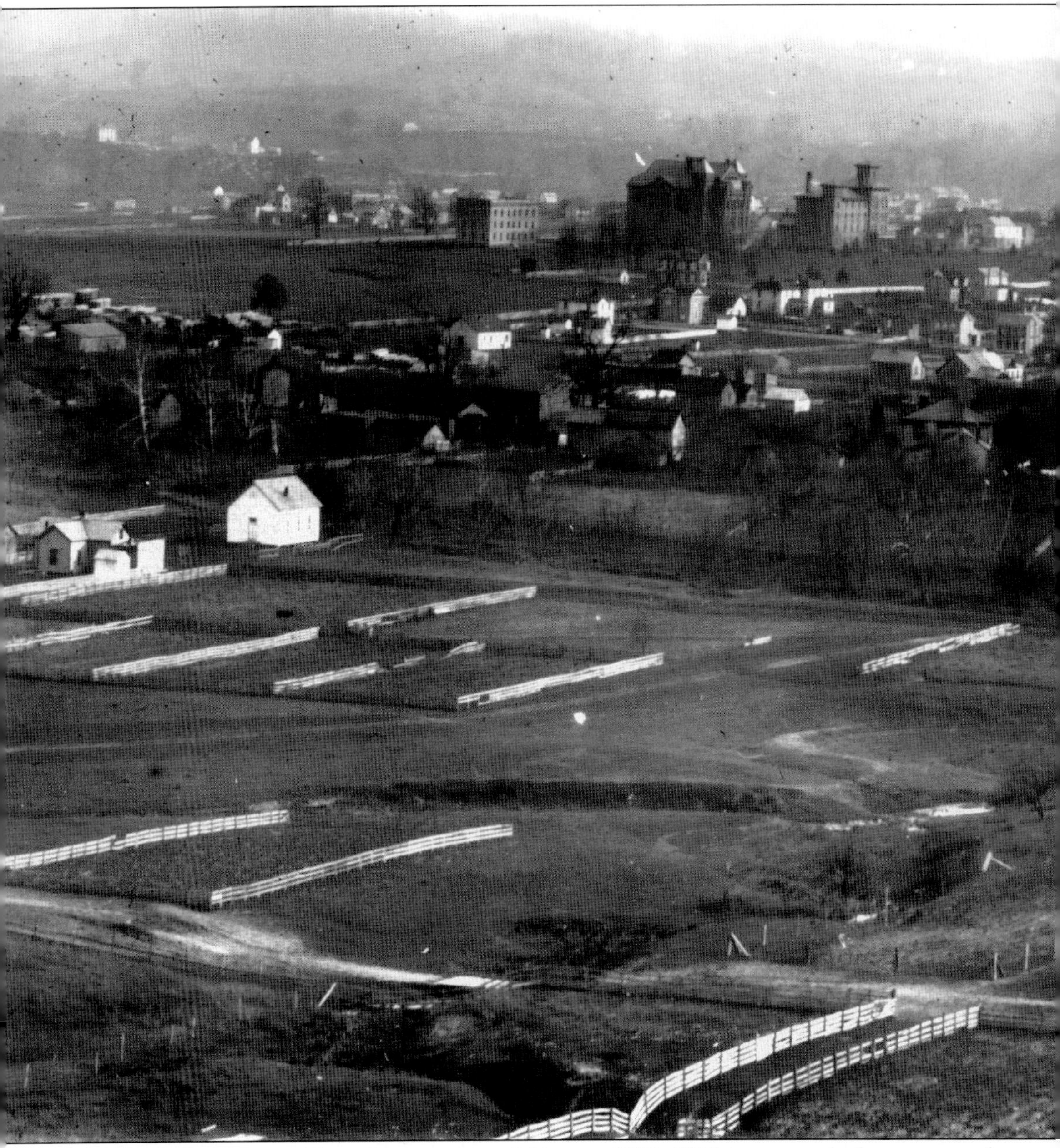

**BIRD'S-EYE VIEW OF EAST BUCKHANNON.** This rare 1902–1905 image made from a recently found glass negative shows the eastern half of Buckhannon looking toward the south. In the foreground is the white fenced farmland that would shortly become "Oklahoma" or North Buckhannon. The small, white, one-room school building at the middle left still stands today. Looking carefully, one can see the two tree-lined streams of water where the Buckhannon River makes its loop and what naturally created a delta. However, in the early 1800s a connecting channel was dug providing for a "millrace" over which the old Farnsworth grist mill/sawmill was set. Pictured just above the school building is the covered bridge, now long gone. Just above the

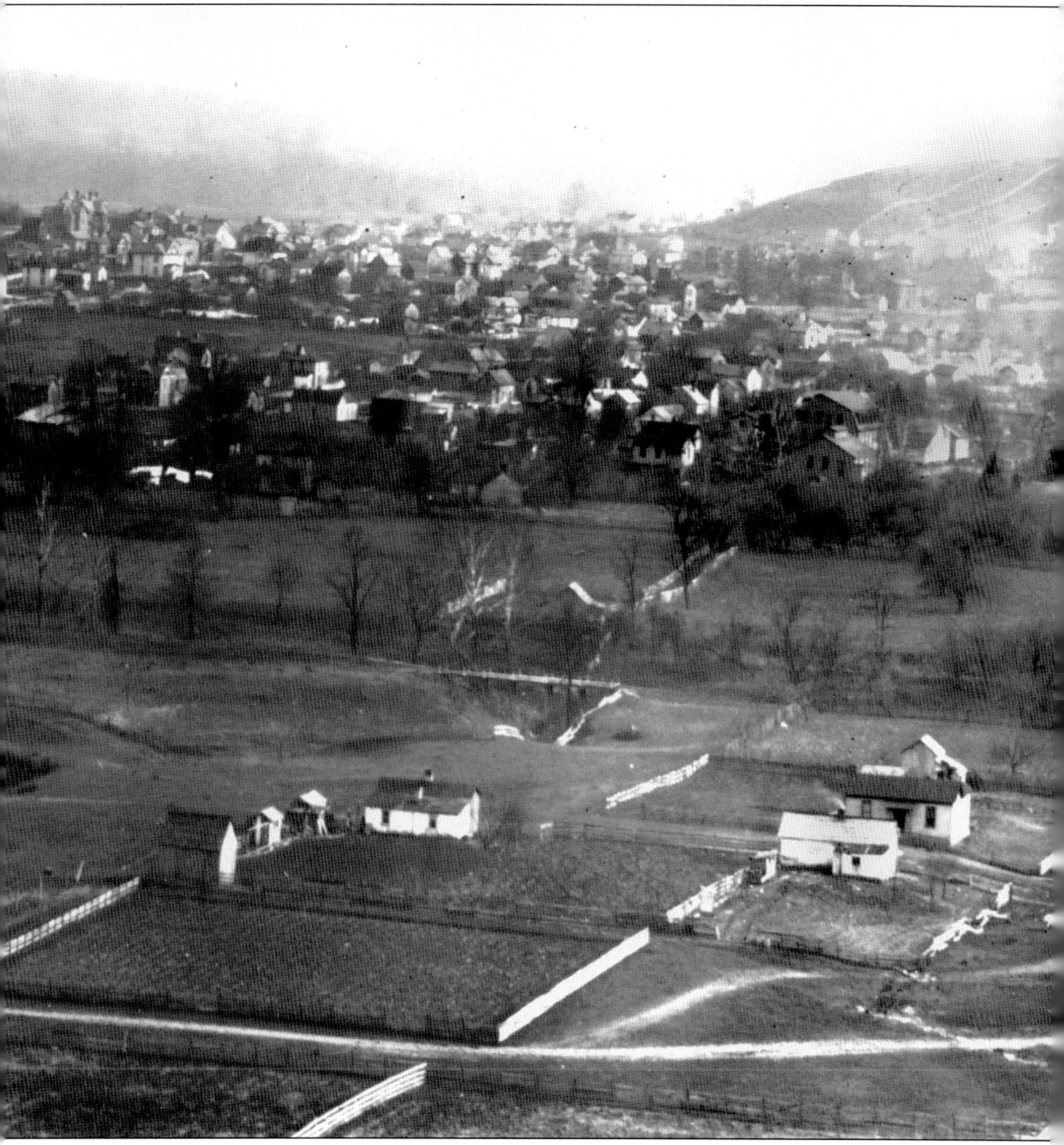

bridge is another small white building, which housed one of Buckhannon's earliest African-American church congregations. The large buildings near the top left are on the campus of WV Wesleyan College. The smaller square one to the left is the "Music Building," built in 1902, and the center one is the old Seminary Building that was destroyed by fire on February 5, 1905. The towered building to the right of the Seminary Building is Agnes Howard Hall, the oldest extant building on campus and the oldest continuously used residence hall on any West Virginia college campus. It has recently been listed in the National Register of Historic Places. (Photo courtesy of UCHS, Noel W. Tenney Collection.)

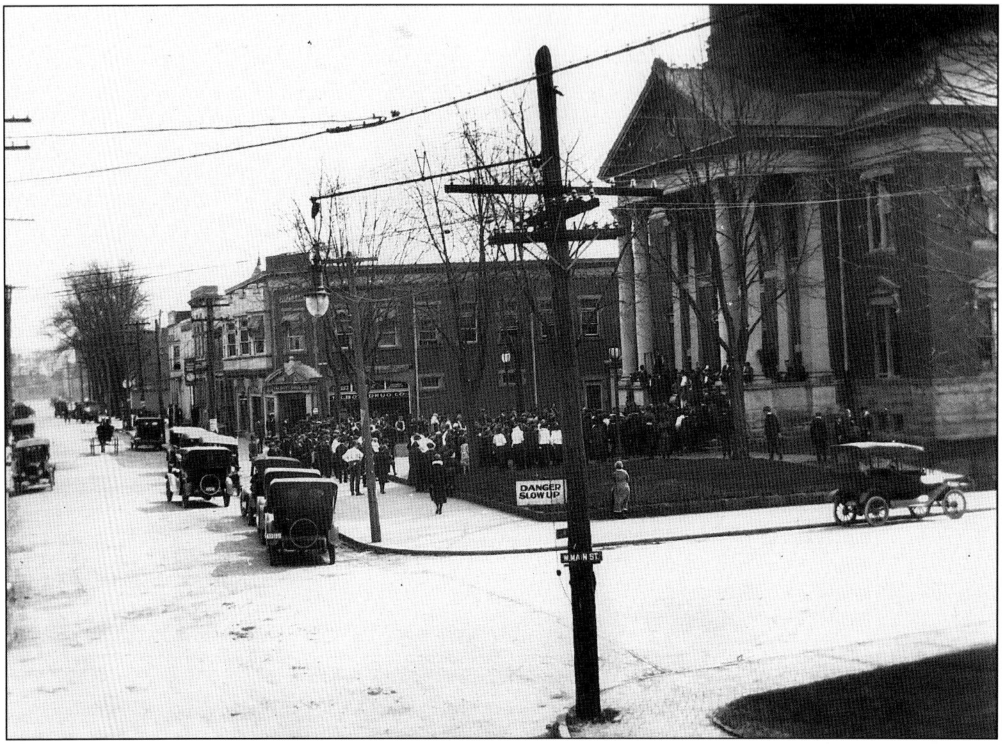


**COURTHOUSE SQUARE.** This early-20th-century Hode Clark photograph shows some social gathering at the courthouse. Note the combination of horse and buggies along with automobiles. Located beside the courthouse is the Talbott Drug Company, which in later years was known as the Poundstone Drug Store. (Photo courtesy of UCHS, Alan Sturm Collection.)

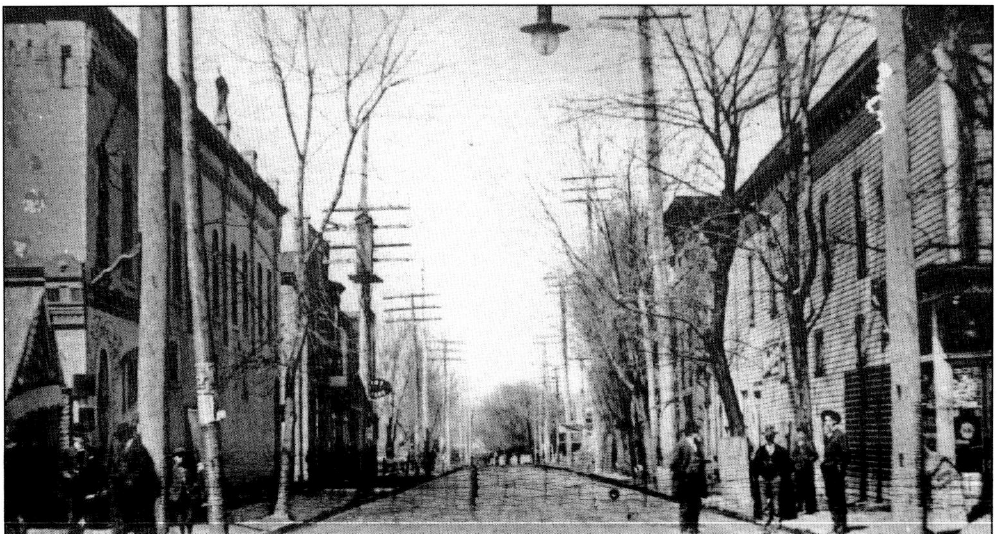

**DEPOT STREET, LOOKING NORTH.** This pre-1910 printed postcard image shows Depot Street with the post office on the left. Further down the street, hotels were situated as well as the Opera House, and of course, at the very end of the street was the railroad depot. (Photo courtesy of UCHS, Betty Hornbeck Van Kirk Collection.)

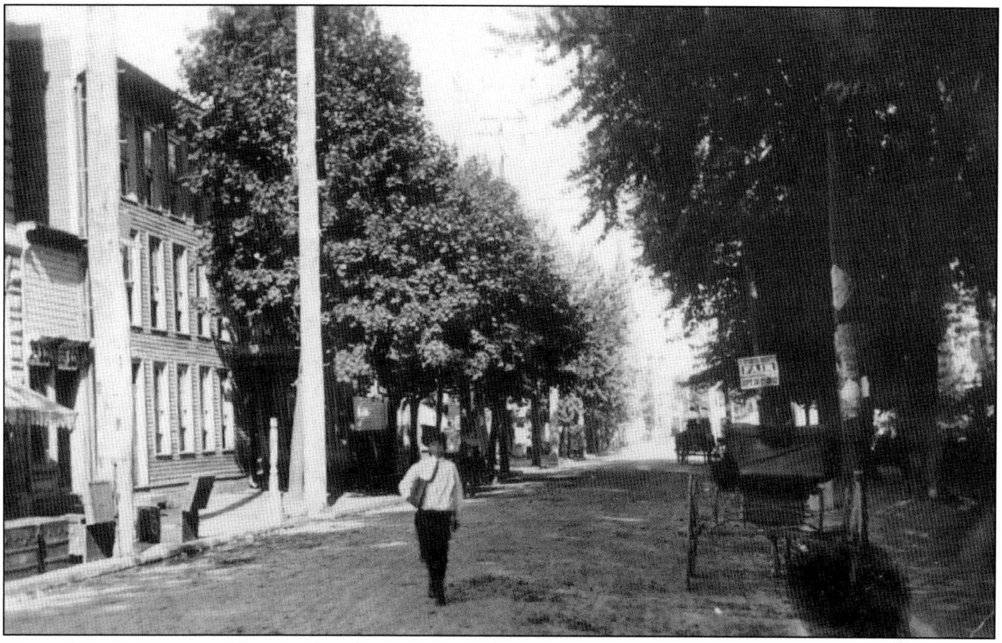


**East Main Street.** This early photo postcard image was taken looking east from the center of Buckhannon's Main Street. The building to the left with the even row windows was the New Valley Hotel. The north wing of this building was standing during the Civil War, and Marcia Sumner Phillips recounted many episodes that took place there as she wrote in her journal from her home next door. The schoolboy has just passed the street sign advertising the "Upshur County Fair," which was begun in the early 20th century. (Photo courtesy of UCHS, Jim Amlung Collection.)

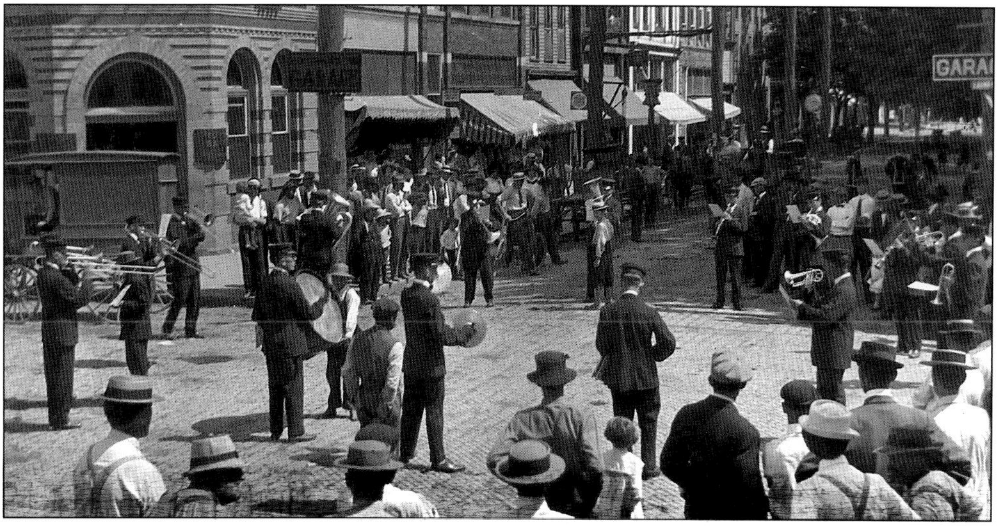

**Corner of Main and Kanawha Street.** The Buckhannon Brass Band performs in the heart of town in this Hode Clark treasured photograph. The People's Bank on the corner at left was only two years old and the G.O. Young Drugstore, with the apothecary street sign, had just opened. By using a perpetual calendar, the date on the street poster shown on the right, as well as pertinent historical information, the year of this image has been established as 1912. (Photo courtesy of UCHS, Alan Sturm Collection.)

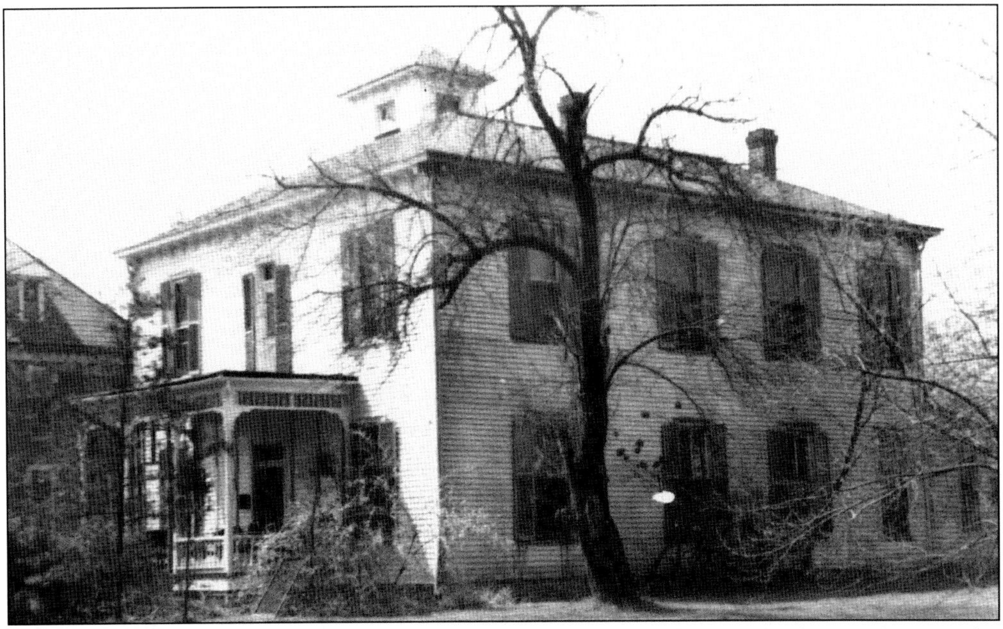

**HIGGINBOTHAM HOUSE.** This was the home of Coleman Cabell Higginbotham, a lawyer who practiced in Buckhannon for many years and brother to Col. John Carleton Higginbotham, Civil War soldier. Coleman married Mary Ida Day from Virginia and they had six daughters, Mary, the artist, being the most notable. This house stood at 65 South Kanawha Street and was given to the Church of the Transfiguration Episcopal in 1965. It was replaced with the current "A" frame church building at that time. (Photo courtesy of UCHS, Church of the Transfiguration Episcopal Collection.)

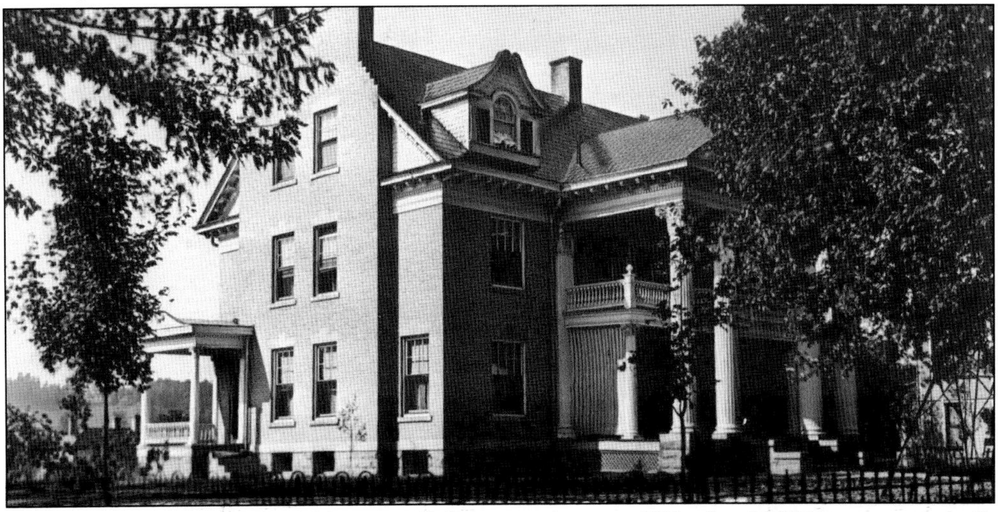

**MCWHORTER HOUSE.** "Gray Chimneys," the most elegant of "Quality Hills" homes, was built in 1907–1908 with 22 rooms and a fireplace in each. With Indiana limestone foundation and steps, curly birch in the stairway, woodwork of mahogany, and quarter-sawn oak, the building cost $15,000. Judge J.C. McWhorter was born in 1866, became a lawyer and formed a partnership with U.G. Young in 1897. McWhorter was elected in 1904 as judge of the Twelfth Judicial Circuit and served until 1913. He also authored the historic romance novel, *Scout of the Buckongehonon.* (Photo courtesy of UCHS, Phyllis Miller Collection.)

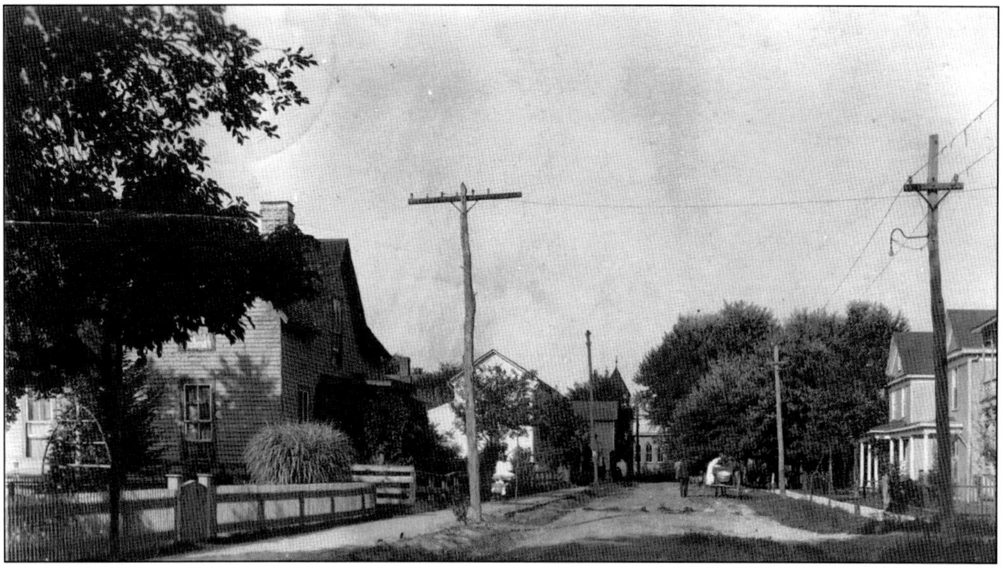

**FRANKLIN STREET.** This real photo postcard was taken November 26, 1912. The view looks east toward the courthouse area, and at the very end of the street is the Simpson AME Church. The small African-American community in Buckhannon was originally centered on Franklin Street where the school and church were located. (Photo courtesy of UCHS, Phyllis Miller Collection.)

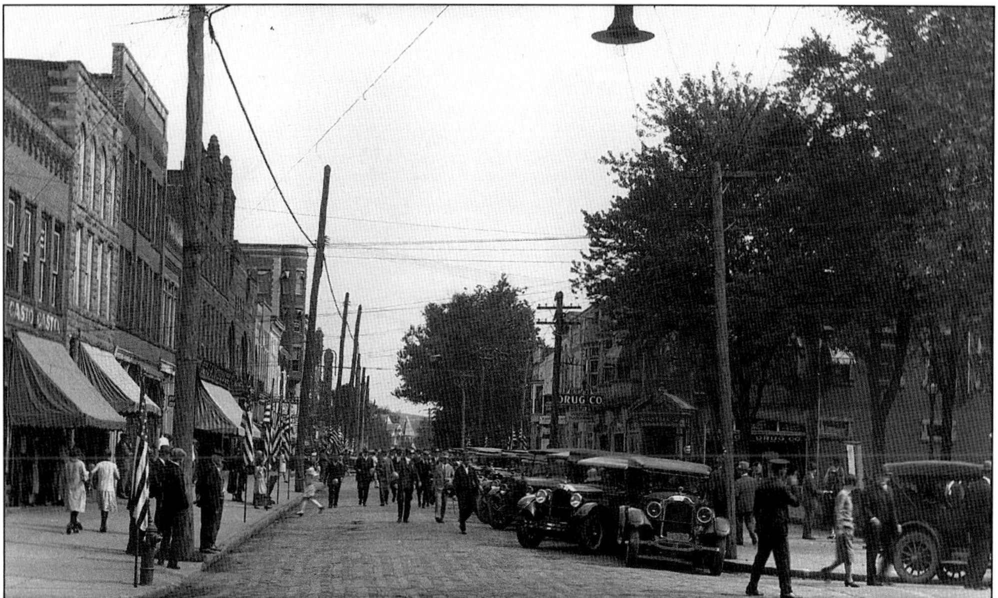

**BUCKHANNON MAIN STREET PARADE.** This eastward-looking Hode Clark photograph was taken between 1915 and 1928 and captured what was most likely a Fourth of July parade. Businesses on the left side of the street include Casto and Casto, as well as Murphy's 5 & 10 in the Farnsworth building. Further down on the left, one can view the three-story electrically lighted sign on the G.O. Young Drug Store. It was installed in 1915 and was advertised as being the "largest lighted sign between Washington D.C. and Chicago." (Photo courtesy of UCHS, Alan Sturm Collection.)

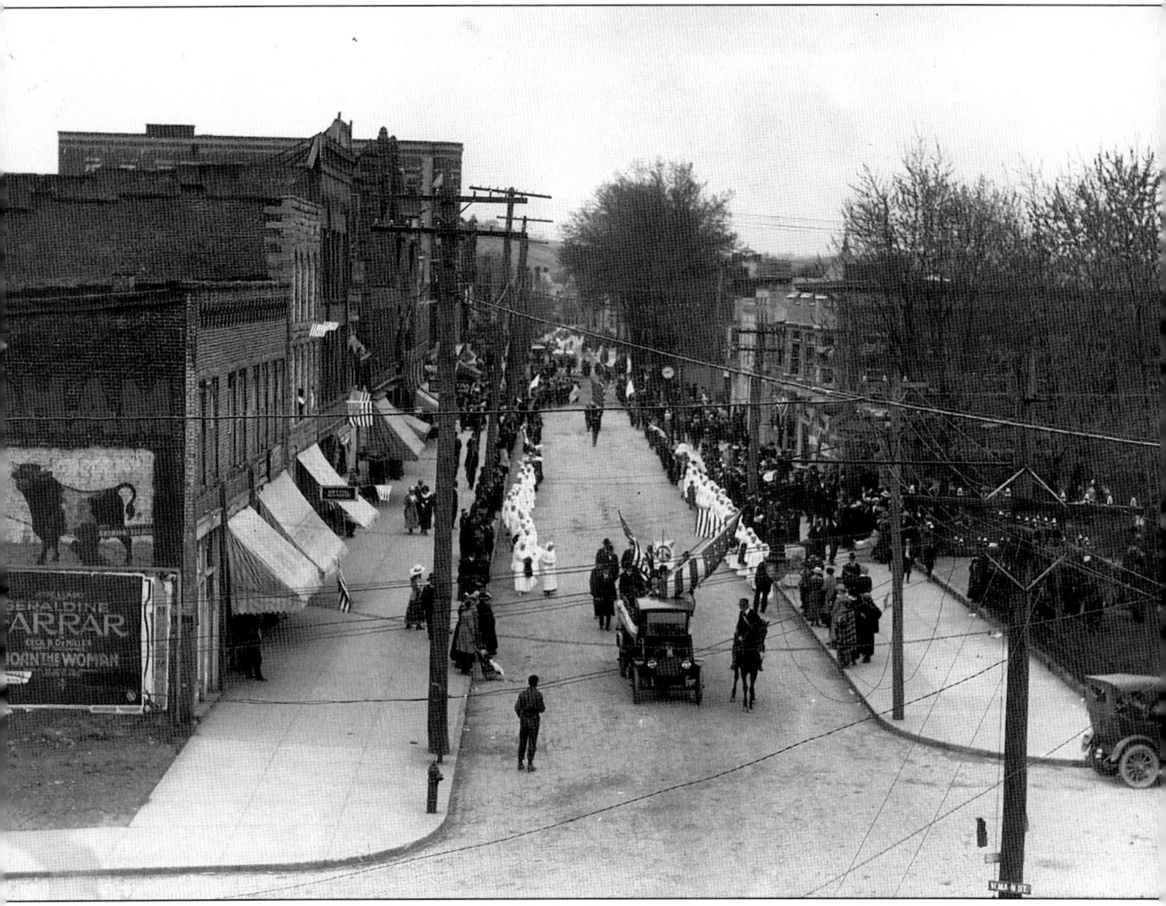


**ARMISTICE DAY PARADE.** This Hode Clark photograph was taken in 1918 and shows nurses marching in a victory parade after World War I. It also shows the power poles and wide sidewalks that all disappeared in 1928 with the re-paving and widening of Main Street. The courthouse square is to the bottom right and the scene looks east. (Photo courtesy of UCHS, Alan Sturm Collection.)

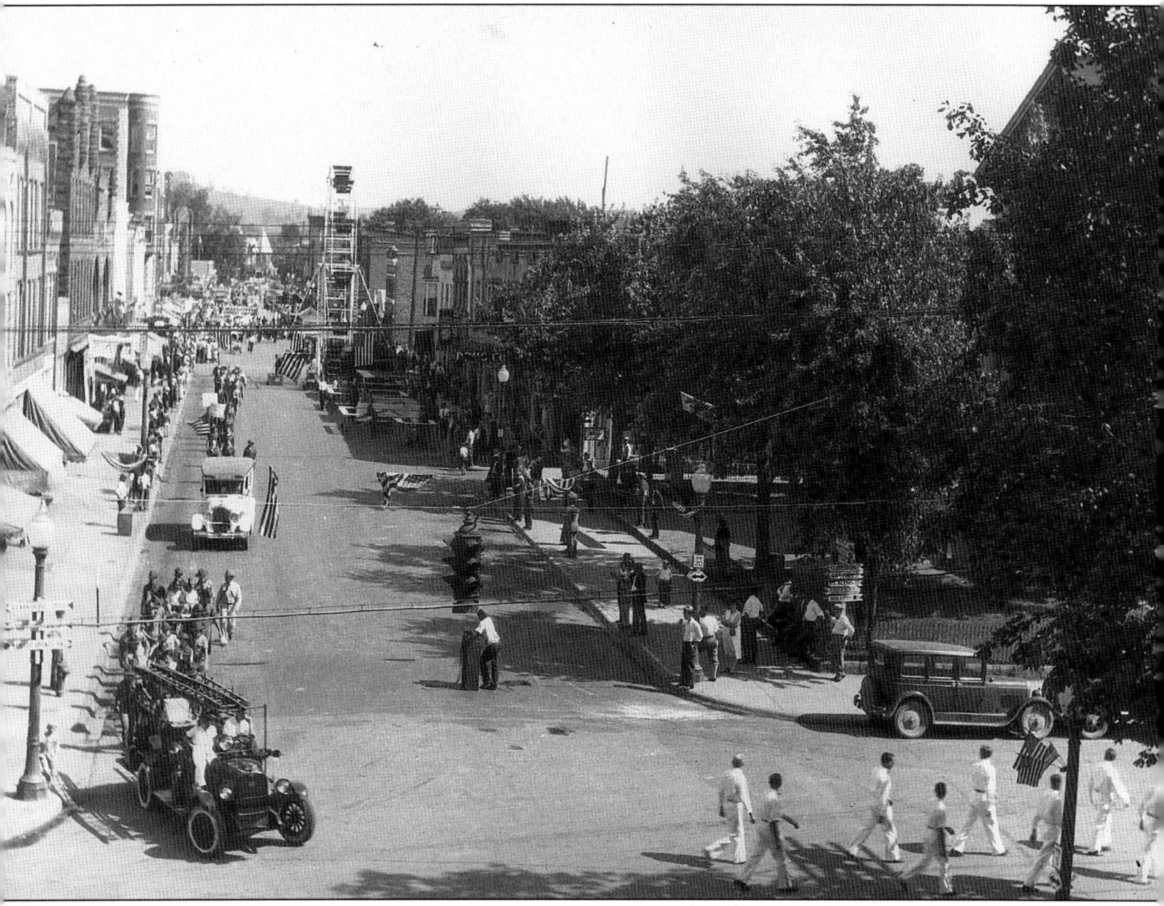

**BUCKHANNON'S MAIN STREET AFTER 1928.** In contrast to the photograph pictured on page 20, this post-1928 image shows a widened main street with less sidewalk and the absence of utility poles and lines. This is very likely an early Strawberry Festival parade in the 1930s. In viewing Buckhannon Main Street scenes, certain structures and features may be observed for dating purposes. The present courthouse and Talbott Drug Company were built in 1899, the tall bank building on the far rear left was built in 1910, and G.O. Young installed his electrically lighted sign in 1915. In 1928 the street was repaved and widened and the utility lines removed. (Photo courtesy of UCHS, Alan Sturm Collection.)

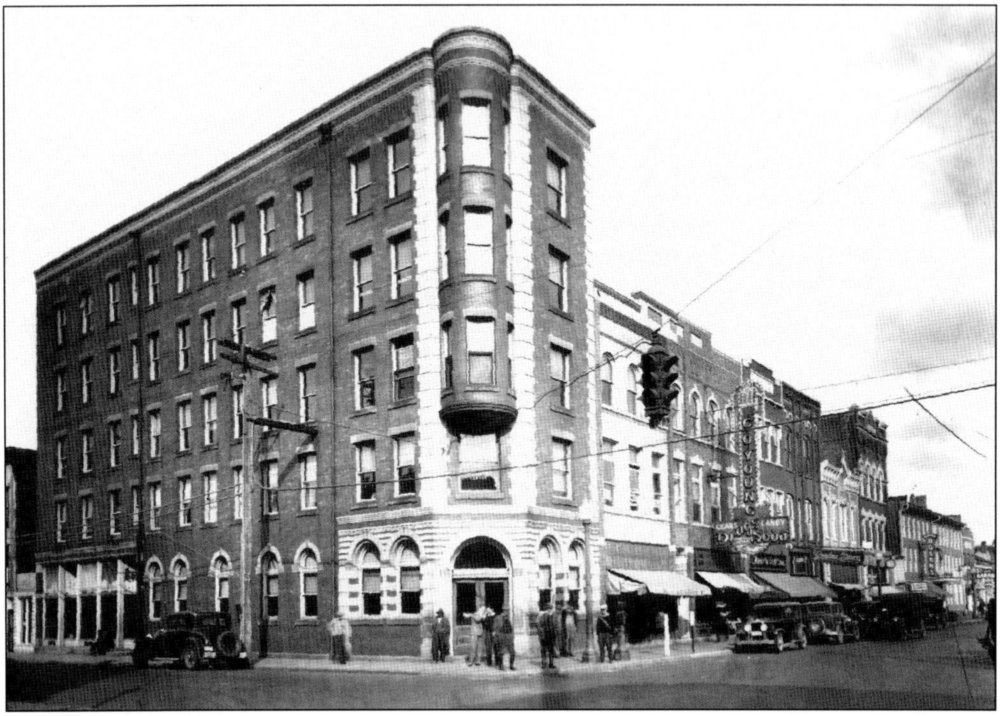

**TRADER'S BANK.** This late 1930s Main Street photograph shows the bank building on the corner of Main and Kanawha Streets. The building was constructed in 1910 at a cost of $50,000 and originally housed the People's Bank, which closed in the early 1930s. Looking further down toward East Main Street one can see other businesses, including G.O. Young Drug Store, Murphy's, Leader Store, Liberty Lunch, Rosen's, the New Valley Hotel, and the Chevrolet Garage. (Photo courtesy of UCHS, permanent collection.)

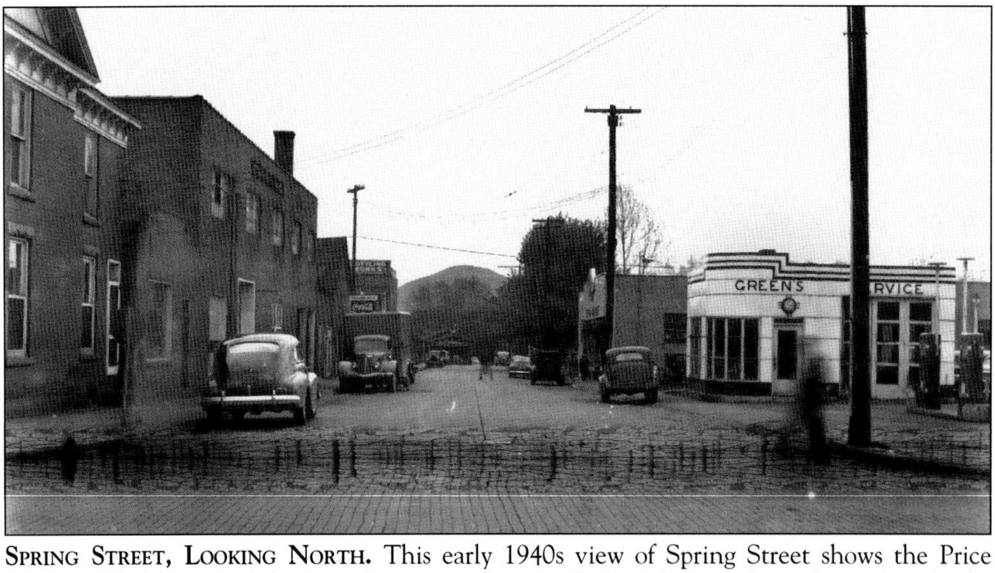


**SPRING STREET, LOOKING NORTH.** This early 1940s view of Spring Street shows the Price Bottling Works on the left, Green's service station and the A& P on the right, and at the far back, the Land-O-Hills Creamery where Kasten's is located today. (Photo courtesy of UCHS, WV Wesleyan Collection.)

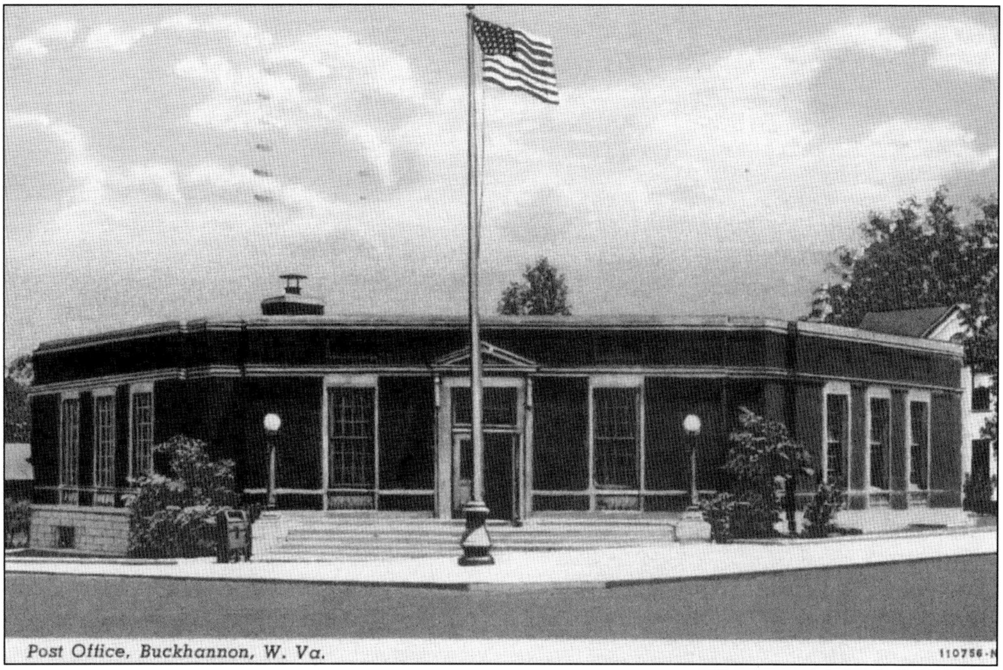


**OLD POST OFFICE.** This linen postcard depicts the Buckhannon post office when it was located on the corner of Main and Florida Streets. The Buckhannon post office was first established in 1804 with John Jackson as postmaster. In 1916 this building was constructed on the lot where the Buckhannon Methodist Episcopal church had been located. In 1966, the new post office was dedicated on Spring Street, and this building then became Buckhannon's city hall. (Photo courtesy of UCHS, Phyllis Miller Collection.)

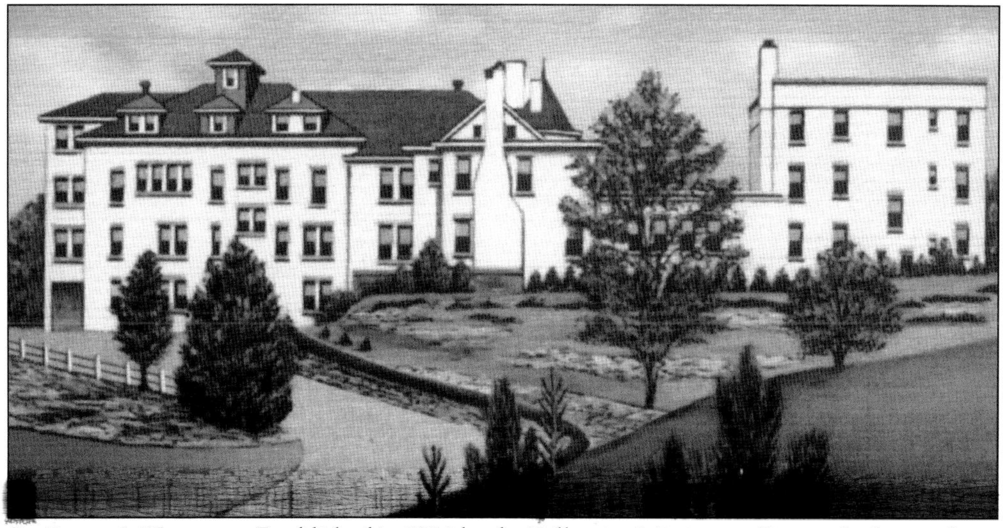

**ST. JOSEPH'S HOSPITAL.** Established in 1921 by the Pallottine Missionary Sisters, the hospital was originally housed in the old Barlow home, located in the center of this complex. Enlargements to the building began in 1924, again in the mid-1960s, and finally in the 1980s. The old structure pictured here was demolished in 1966 to construct the new building except for the square unit at the far right, which still serves today as office space. (Photo courtesy of UCHS, Phyllis Miller Collection.)

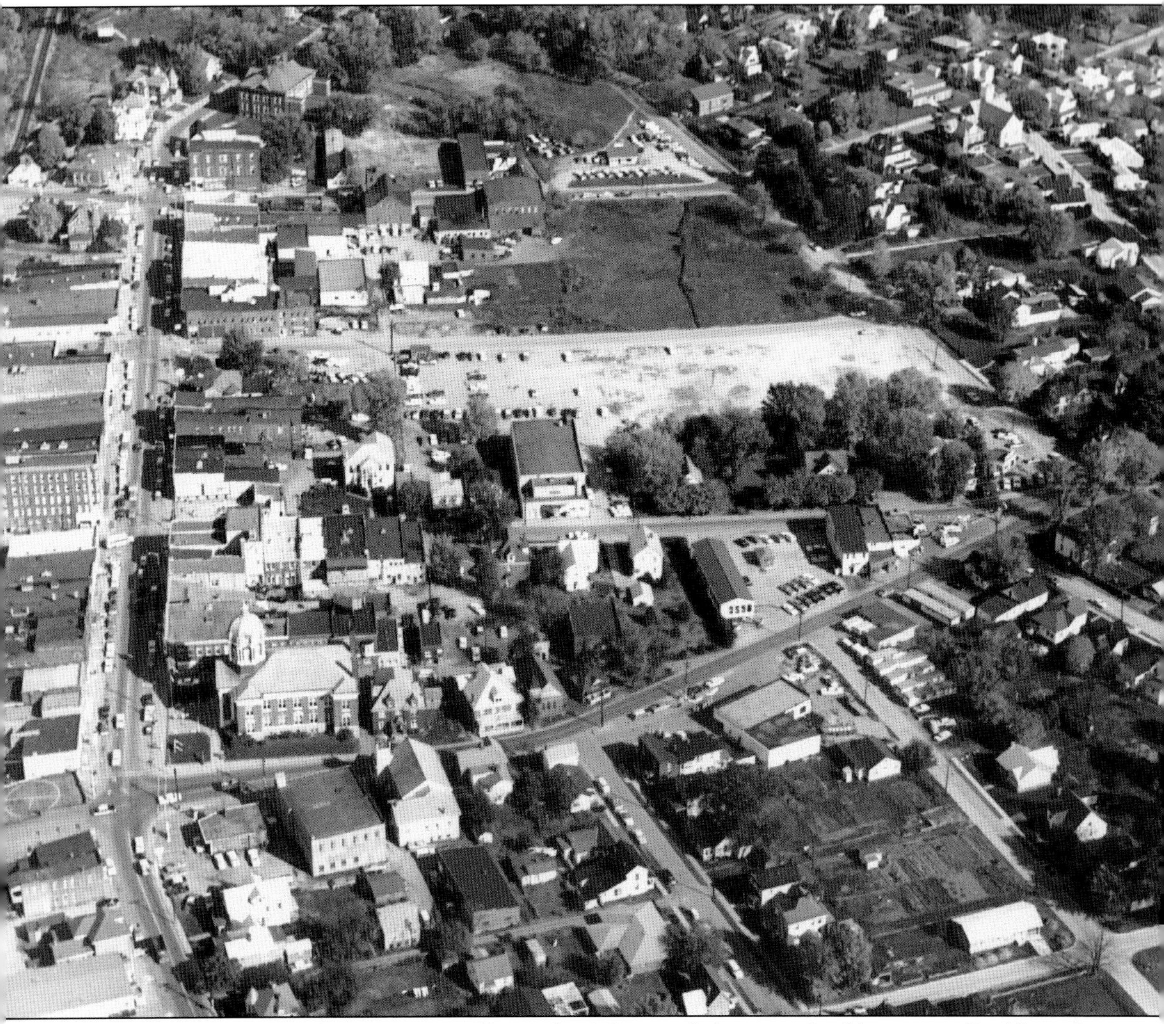

**BIRD'S-EYE VIEW OF BUCKHANNON.** This early 1960s aerial photograph of downtown Buckhannon shows Main Street running from top to bottom along the left edge with the courthouse located at the lower left. Points of interest included here are the north pointing compass atop the Upshur Building diagonally across from the courthouse, the large empty lot in the upper center where the new post office would soon be built, and the old African-American Simpson AME Church located at the end of Franklin Street and behind the courthouse. Where today's courthouse annex stands, the Poundstone Drug Store building used to stand; it was destroyed by fire a few years after this photograph was taken. (Photo courtesy of. UCHS, WV Wesleyan Collection.)

## *Two*

# UPSHUR COUNTY COMMUNITIES

*Abbott, Adrian, Alexander, Alton, Arlington, Atlas, Bean's Mill, Bridge Run, Brooks Hill, Buckhannon, Canaan, Carter, Cos, Craddock, Daysville, Deanville, Eden, Excelsior, Ellamore, Evergreen, Fairview, Fishing Camp, Flat Rock, French Creek, Frenchton, Gaines, Goodwin, Gormley, Gould, Hackers Creek, Hampton, Heaston Ridge, Hemlock, Hesper, Hickory Flat, Hinkle, Hinkleville, Hodgesville, Holly Grove, Imperial, Indian Camp, Ivy, Kanawha Head, Kedron, Kesling Mill, Lantz, McCue, Natural Bridge, Nebo, Newlon, Palace Valley, Queens, Red Knob, Red Rock, Reger, Rock Cave, Rocky Ford, Sago, Sand Run, Selbyville, South Buckhannon, Stillman, Tallmansville, Ten Mile, Tennerton, Teter, Vegan, Yokum, and Zion are all place names in Upshur County—some familiar and present, some not so familiar and long gone. The following photographs are representative of many of the county's communities.*

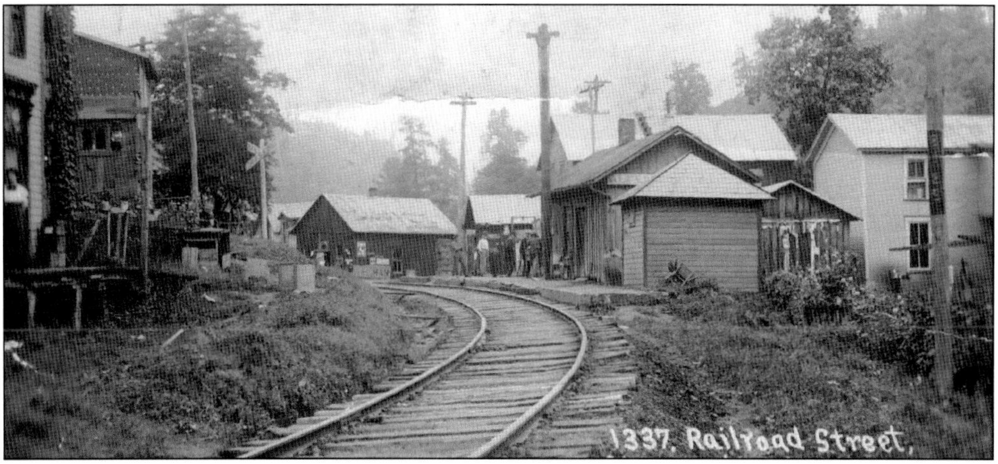


**ALEXANDER.** This postcard of Alexander is postmarked 1910 and addressed to Miss Edna Chaunell. The message reads,"Well dear little Edna, guess will haf to send you a postcard, you surely have forgot Papa all together haven't you. Guess you are very buisy tho. Lovingly Daddie." At this time, Alexander was a booming lumber town even though the writer here also adds, concerning the picture, "This is all of Alexander." Most likely this writer was working in the lumber industry. This Meade District village was named for John M. Alexander, a partner in the Alexander Lumber Company, and there was a post office from 1890 to 1980. (Photo courtesy of UCHS, on loan from Doris Hammon.)

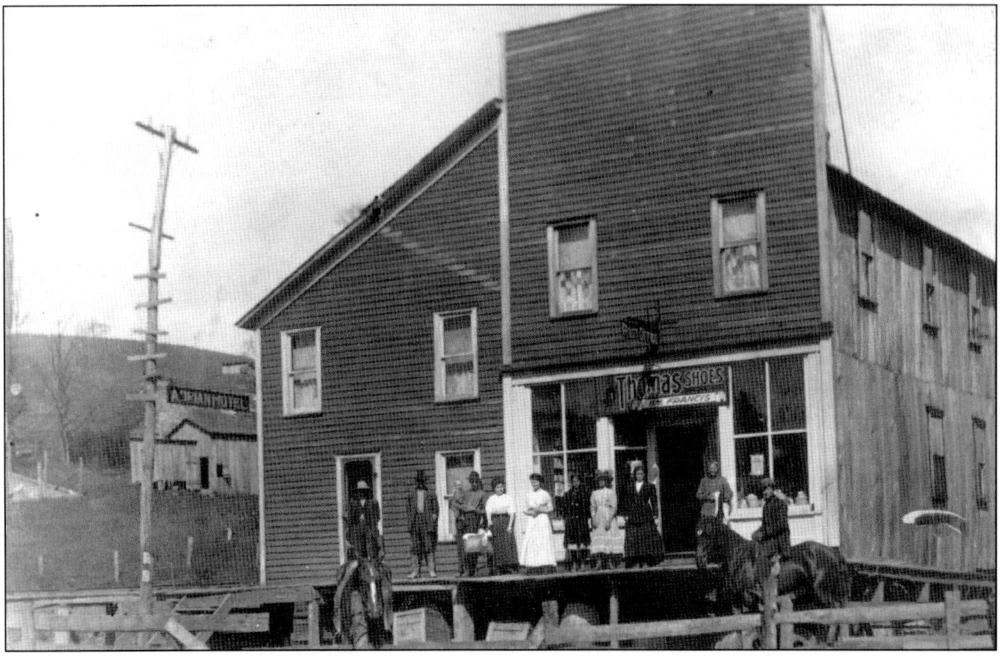


**ADRIAN HOTEL.** This 1911–1914 photograph shows unidentified people in front of the two-story building that housed the Adrian Hotel, post office, and William A. Francis general merchandise store. During the heyday of Adrian, several coal mines were in operation in the community. The post office was first established in 1887–1891 and reopened in 1904. (Photo courtesy of UCHS, Willa Score Collection.)

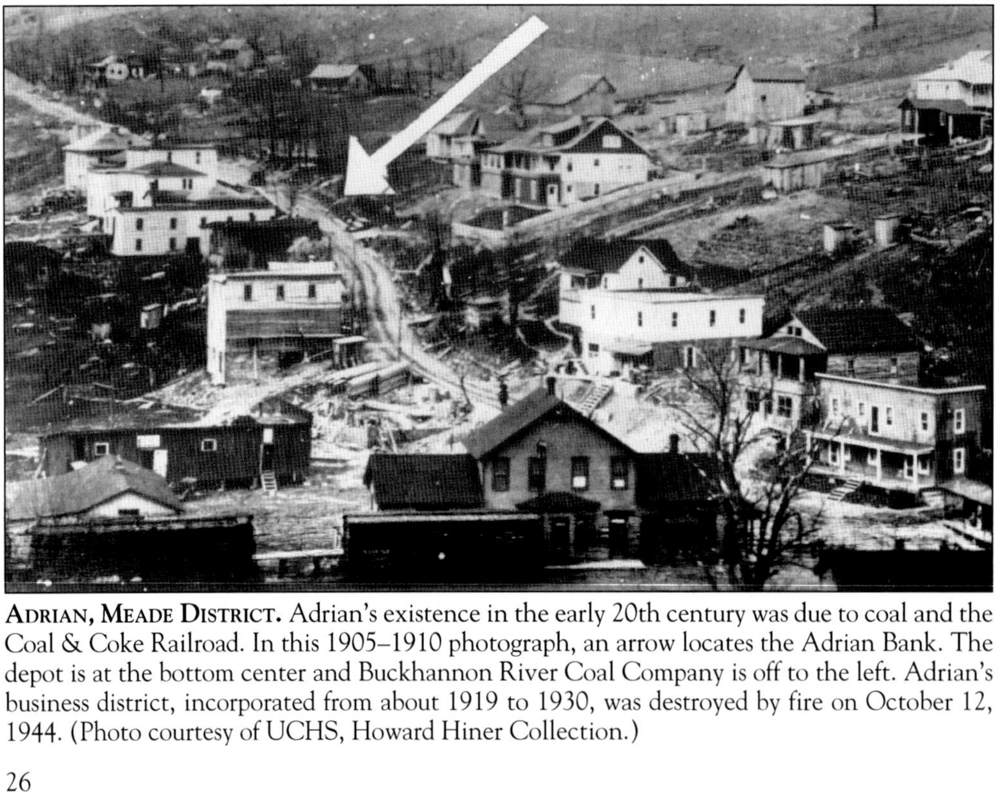

**ADRIAN, MEADE DISTRICT.** Adrian's existence in the early 20th century was due to coal and the Coal & Coke Railroad. In this 1905–1910 photograph, an arrow locates the Adrian Bank. The depot is at the bottom center and Buckhannon River Coal Company is off to the left. Adrian's business district, incorporated from about 1919 to 1930, was destroyed by fire on October 12, 1944. (Photo courtesy of UCHS, Howard Hiner Collection.)

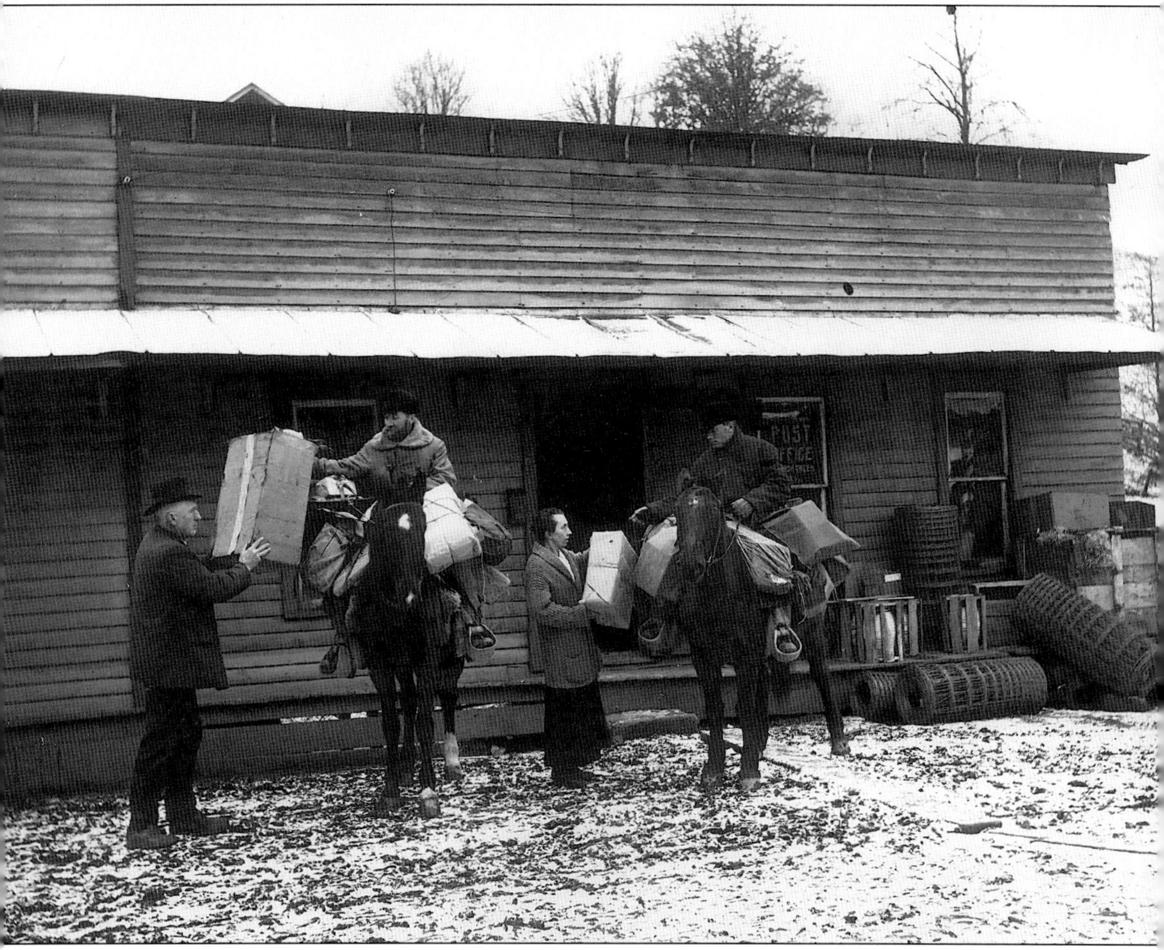


**FRENCH CREEK POSTAL SERVICES.** Pictured in 1919 in front of the French Creek post office are, from left to right, H.B. Darnall, postmaster; Henry Otis Talbott, rural carrier; Mrs. H.B. Darnall (Ellie N. Hefner Darnall); and Ellias W. Brooks, rural carrier. This settlement was formed in the early 1800s by a large group of New England Presbyterian settlers with family names such as Gould, Young, Phillips, Burr, Sexton, Brooks, and Loomis. The post office, the second in the county, was established in 1822 and was named for the stream of water that flows through the village. The community was also known as Meadeville as it is located in Meade District. Local tradition also indicates that during the Civil War the village was known as "Snatchburg" because everyone was grabbing and snatching what was available. (Photo courtesy of UCHS, Fred Brooks Collection.)

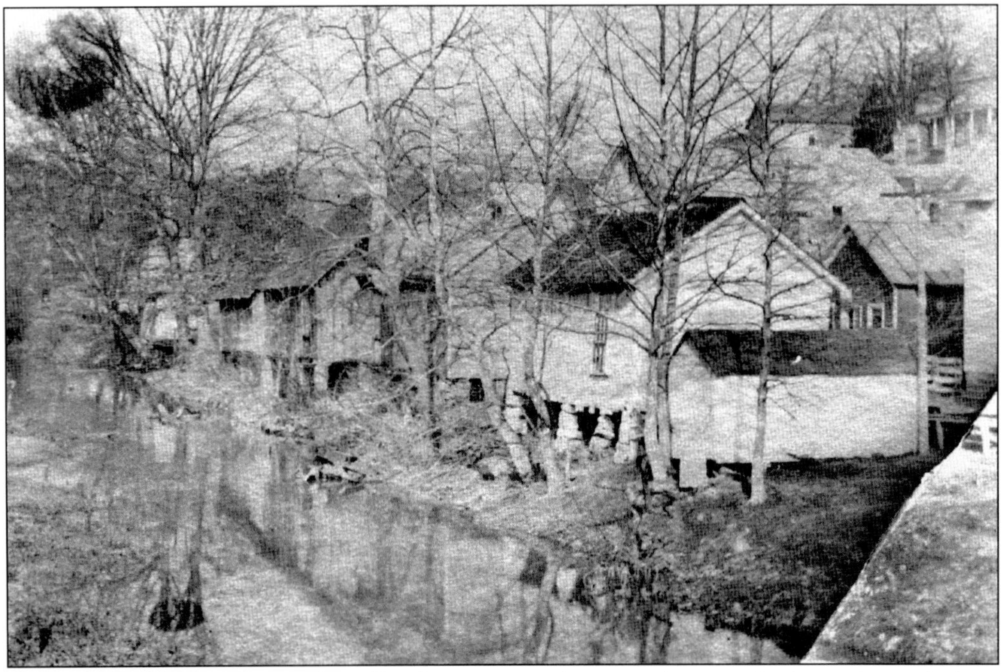

**French Creek Businesses.** The village's prosperous business district, which was located along the creek on Slab Camp Road, was destroyed by fire in June 1911. Also destroyed was the Methodist church building. At about the same time, the old Buckhannon ME Church was being dismantled to make room for the new post office (now used as city hall) and so most of that building was used to rebuild the French Creek Methodist Church. (Photo courtesy of UCHS, Noel W. Tenney Collection.)

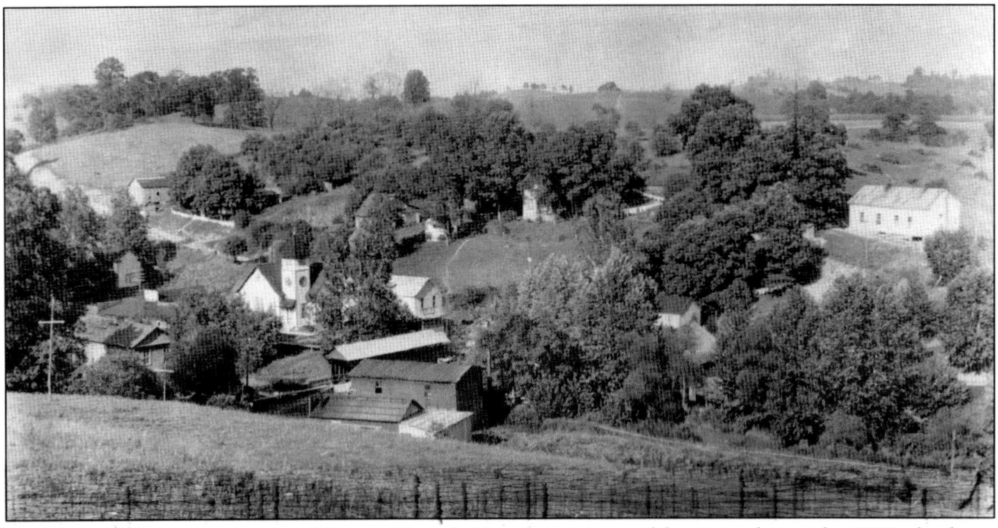

**Bird's-eye View of French Creek.** French Creek is pictured here in the early 1900s looking northeast toward Buckhannon. Note the Methodist Church on the middle left side with the old covered bridge just to its right. At the far right is an early French Creek school building. In 1916 the French Creek Pioneer Descendants organization was formed to celebrate and perpetuate the historical significance of the community's early settlement. This organization is still active today. (Photo courtesy of UCHS, Noel W. Tenney Collection.)

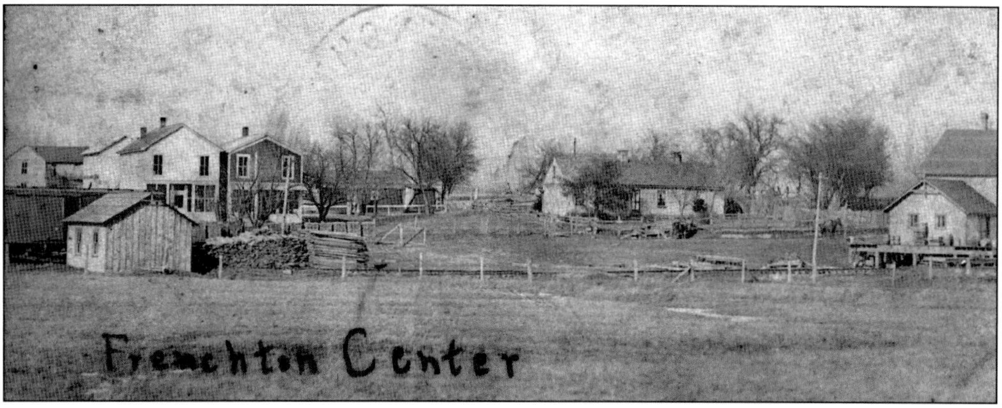


**FRENCHTON.** Pictured on this *c.* 1909 postcard is "Frenchton Center." The original name of the village was Beechtown, supposedly because Native Americans lived there in huts made of beech bark. This Banks District post office was established in 1837. (Photo courtesy of UCHS, Doris Orsburn Collection.)

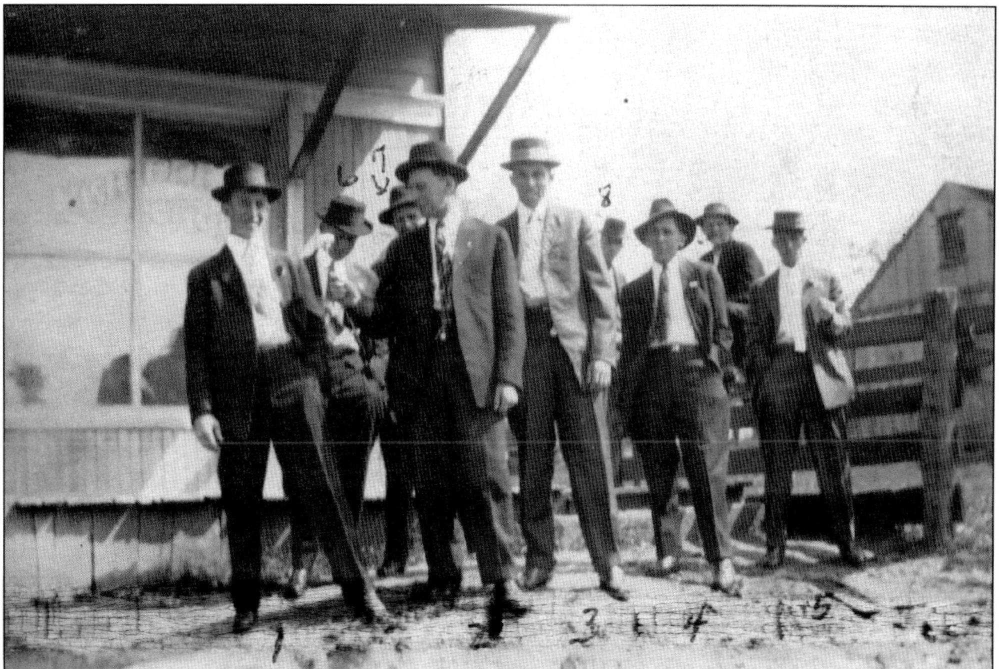

**FRENCHTON YMCA.** Pictured in this real photo postcard taken on Main Street and dated 1915 are, from left to right, (front row) Ed Rusmissell, Burley Rawson, Bill Wilson, Lester Bennett, and Orvill Brown; (back row) Claud Brown, Overton Harper, John Wilson, and unidentified. (Photo courtesy of UCHS, Doris Orsburn Collection.)

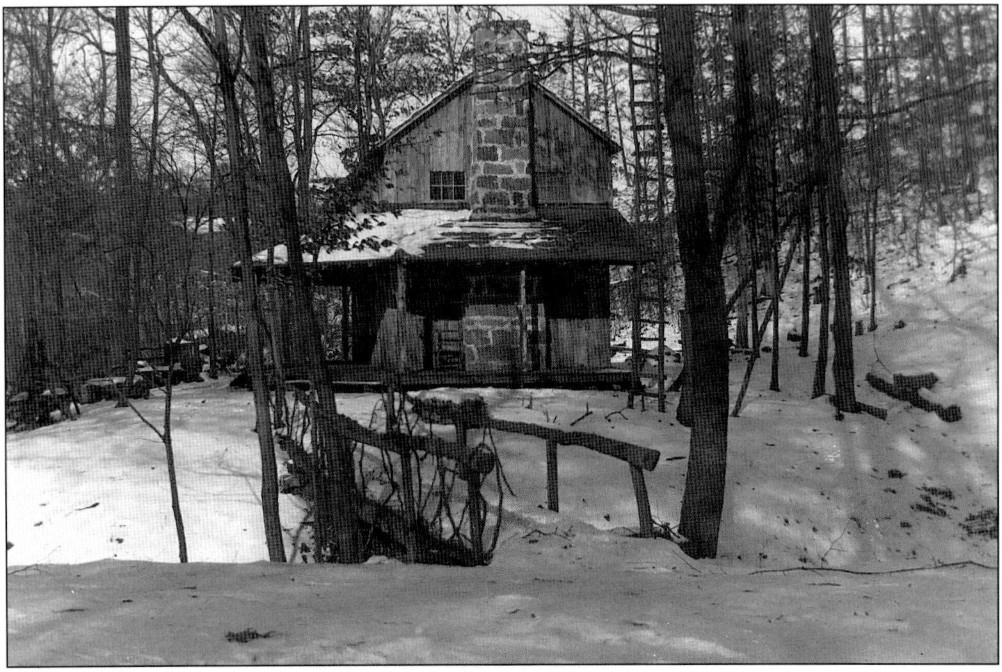

**Camp Beechwood.** Summer camps along the Buckhannon River were very fashionable during the early 20th century. Names like "Camp Coquina," "Chippewa Lodge,"and "Beechwood Inn," were the rave. Quoting from the guest book of the "Chippewa Lodge," we read, "Brought down to the little camp by the Latham Tribe on a stormy night, June 18, 1921. May you hold only happy memories of joyous hours, spent with those whose names are inscribed herein." (Photo courtesy of UCHS, Alan Sturm Collection.)

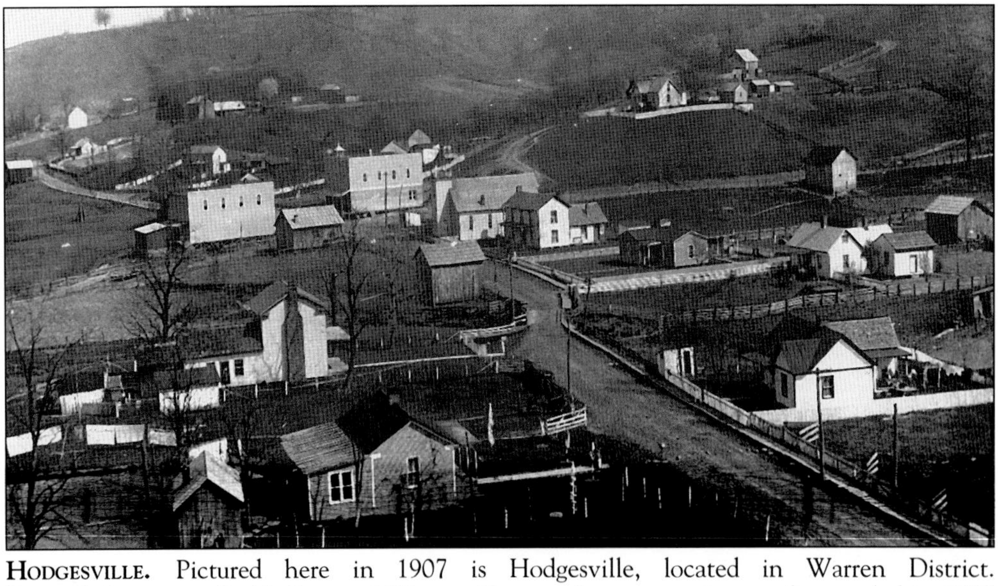

**Hodgesville.** Pictured here in 1907 is Hodgesville, located in Warren District. Formerly known as Peck's Run and Warren Center, the community was first settled in 1820 by Nathaniel Peck. In 1846, John Hodges established a mercantile business. In the early 20th century, the area became a major coal mining center. (Photo courtesy of UCHS, Robert Marple Collection.)

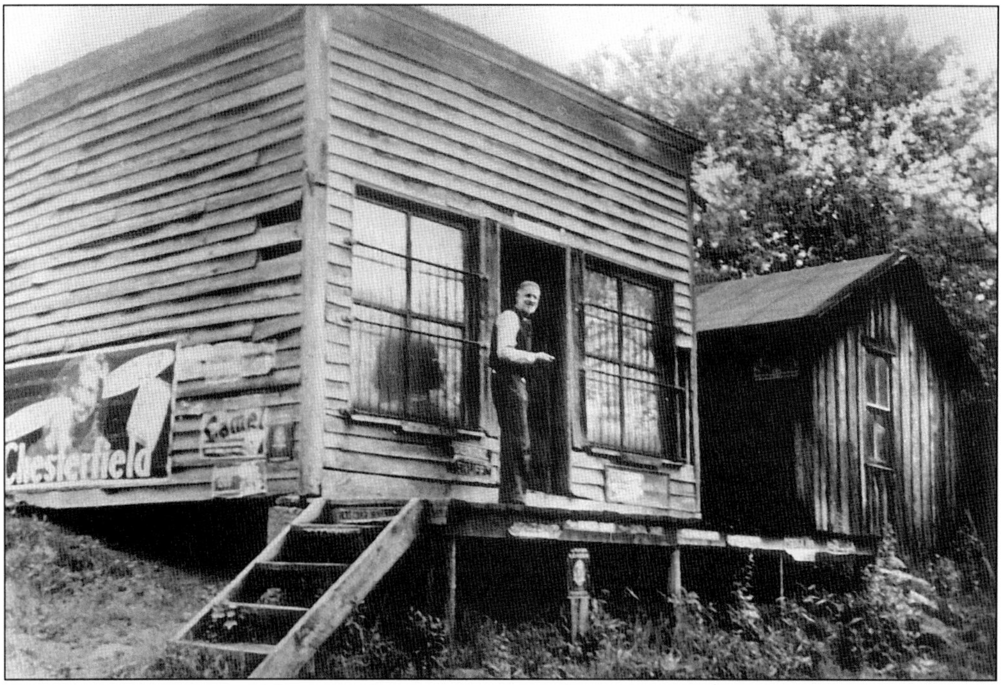


**Kedron Store.** Pictured here is Clint Simmons on the porch of his store building in Kedron, c. 1930. This community is located in Washington District near the Mt. Union Methodist Church. There was a post office from 1891 to 1895, and tradition says that William Steele gave it the Biblical name at that time. The Kedron gristmill was built by George Steele Sr. in 1886. (Photo courtesy of UCHS, Sheila Tenney Thomason Collection.)

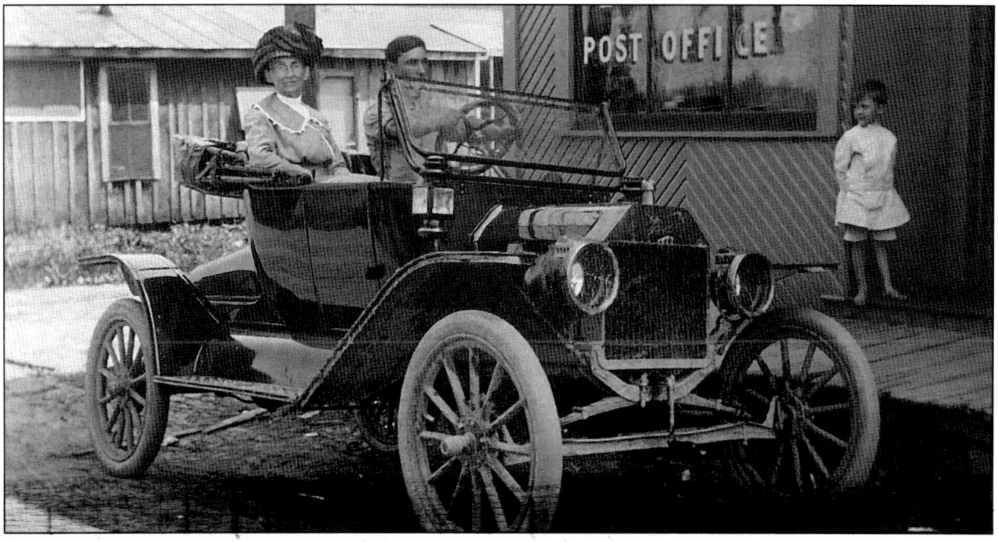


**Lorentz Post Office.** Pictured here are members of the W.B. Miles family in their new automobile at the local post office, c. 1916. The third oldest post office in Upshur County was established here in 1824 as "Lorentz' Store." The village was named for Jacob Lorentz, an early business man and blacksmith who carried his goods over the mountains from Cumberland, Maryland and Staunton, Virginia on pack horses. (Photo courtesy of UCHS, Ralph Miles Collection.)

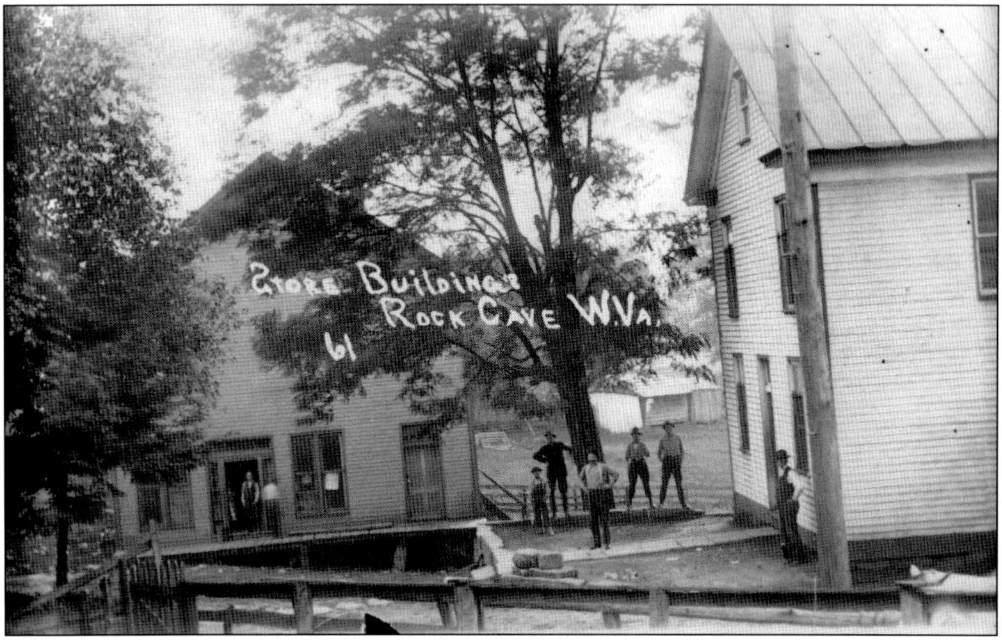


**Rock Cave.** Pictured here are two views of Rock Cave in Banks District. The community was also known as Rude's Mill, Bob Town, and Centerville. According to tradition, the original name was Bob Town in honor of Robert Curry and then Rude's Mill for the first postmaster, Edwin D. Rude in 1848. In 1859 the name was changed to Rock Cave, believed to have been a postal department mistake as the name submitted was Rock Lava, proposed because of stones, apparently lava and volcanic, found on Straight Fork Run. The area was most notably known as Centerville, and it was there on September 12, 1863 that the 70 members of the Upshur Militia were taken captive by Confederate soldiers. Seven of them escaped, 25 were paroled, and the rest died in Southern prison camps, some at dreaded Andersonville. Twenty-seven widows and 83 children were left behind. (Photos courtesy of UCHS, Lisa Wilson Collection.)

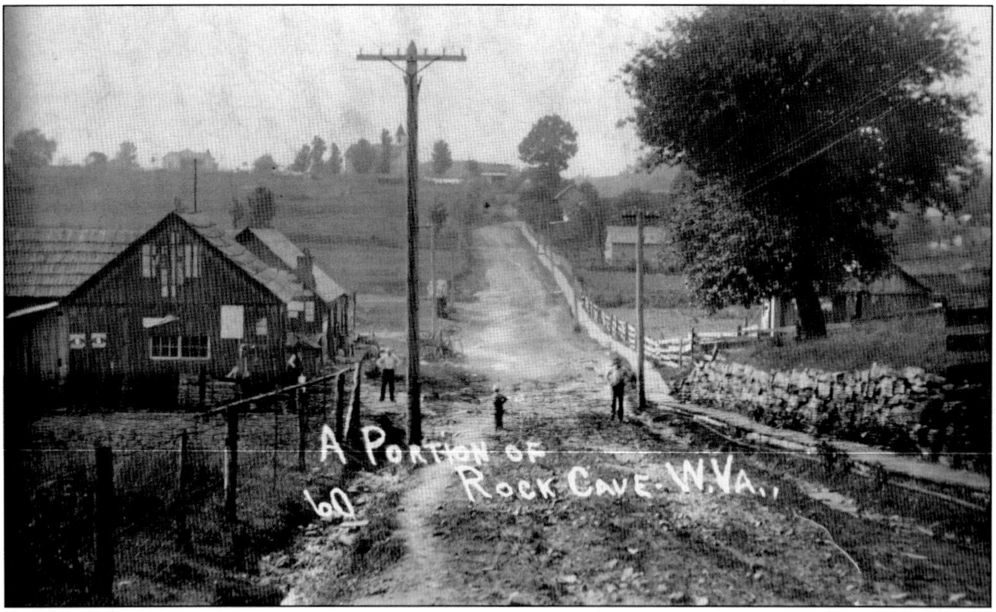

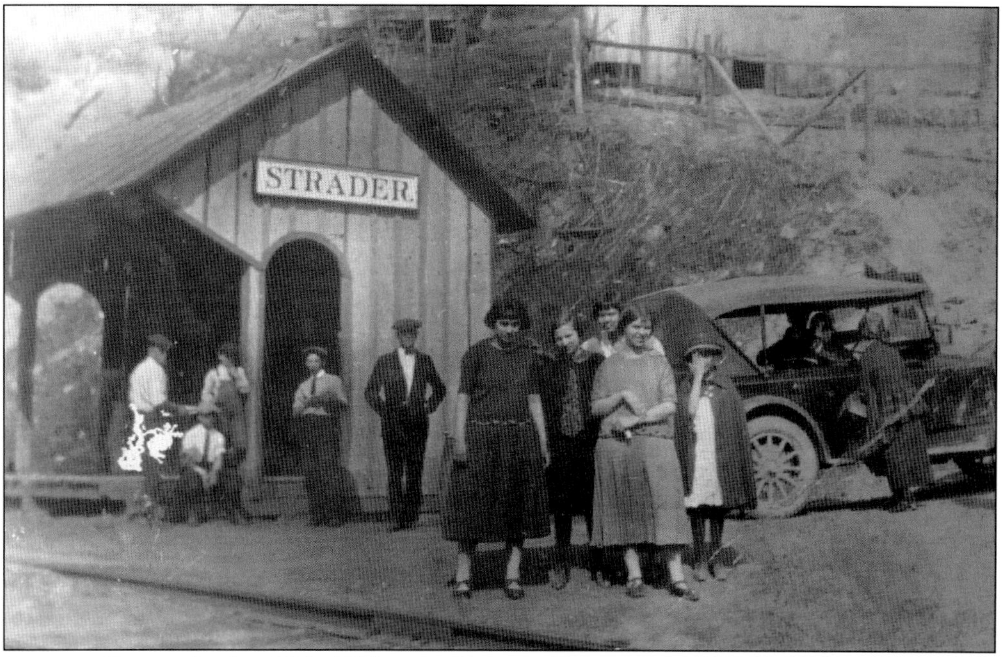


**STRADER DEPOT.** In the 1920s, Tallmansville was also known as the Strader stop on the Coal & Coke Railroad. The station was located near the Robert E. Tenney store and home. The Tallmansville post office was housed in his store and Tenney was the postmaster from 1906 until the mid-1940s. Tallmansville was named in honor of Benjamin Tallman, the first postmaster in 1869. (Photo courtesy of UCHS, Leila Tenney Ours Collection.)

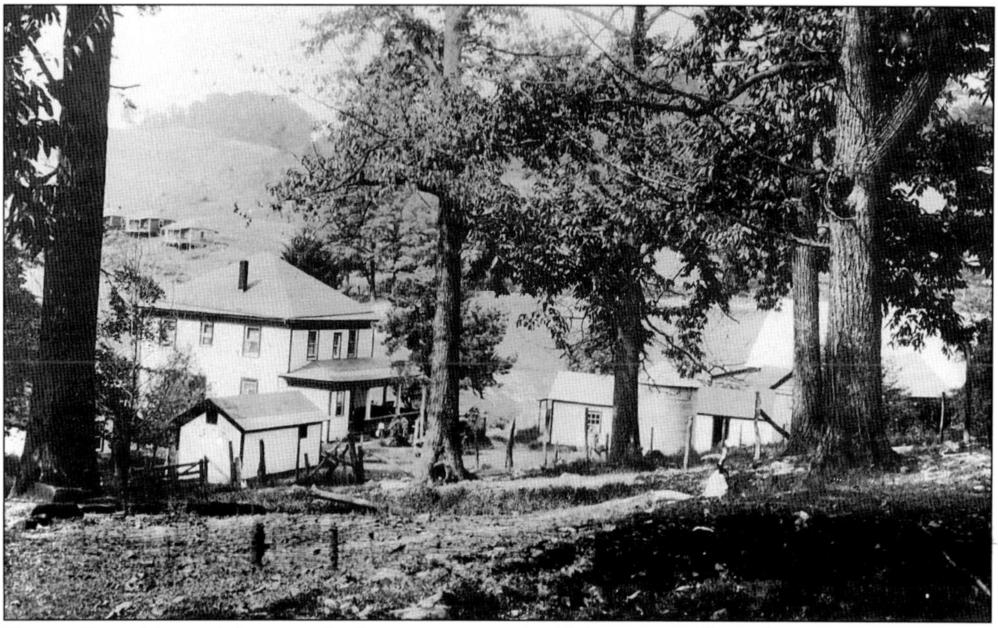

**FLOYD REED FARM.** This stately farm was an early-20th-century showplace in Tallmansville, Washington District. This image was taken in the 1920s looking through a grove of Native American Chestnut trees. In the background a segment of "string town," Greenmar Coal company houses, can be seen. (Photo courtesy of UCHS, Marjorie Craven Miles Collection.)

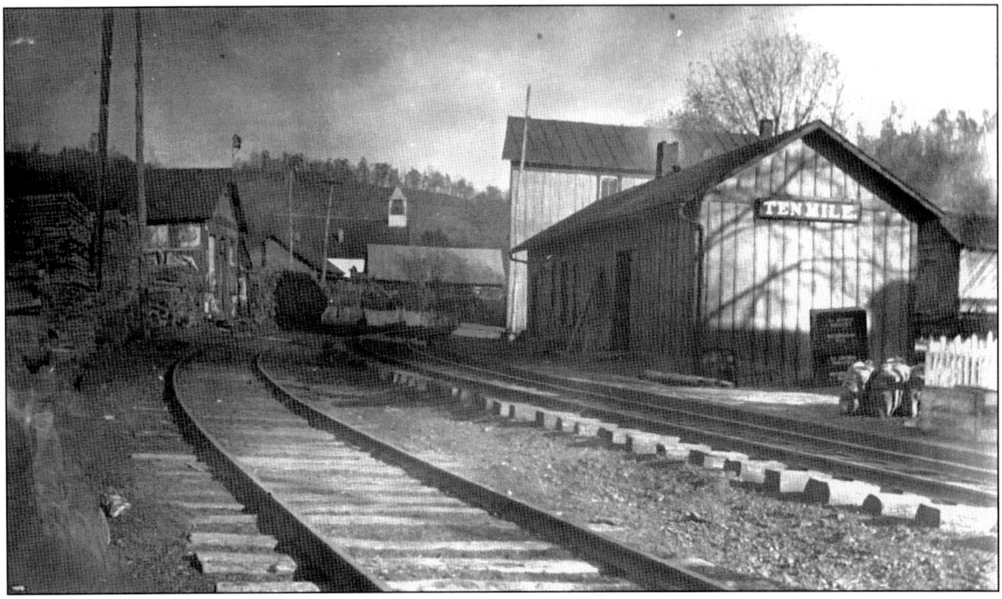


**Ten Mile Depot.** This village was divided by the Buckhannon River and was situated along the riverbank in both Meade and Washington Districts. The Baltimore & Ohio Railroad depot, pictured in this early-20th-century photograph, was situated in Meade District. The Ten Mile Methodist Church is visible in the background and is the only building pictured here to survive to today; most of the area was destroyed by fire in 1948. The post office was in existence from 1899 to 1957, and the name Sellars was also attached to this community. (Photo courtesy of UCHS, Joe Tenney Shingleton Collection.)

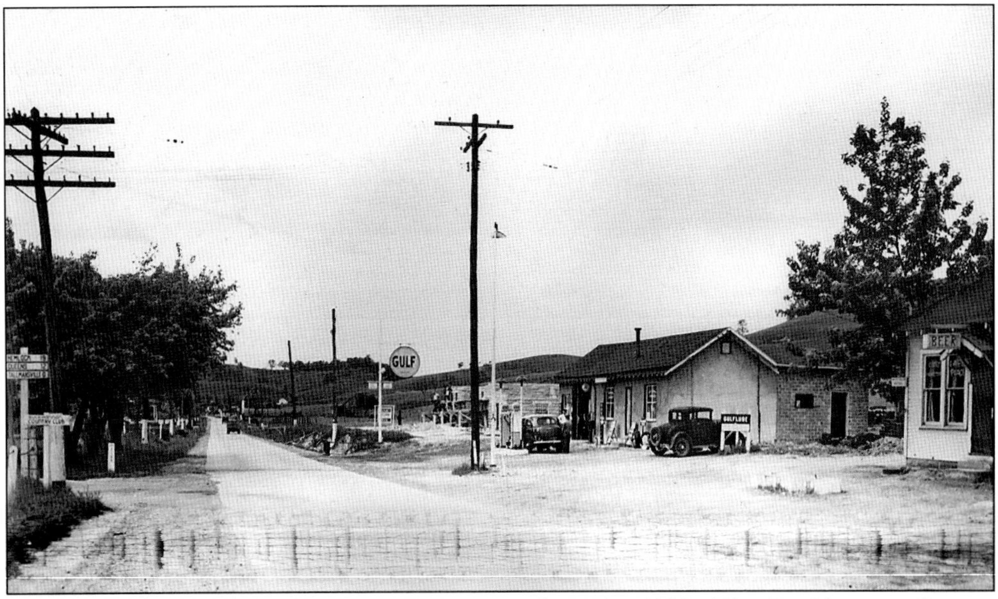


**Tennerton.** Pictured are the Tennerton crossroads in the 1930s. This Buckhannon District village was named for John Kinley Tener who established the Steimer Glass Company here in 1903. Note the Scott's Service Station on the right and the Tallmansville road on the left. The WPA state road building was just being constructed when this photograph was taken. (Photo courtesy of UCHS, Brent Scott Collection.)

# *Three*

# Upshur County Personalities

*Upshur County has produced many important and recognized individuals. Daniel D.T. Farnsworth, second governor of West Virginia, was a member of the Buckhannon family who originally owned all of the property where the city now stands, having traded a major portion of Staten Island, New York for this local property. Arthur B. Waugh, native of Gaines, won a Pulitzer Prize for journalism in 1935. Pare Lorentz was well known as President Roosevelt's "New Deal" documentary filmmaker with his* The Plow that Broke the Plain *and* The River. *Jean Lee Latham received the Newberry Award for* Carry On, Mr. Bowditch *in 1956. Contemporarily, Stephen Coonts and Jayne Anne Phillips are internationally recognized authors. Annie Latham Bartlett was well known for her sculptural works and exhibited at the New York World's Fair in 1939. Her father, Col. George R. Latham, served as consul to Australia in the 1860s. Charles Harper, known internationally for his silkscreen prints, is from Frenchton. Warren Jackson and Laura Jackson Arnold, siblings of "Stonewall," rest eternally here in Upshur County. Pictured in this chapter are some of the county's great personalities as well as some who, like the most of us, are of the common masses.*

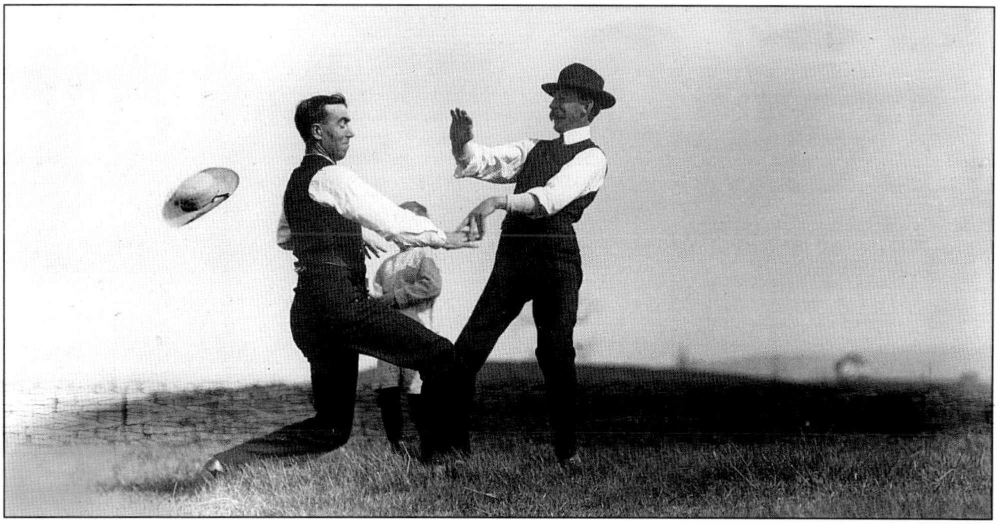

**Mock Fight in French Creek.** Pictured in this c. 1919 Fred Brooks photograph, from left to right, are Lynn Brooks, an unidentified child, and A.B. Brooks, making quick work of their mock fight. (Photo courtesy of UCHS, Fred Brooks Collection.)

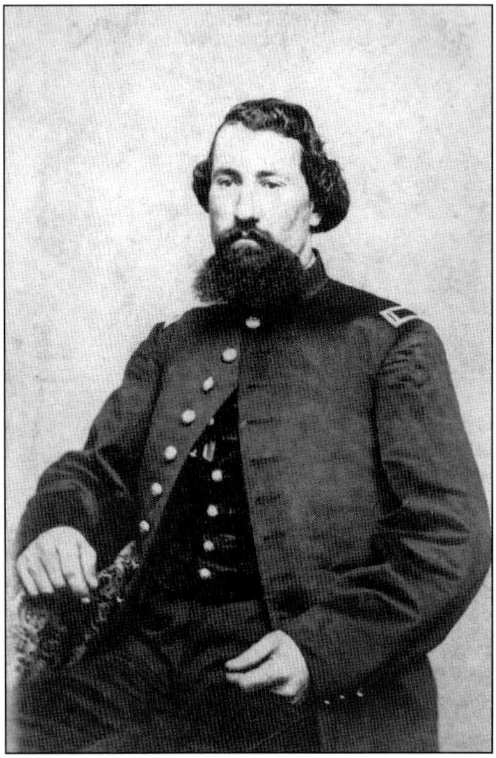

**Capt. George Sexton.** The William and Sallie Jackson Sexton family came to French Creek in 1848, and it was there that young George grew up. During the Civil War he served in the Union army and is pictured here by Wheeling photographers, Wykes & Brown, as a first lieutenant in Company I, 3rd West Virginia Cavalry. He also served as a staff officer under Sheridan, Custer, and others. He died in Buckhannon on November 16, 1916. (Photo courtesy of UCHS, permanent collection.)

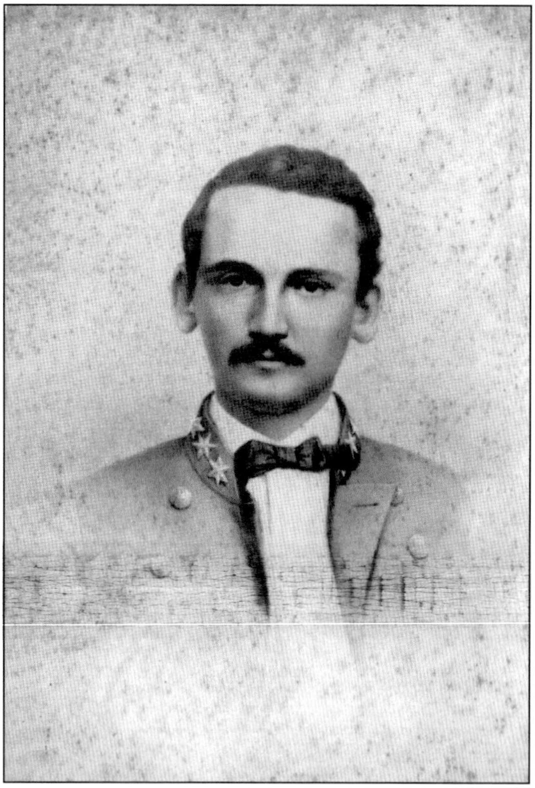

**Col. John Carlton Higginbotham.** Born November 11, 1842, he arrived in Upshur County with his parents in 1848. He was a student at Lynchburg Military Institute when the Civil War began. Higginbotham raised the only Confederate company from Upshur County, the "Upshur Grays," and served as its captain. Promoted to major and lieutenant colonel, he was wounded at the battles of Rich Mountain, McDowell, Cedar Mountain, and Second Bull Run. He was promoted to colonel of the 25th Virginia Infantry Regiment on January 28, 1863, wounded at Gettysburg, and killed in action at Spottsylvania Courthouse, Virginia on May 10, 1864. (Photo courtesy of UCHS, Church of the Transfiguration Episcopal Collection.)

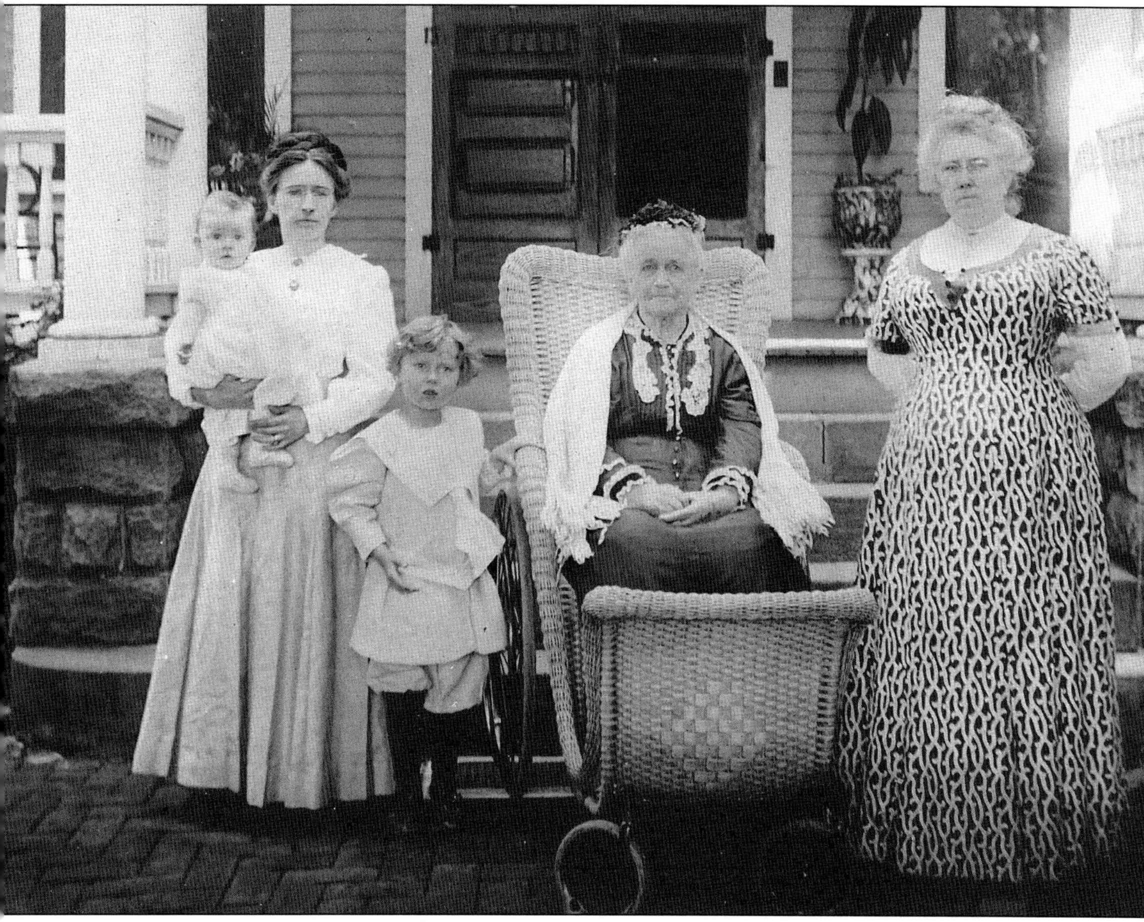

**LAURA JACKSON ARNOLD.** Laura Jackson Arnold, sister to the noted Civil War Confederate general Thomas J. "Stonewall" Jackson, is pictured here in a wheelchair in front of her son's home on Kanawha Street in Buckhannon, c. 1910. Throughout the Civil War, Laura attended to soldiers of both sides at her Beverly, Randolph County home; however, her true sympathy always was with the North, much to the dismay of her brother. She died in 1911 and is buried in the Heavner Cemetery. Their brother, Warren Jackson, died young while teaching school here in Upshur County and was buried in a farm cemetery near Hodgesville. (Photo courtesy of UCHS, Darthy Nagle Collection.)

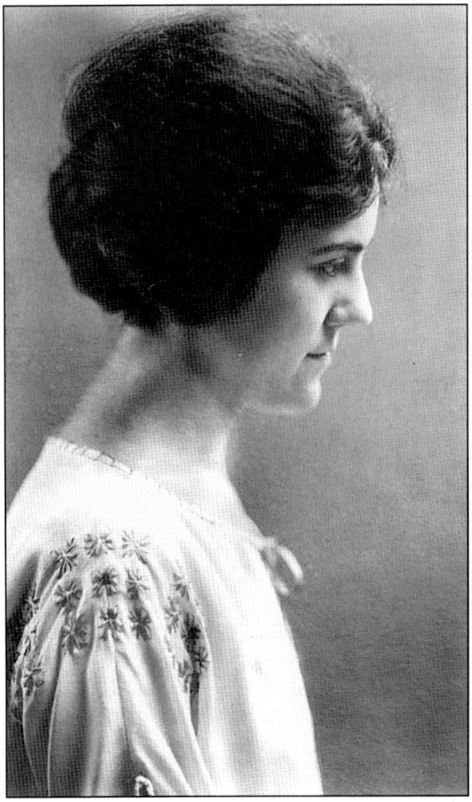

**Lillian Mayfield Roberts, Poet.** This noted West Virginia poet resided in Upshur County for many years during the early 20th century. One of Roberts's most noted works is called "Hill Hunger," and her personal papers are housed at West Virginia University. This formal portrait was photographed by French Creek photographer Fred E. Brooks. (Photo courtesy of UCHS, Fred Brooks Collection.)

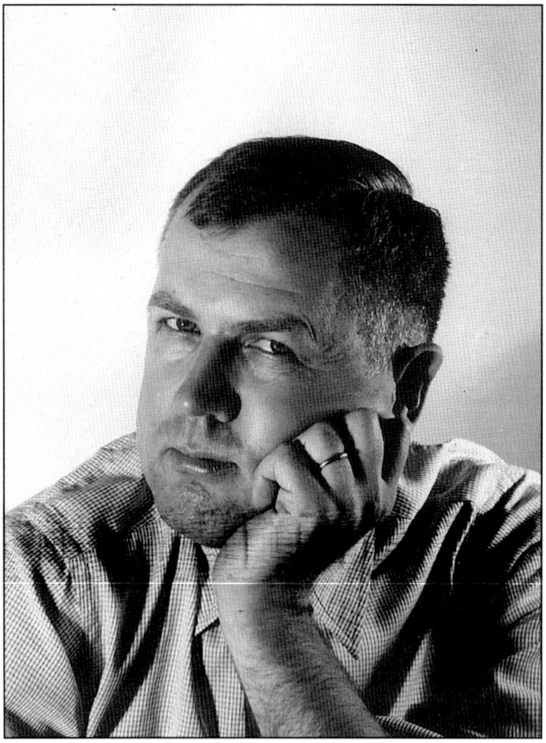

**Charles Harper, Artist.** Upshur County's most noted artist was born at Frenchton in 1922. Following graduation from Buckhannon-Upshur High School, Charles Harper studied at West Virginia Wesleyan College, Cincinnati Art Academy, and the Arts Student League in New York. His work with *Ford Times*, The National Park Service, and as a silkscreen fine artist is internationally known. He resides in Cincinnati, Ohio with his wife, Edie. (Photo courtesy of UCHS, Virginia Bly Hoover Collection.)

**HIGGINBOTHAM LADIES.** Pictured here are Lula and Mary Higginbotham, c. 1909, two of six daughters of a prominent old Buckhannon family. Mary was nationally noted as a very fine painter, specializing in oil and pastel portraits. Because of her family's Southern connections, she also did portraits of Civil War figures such as General Lee. (Photo courtesy of UCHS, Church of the Transfiguration Episcopal Collection.)

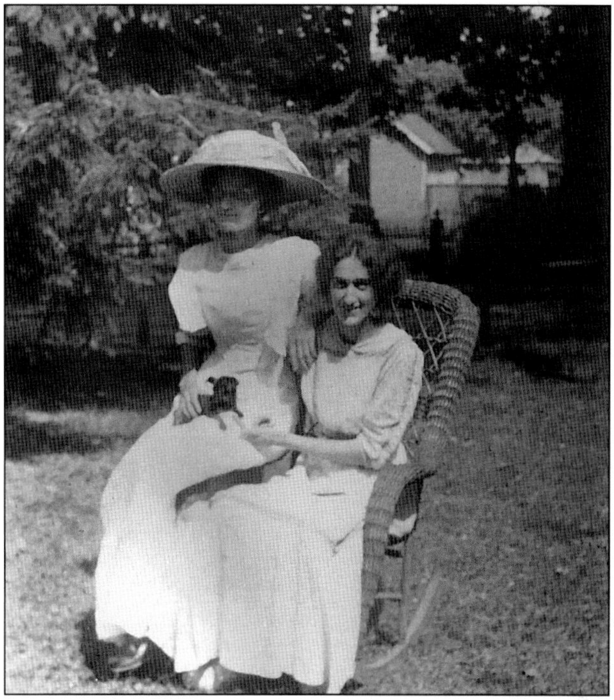

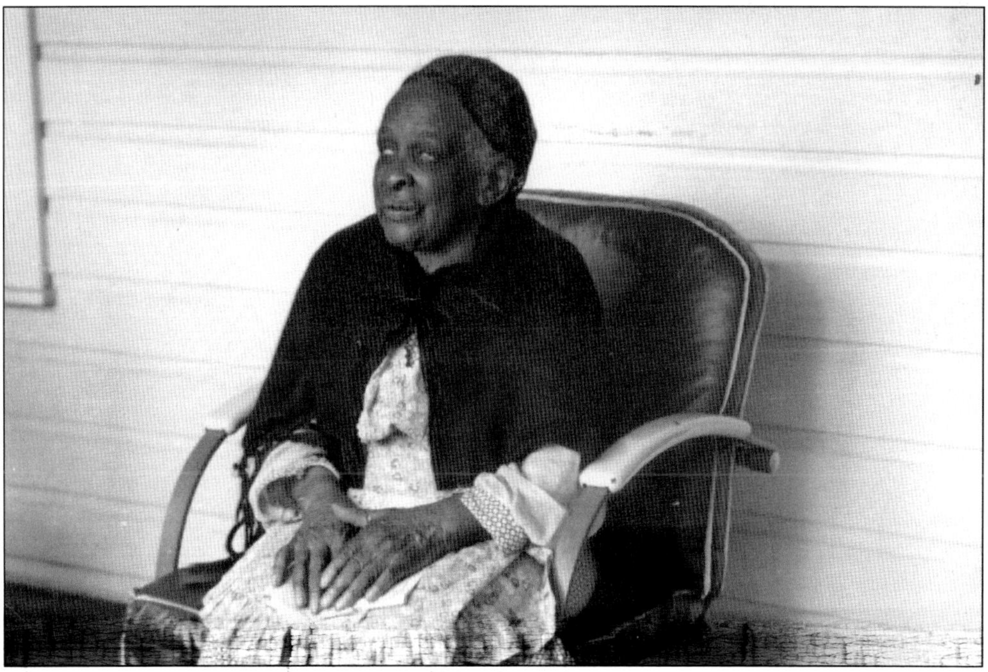

**ELIZA MUMFORD.** Born into slavery in Highland County, Virginia in 1849, Eliza Mumford was given her freedom "in the second year of the war . . . and the ole missus . . . told us to go where we wanted to go." She arrived in Buckhannon in September 1865 and stayed with various families. Her later days were spent with the Higginbotham family on Kanawha Street. Eliza Mumford died in 1948 at the age of 99 years and is buried in the Heavner Cemetery. (Photo courtesy of UCHS, Church of the Transfiguration Episcopal Collection.)

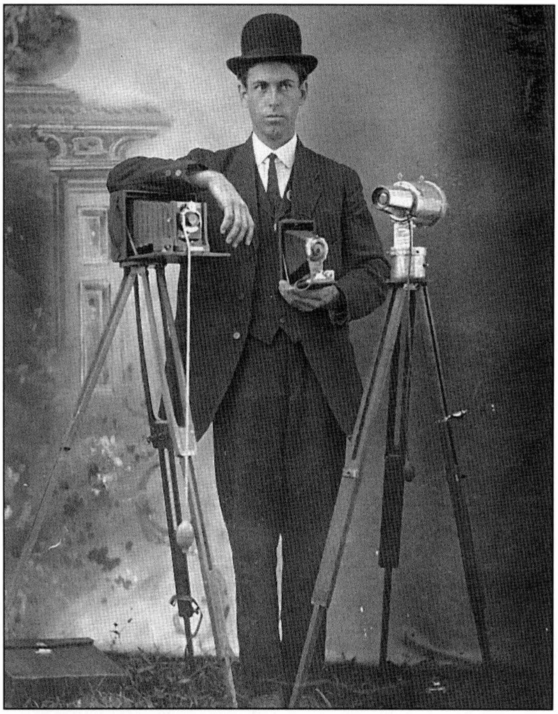

**James Arthur Simmons, Photographer.** Born January 27, 1881, photographer James Arthur Simmons recorded the Sand Run, Upshur County history as well as oddly shaped trees, natural bridges, waterfalls, and rock formations. He served as postmaster at Sand Run from 1908 to 1949, as well as a Coal & Coke Railroad ticket agent and storekeeper. He attended Mountain State College in Parkersburg and studied photography in Marietta, Ohio. He was married to Laola Edith Shipman, and they were the parents of six children. Simmons died on July 30, 1967.(Photo courtesy of UCHS, Sheila Tenney Thomason Collection.)

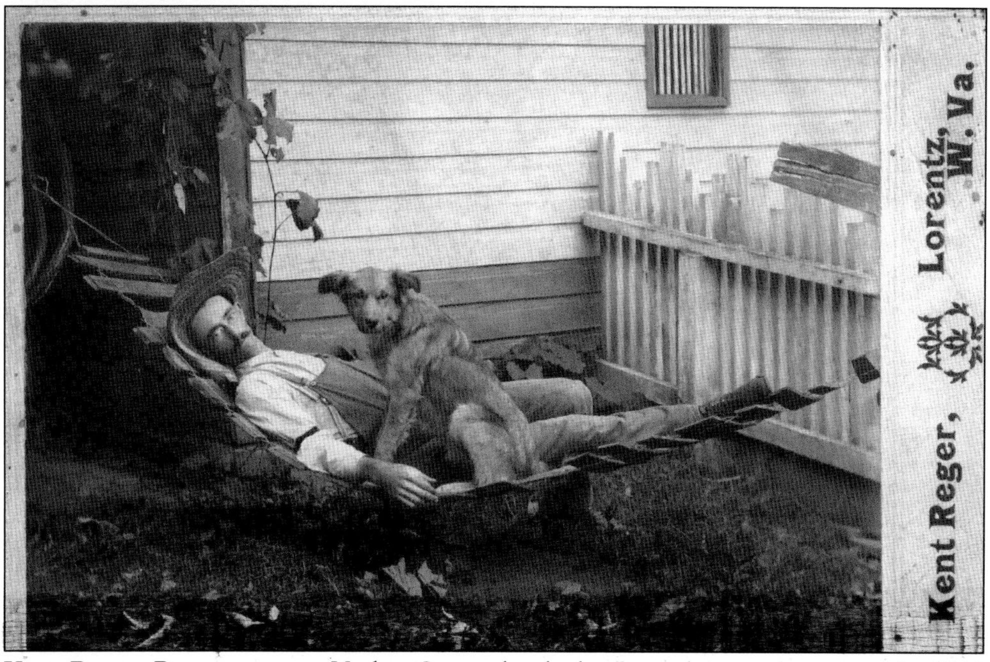


**Kent Reger, Photographer.** Upshur County has had various photographers since the Civil War days. Their names have included H.D. Murphy, L.S.S. Farnsworth, Foreman, MacAvoy, Clark, Ridenour, Berry, Casto, Gawthrop, Simmons, as well as John H. Glauner, Howard Hiner, Wilton Ray Tenney, and Kent Reger, and these individuals have captured hundreds of images here in Upshur County. This self-portrait of Reger was made in the early 20th century. (Photo courtesy of UCHS, Juanita Reger Collection.)

**G.O. YOUNG, DRUGGIST.** George Orville Young was born December 26, 1873 and graduated from the Scio College of Pharmacy in June 1896. He opened his first store here in 1902 and moved into his landmark building in 1911, which is today Miller's Pharmacy on Main Street, Buckhannon. The G.O. Young Drug Store was known far and wide for the array of pharmaceuticals produced, the homemade ice cream, and the beautiful and elegant store interior. Young also participated in big game hunting expeditions in Canada and Alaska and wrote about those experiences in his *Alaskan Trophies Won and Lost*. He died in 1958. (Photo courtesy of UCHS, Sally Young Waddell Collection.)

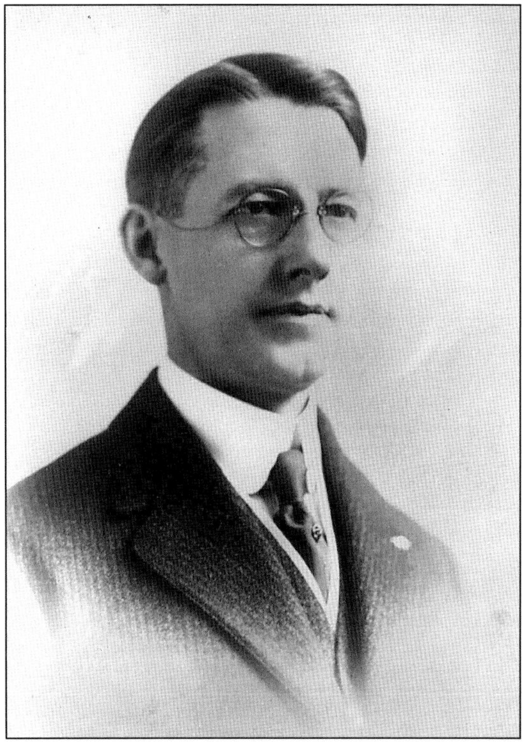

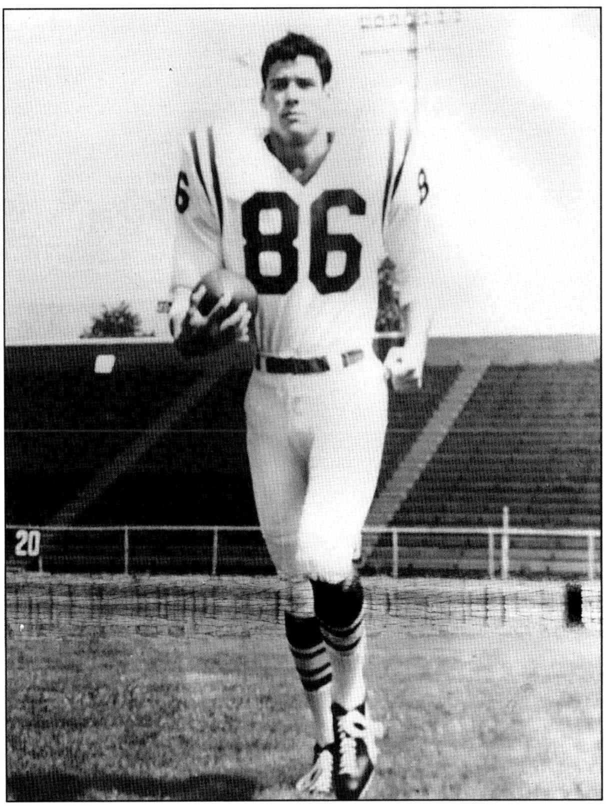


**JOHN PATTON YOUNG.** Born in 1950 in Upshur County to Floyd Patton and B. Elizabeth Young, John Patton Young was a member of the Marshall University football team that was tragically killed when their plane crashed in Huntington, November 14, 1970. Their story was recently told in a documentary film called *From Ashes to Glory*. He was a great nephew of G.O. Young, druggist. (Photo courtesy of UCHS, Sally Young Waddell Collection.)

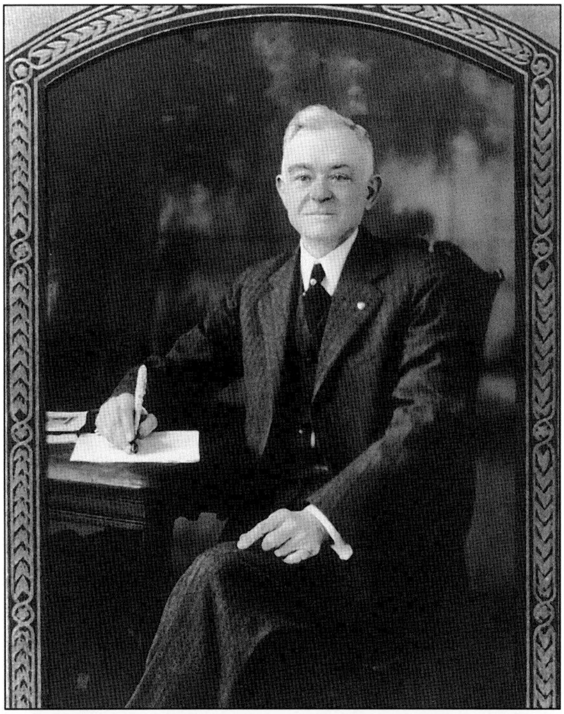

**A.P. RUSSELL, BUSINESSMAN.** Asbury Patrick Russell was born June 11, 1863 and died September 7, 1945. His store on South Kanawha Street, then known as Depot Street, was established around 1900 and flourished as a major wholesale and retail business until his death. Russell bought large lots of various agricultural products, especially ginseng, and sold them in New York to Chinese buyers. (Photo courtesy of UCHS, Milford Reger Collection.)

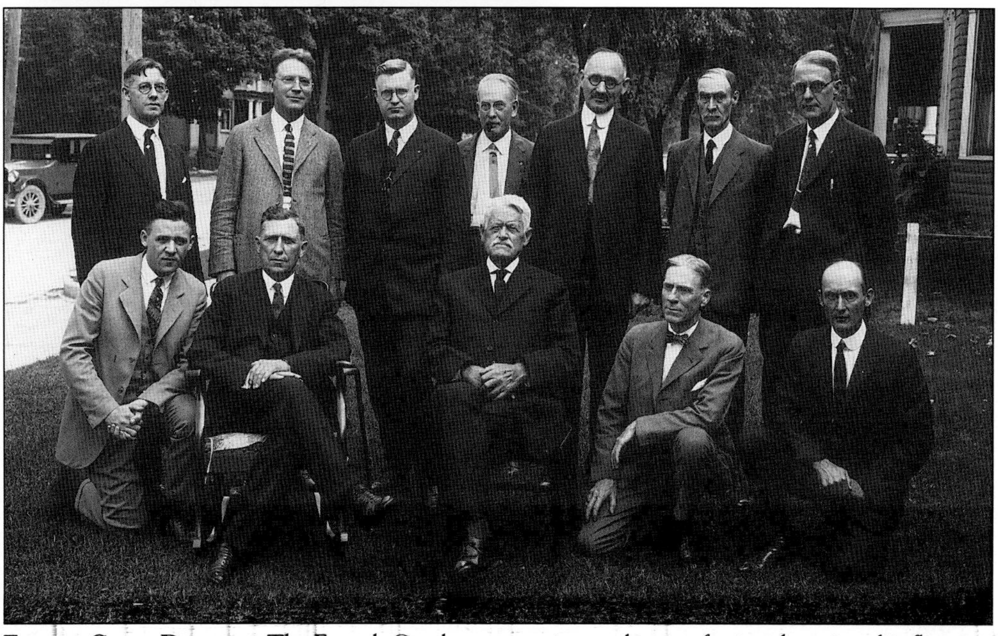

**FRENCH CREEK DOCTORS.** The French Creek community was known for its educational influence, which is demonstrated by this illustrious 1930s photograph of doctors who were all natives of French Creek. Pictured, from left to right, are (front row) Basil Page, G.O. Brown, Jefferson J. Morgan, William Winfred Vance, and Homer O. VanTromp; (back row) G.O. Young, Oscar Beer, French Farnsworth, Nathan B. Bird, Lowry Page, O.L. Perry, and Dellett Bronson. This photograph was taken at Dr. Morgan's home on Meade Street in Buckhannon. (Photo courtesy of UCHS, Fred Brooks Collection.)

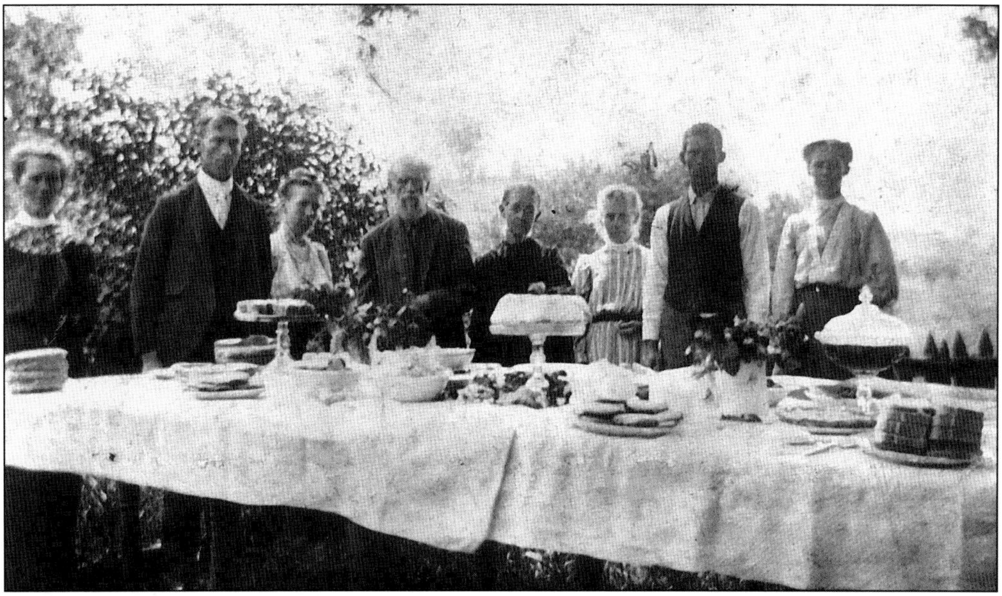

**ARMSTRONG FAMILY REUNION.** This 1912 photograph was taken at a family gathering in French Creek. Pictured, from left to right, are Dora Armstrong Lance, ? Marple, unidentified, Harvey Armstrong, Peggy Armstrong, unidentified, unidentified, and ? Marple. (Photo courtesy of UCHS, Willa Score Collection.)

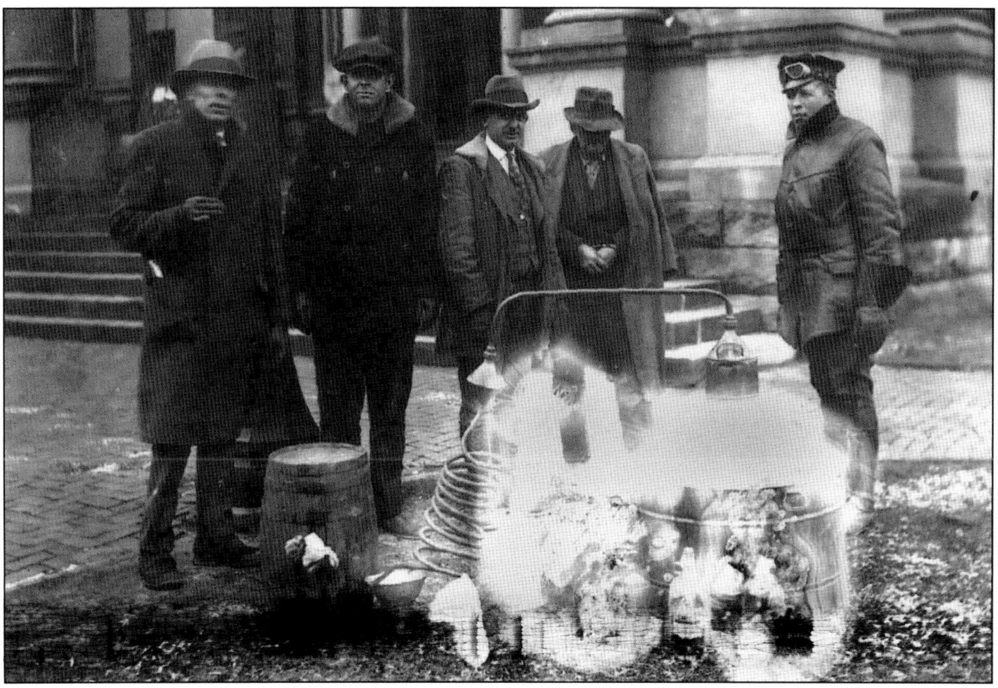

**RAID ON THE BOOTLEGGERS.** This c. 1928 courthouse plaza scene depicts the outlawed bootlegger and his equipment. Pictured, from left to right, are Sheriff Morgan Bailey; State Prohibition Officer Bruce Lambert; Deputy Sheriff Weese Harper; Pat Bailey in handcuffs (the moonshiner and brother to the sheriff); and State Trooper Fred Currence. (Photo courtesy of UCHS, Jean Harper Rylands Collection.)

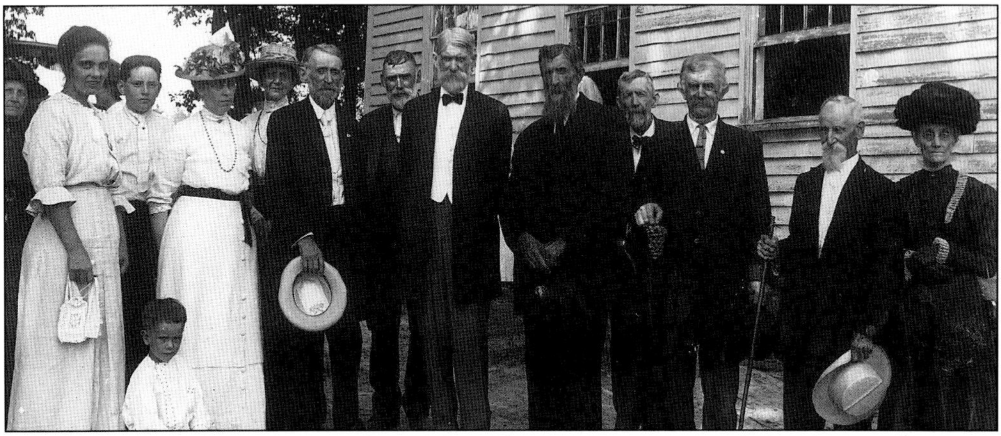

**French Creek Personalities.** This early-20th-century group stands by the French Creek Presbyterian Church. Members of the group are, from left to right, young Arthur Gould in the white shirt, Ida Cooper Gould, Amie Morgan, S. Hall Young, Chandler Gould, William O. Phillips, Layton Gould, Spencer Phillips, unidentified man with grapes, Maranda Rexroad, and Electra Phillips. S. Hall Young was a famous missionary and minister in Alaska. Electra Phillips, as a young girl during the Civil War, traveled alone through enemy territory to the Eastern Panhandle of West Virginia to rescue her wounded Union soldier brother, Franklin, from a Confederate prison. (Photo courtesy of UCHS, Fred Brooks Collection.)

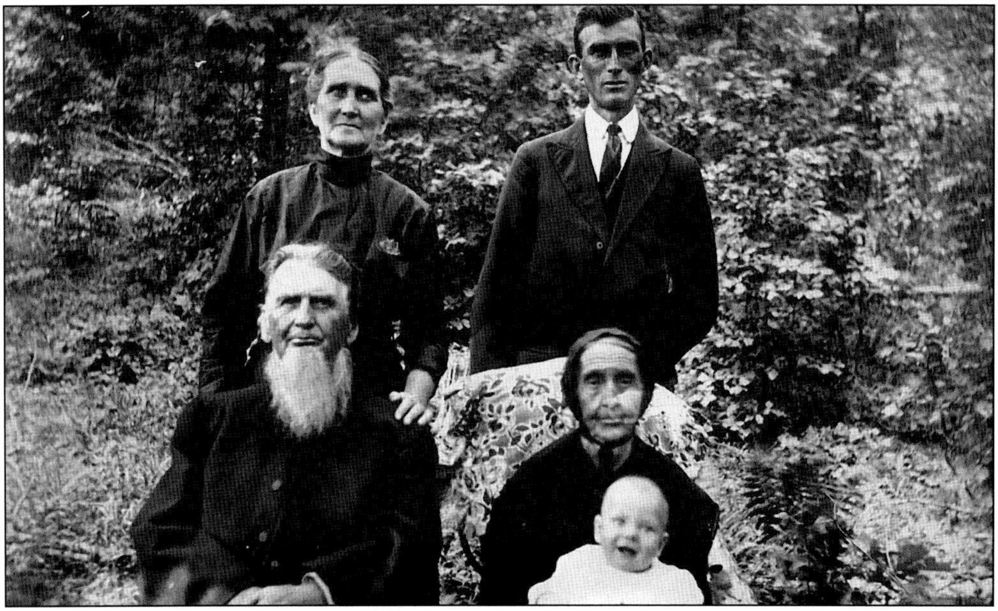

**Five Generations.** This *c.* 1918 photograph depicts five generations of one family. Pictured, from left to right, are (front row) Rev. David Miller Sr., "Granny" Elizabeth Reeves Miller Gibson Snell, and baby Charles Arthur Bailey; (back row) Elizabeth Miller Bailey, and Jacob A. Bailey. Granny Snell lead the first group of German Baptists to Upshur County just before the Civil War and gave land for the Sand Run German Baptist (Dunkard) Church and family cemetery. Her son Rev. David Miller was an early minister in this church. Later, the Snell school would be built near the church. Reverend Miller's daughter Elizabeth was the mother of Jacob A. Bailey and the grandmother of baby Charles Arthur Bailey. (Photo courtesy of UCHS, Nora Bailey Bennett Collection.)

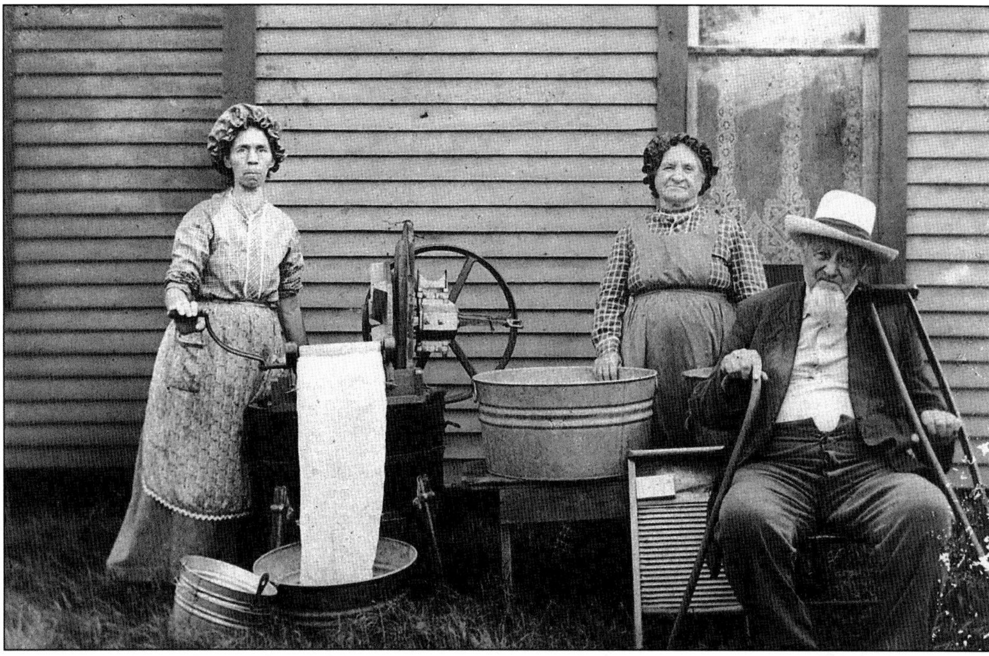

**Washing Day.** This early-20th-century scene shows the mechanics of doing laundry the old-fashioned way. Pictured, from left to right, are Athalena Smith, Fanny Adkisson, and Nathan Allman. (Photo courtesy of UCHS, Charles Waugaman Collection.)

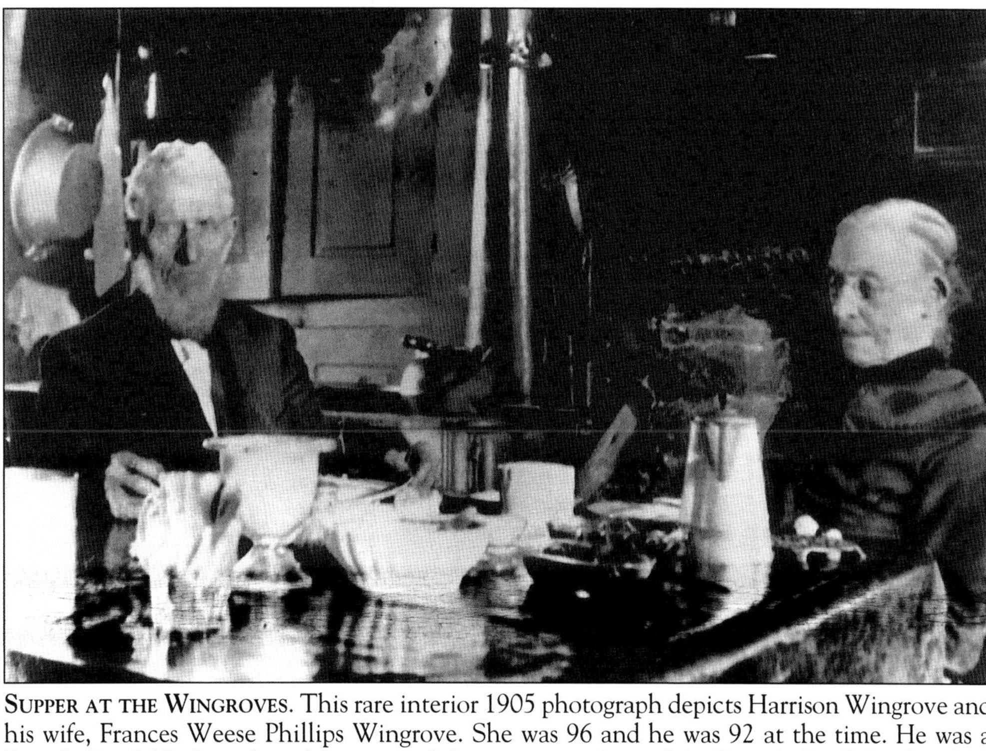

**Supper at the Wingroves.** This rare interior 1905 photograph depicts Harrison Wingrove and his wife, Frances Weese Phillips Wingrove. She was 96 and he was 92 at the time. He was a French Creek blacksmith and farmer, and they were members of the French Creek Presbyterian Church. (Photo courtesy of UCHS, Virginia Bly Hoover Collection.)

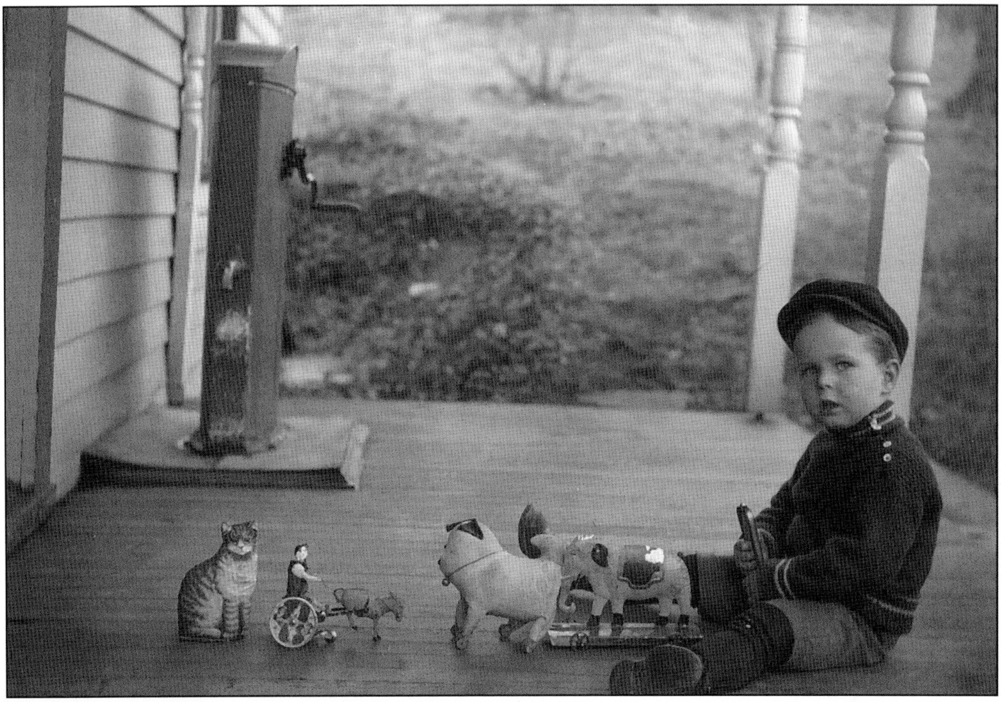

**Dr. Maurice Brooks as a Child.** Maurice Graham Brooks, son of Fred Brooks, was a professor of wildlife management at West Virginia University. He was also a biologist, forester, ornithologist, and an active conservationist. He was recognized as an authority on the region, and his book *The Appalachians* is highly significant. He is pictured here with his toys at home in French Creek, c. 1905. (Photo courtesy of UCHS, Fred Brooks Collection.)

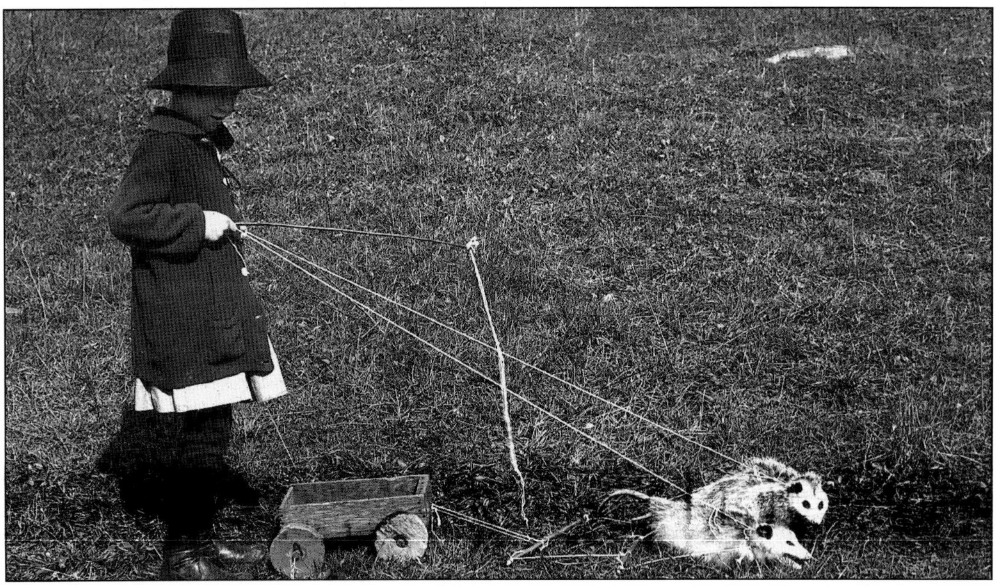

**Dorothy and Her "Possums."** Pictured here, c. 1916, is Dorothy Brooks, daughter of Fred Brooks, with her pet "possums." This is one of many photographs that the great photographer and conservationist Fred E. Brooks made of his children. (Photo courtesy of UCHS, Fred Brooks Collection.)

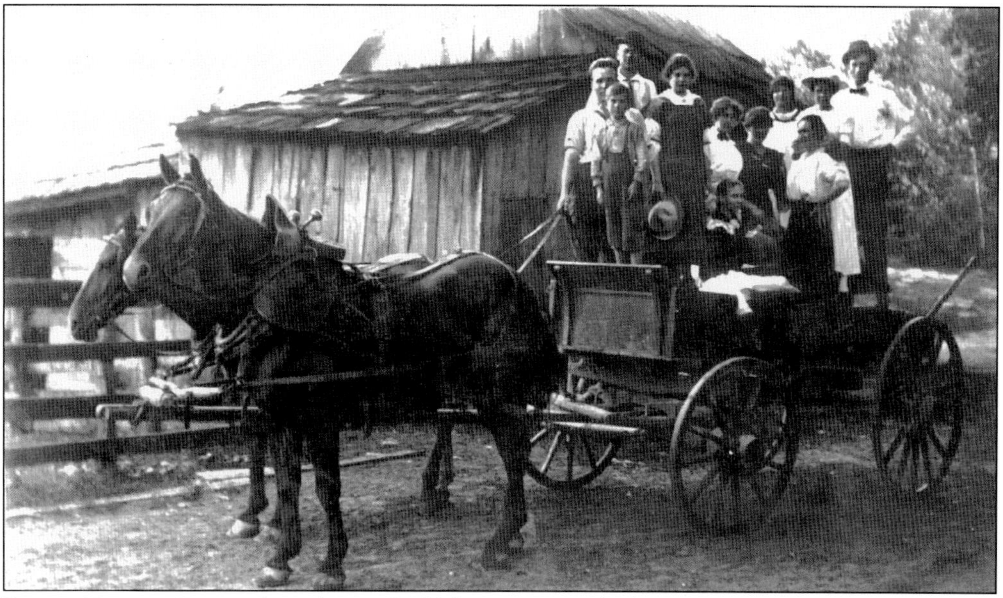

**Bailey Family.** Pictured in this early-20th-century real photo postcard are members of the James Bailey family of Flat Rock in Washington District. Bailey Brothers Undertaking was operated for many years by this family. (Photo courtesy of UCHS, Tom Bailey Collection.)

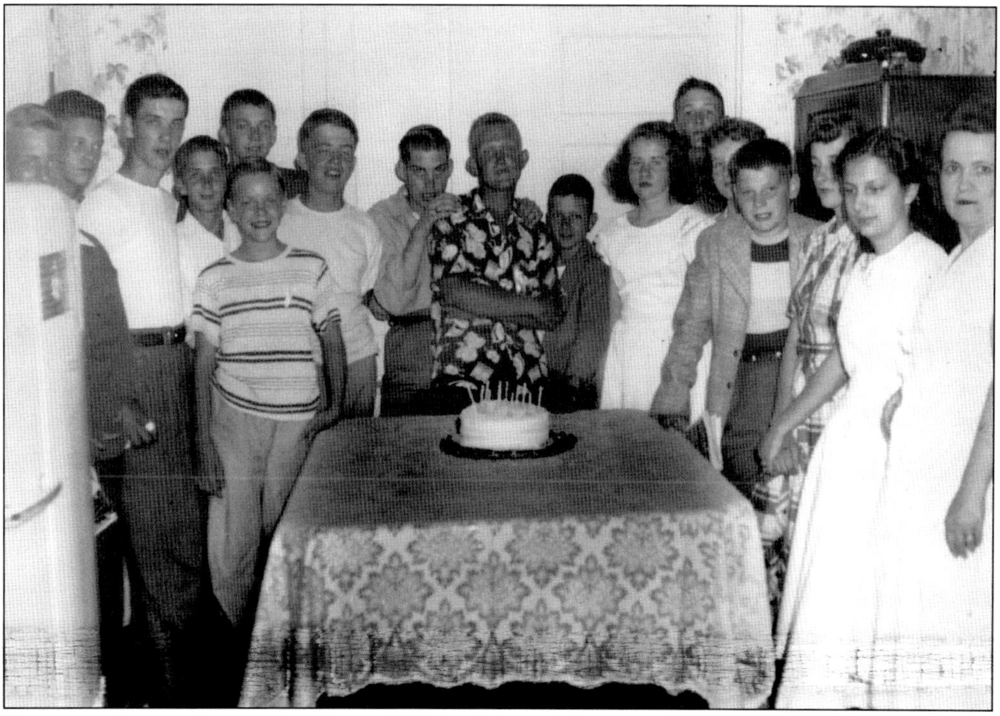

**Birthday Party.** Pictured in this *c.* 1950 birthday celebration, from left to right, are Jim Snyder (behind refrigerator), Don McCoy, Charles Royer, Don Henderson, Dale Groves (behind), Benny Lantz (front, leaning on table), unidentified, Jack Nesbitt, Pete Lantz (birthday boy), Mel Hager, Marie Iden, Louie Hoover, Barbara Iden, Jim Gaston, Linda Hoylman, Sue Shomo, and Lou Lantz. (Photo courtesy of UCHS, Beth Martney Collection.)

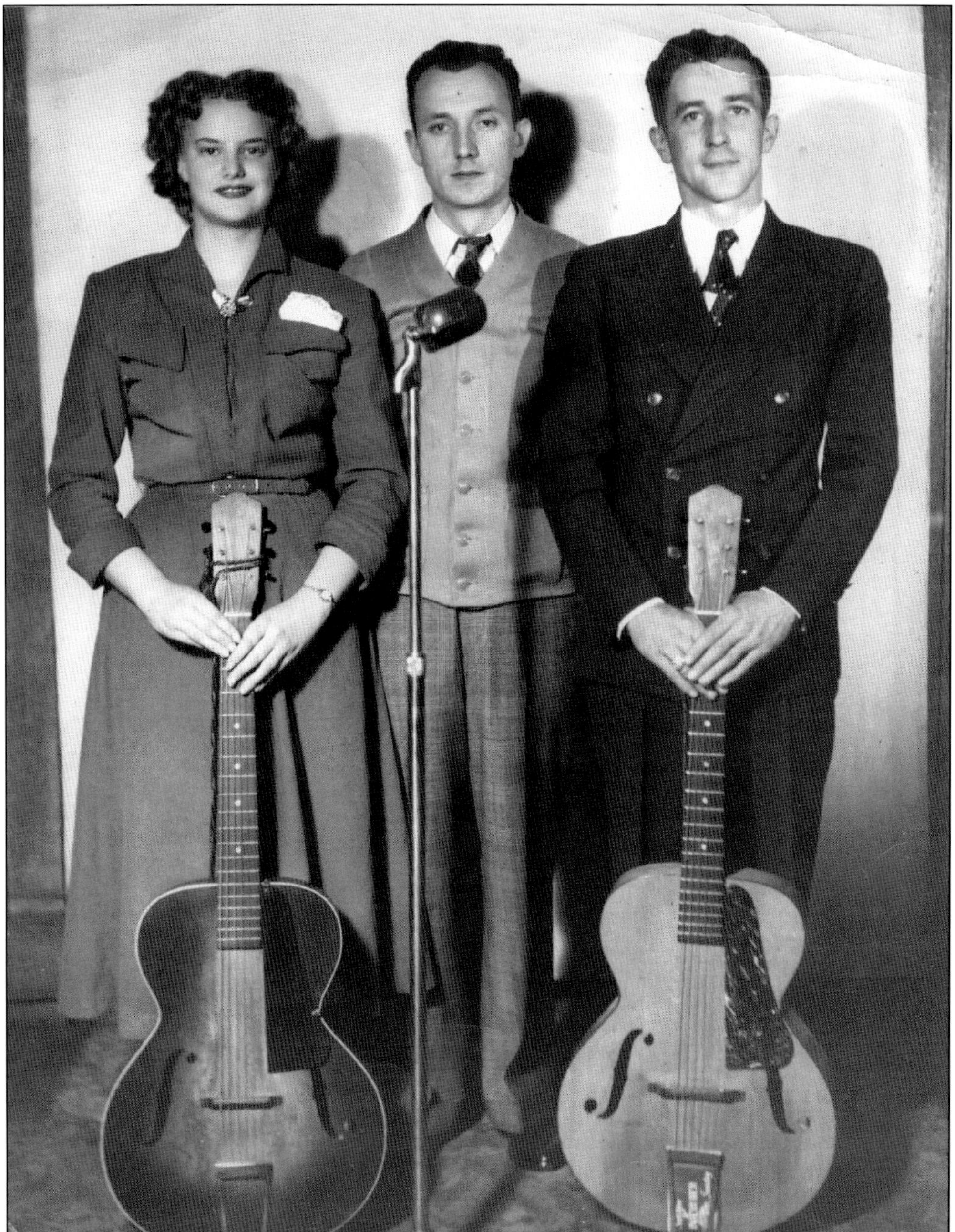

**Gospel Singers.** Pictured in this 1951–1952 photograph by Wilton Ray Tenney are Gilda Woody (left), Gay Bennett (center), and Carius Campbell. Gospel singing was very popular during the early half of the 20th century in this area. The Upshur County Singers Association was established in 1925 with the first "county sing" held in Heavner's Grove with 3,000 people attending. By 1934 the convention had been moved to the Jackson Grove in Tennerton and close to 15,000 attended. "Above the singing which 'must be sacred and in keeping with the day' rises the sound of laughter and a thousand conversations," states the WPA project, *West Virginia: A Guide to the Mountain Sate*. (Photo courtesy of UCHS, Beth Martney Collection.)

# *Four*

# CHURCHES AND RELIGION

*The earliest denominations into Upshur County were the Baptists and Methodists. Following those were the Presbyterians, United Brethren, Dunkards, and Catholics. By far the Methodists outnumbered all of the other denominations with both a Methodist Episcopal and Methodist Protestant congregation in practically every community of the county. There were a few Methodist Episcopal South or Southern Methodist congregations along with the African Methodist of the black community. The first Buckhannon Methodist was called the "Old Carper Church." The Baptists established their congregation in 1786 as a mission of the Bridgeport Simpson Creek Baptist. The Presbyterians pretty much started with the New Englanders. The Dunkards arrived shortly before the Civil War from the Shenandoah Valley of Virginia. The United Brethren first began meetings in the early 1850s and, in recent years, combined with the various Methodist denominations to create the United Methodists. Although some of the above denominations have disappeared, many others are to be found in Upshur County today.*

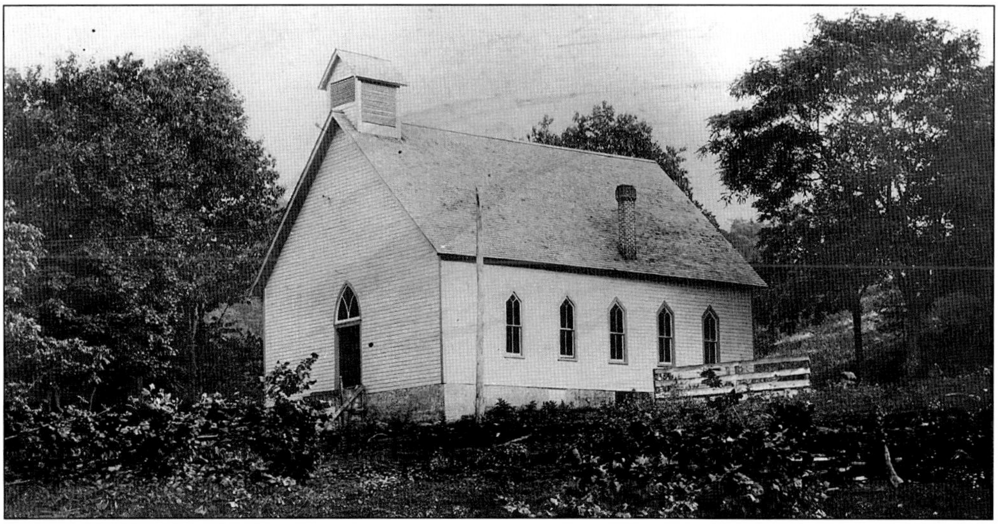

**ALEXANDER ME CHURCH.** This image shows the typical rural-style church buildings, found throughout Upshur County, with their simple end gable construction, steeple, and gothic windows. This c. 1930 photograph shows the Alexander Methodist Episcopal Church just before it was destroyed by fire. (Photo courtesy of UCHS, Ruth Taylor Collection.)

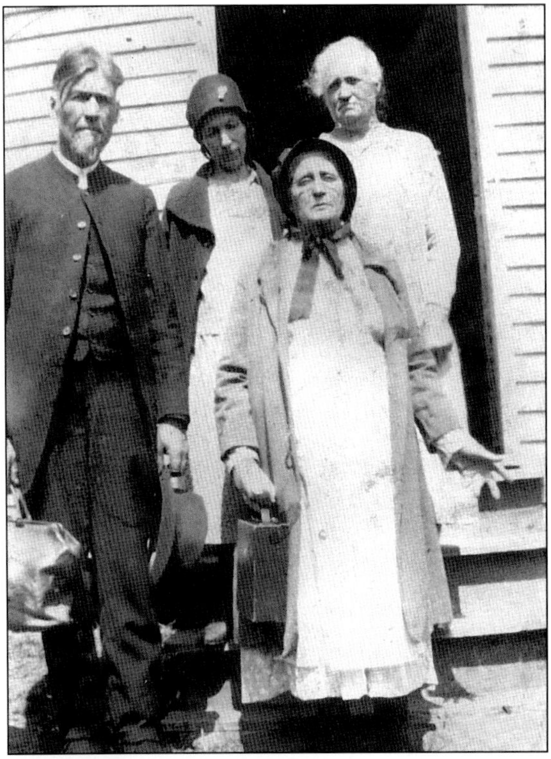

**Dunkards.** Members of the Beans Mill German Baptist Church (also commonly referred to as the Dunkards) in 1919, from left to right, are Reverend Rowe, Emma Wyatts, Dora Wamsley, and Elbana Bean. This denomination first came to Upshur County just prior to the Civil War and established churches at Sand Run, Goshen, Buckhannon, and Indian Camp. In 1902 the Indian Camp congregation was moved to Beans Mill. (Photo courtesy of UCHS, Millie Lewis Collection.)

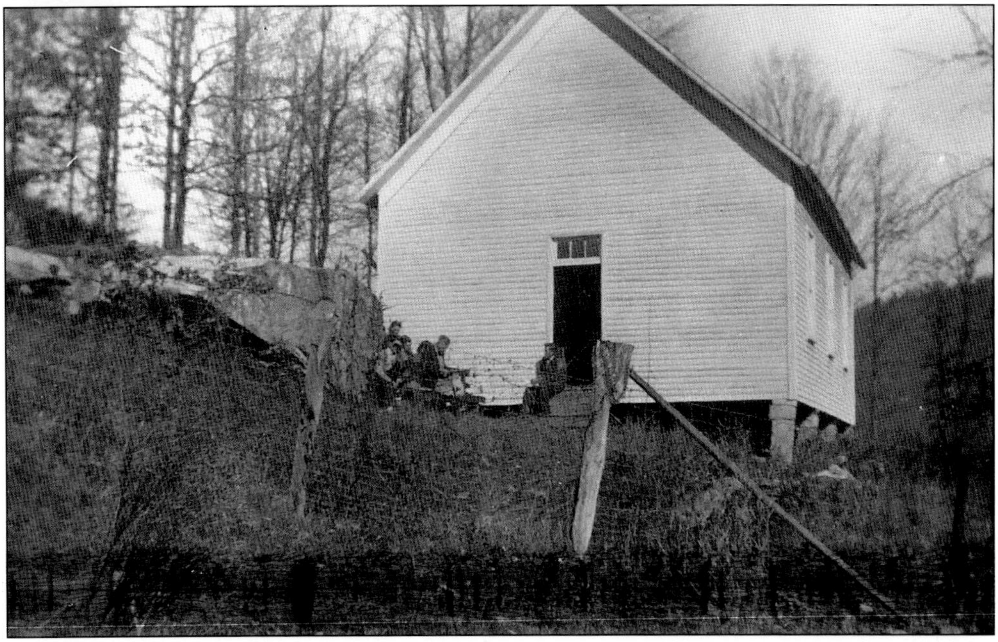

**Beans Mill Dunkard Church.** Picture here, *c.* 1919, is the simple end gabled church of the Beans Mill German Baptists located in southern Upshur County. While most rural church buildings of that era had two front doors, separate for men and women, this congregation used only one entrance, perhaps signifying equality between the sexes. (Photo courtesy of UCHS, Millie Lewis Collection.)

**Old Baptist Church.** This was the second building used by the Buckhannon Baptist congregation. The church was established in 1786 and their first building was of logs. It was built in 1814 and located near Finks Run in what is now known as the old Baptist Cemetery lot. The building pictured here was constructed c. 1850 on North Locust Street. During the Civil War it was commandeered by the Federal government as a food commissary and hospital. During the war years, the minister of this church Rev. Matthew Maddox was charged with preaching "Southern doctrine" and died in prison camp at Camp Chase in October, 1863. (Photo courtesy of UCHS, Betty Hornbeck Van Kirk Collection.)

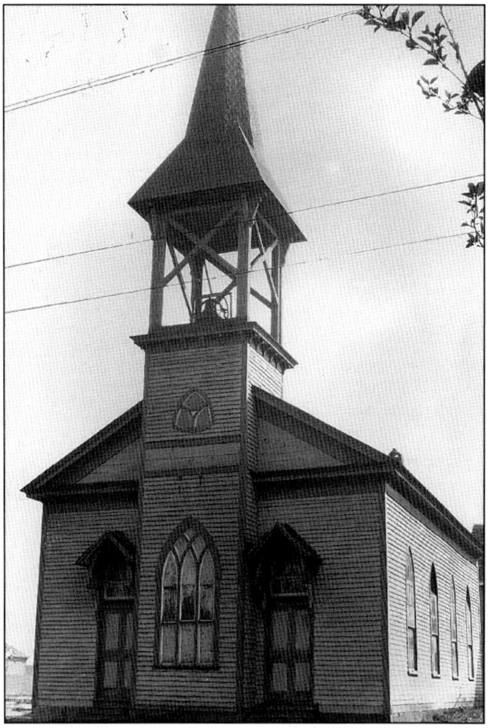

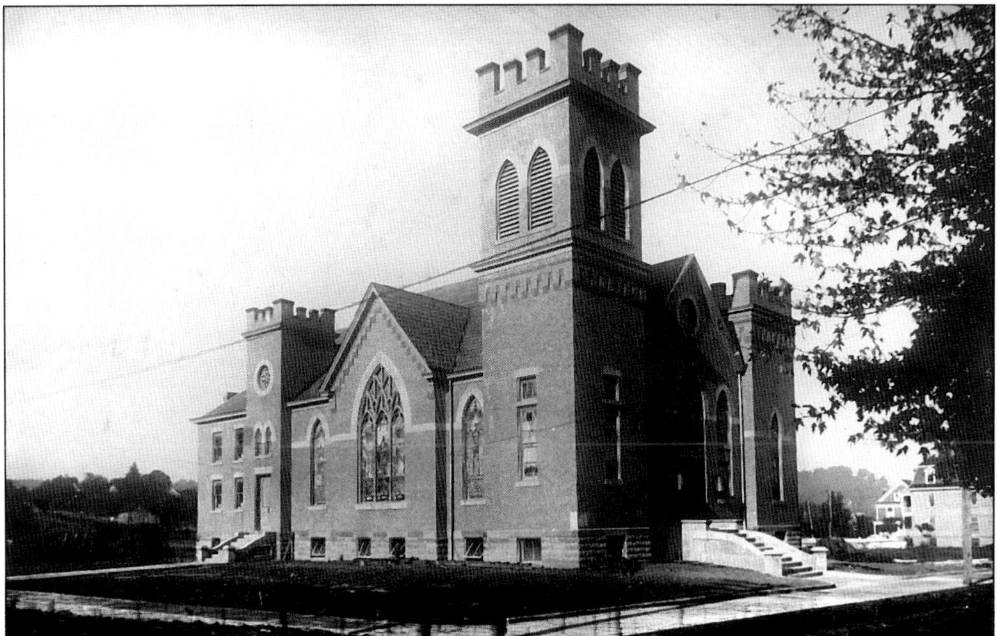

**New Baptist Church.** Pictured here is the new and third Buckhannon Baptist Church under construction in 1911. It is located on South Florida Street. This congregation was first organized out of the Simpson Creek Baptist Church in Bridgeport. Organizing members of this early congregation were Jacob and John Hyre, Jacob and John Brake, and Major Jackson. (Photo courtesy of UCHS, Matt Edmiston Collection.)

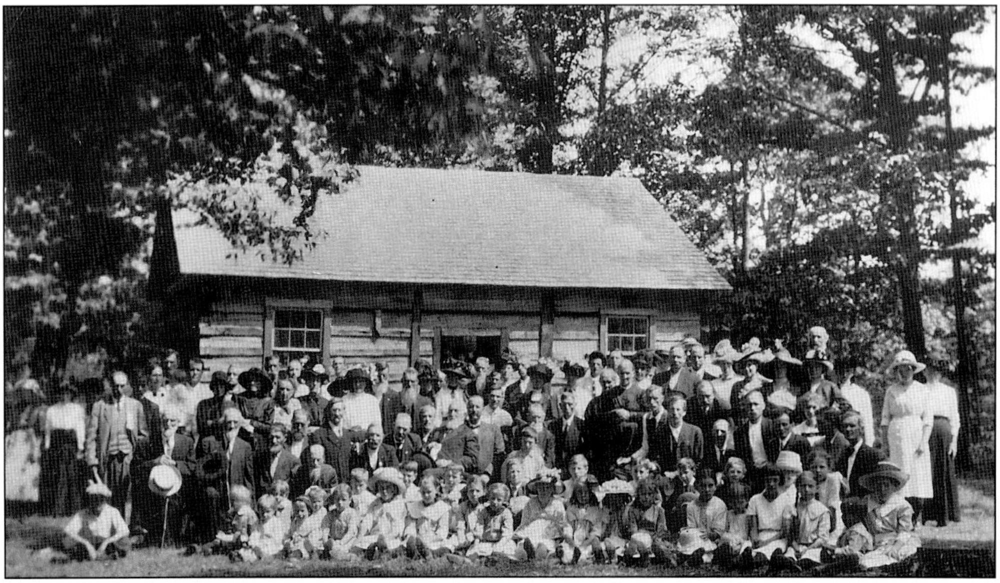

**Old Indian Camp EUB Church.** This reunion group photo was taken during the 1920s in front of the old church building. The Indian Camp Evangelical United Brethren congregation was first organized in 1864. Until this building was constructed in 1865, services were held under the historic Indian Camp Rock, which is nearby. The building was used until 1889 when a wooden structure was built some distance away. The third building, made of brick and tile, replaced the second one in 1954. (Photo courtesy of UCHS, Brian Huffman Collection.)

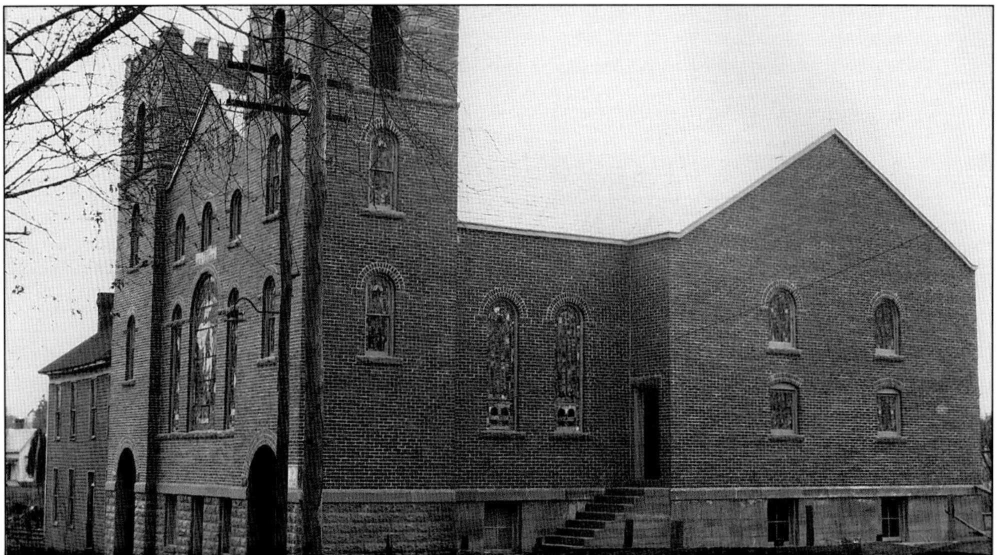

**Buckhannon EUB Church.** The Buckhannon congregation began as class meetings in various homes in the early 1850s when the denomination was called United Brethren in Christ. The first wooden building was constructed in 1873 on South Florida Street. In 1909, when this Hode Clark photograph was taken, the original wooden structure was "turned halfway around, a basement put under it, an addition put on the rear of the building, and then covered with brick." This congregation later joined to create the United Methodist denomination. (Photo courtesy of UCHS, Alan Sturm Collection.)

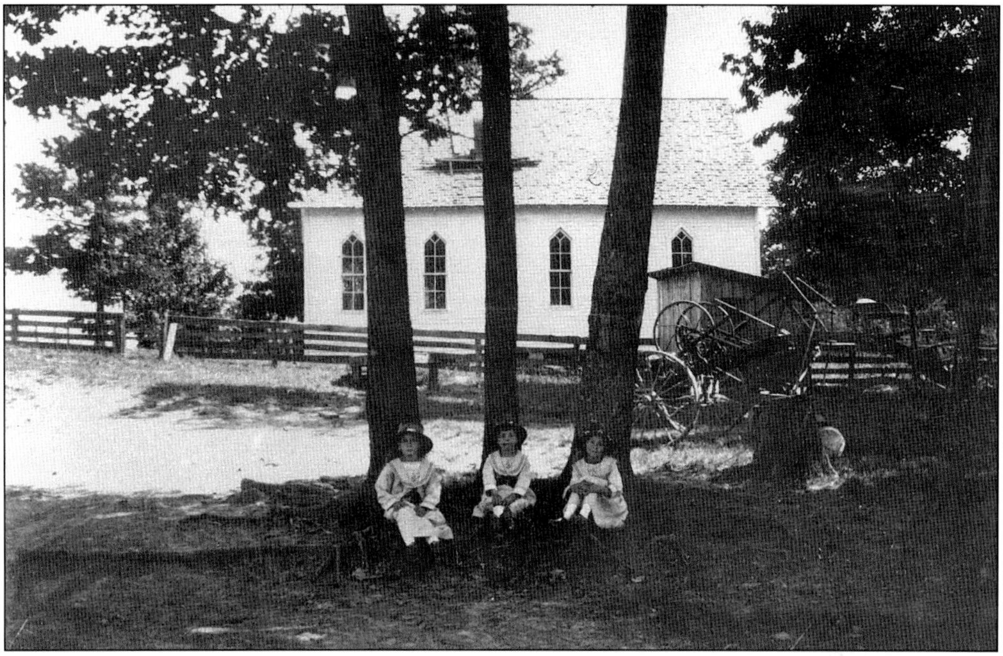

**CHILDREN AT MT. UNION.** Pictured in this *c.* 1920 James Arthur Simmons photograph are his daughters, Leota (left), Geraldine (center), and Pauline Simmons. In the background is the Mt. Union ME Church building, which was constructed in 1893. The original congregation first met in a log building across the road. That area today is the second largest cemetery in Upshur County. (Photo courtesy of UCHS, Sheila Tenney Thomason Collection.)

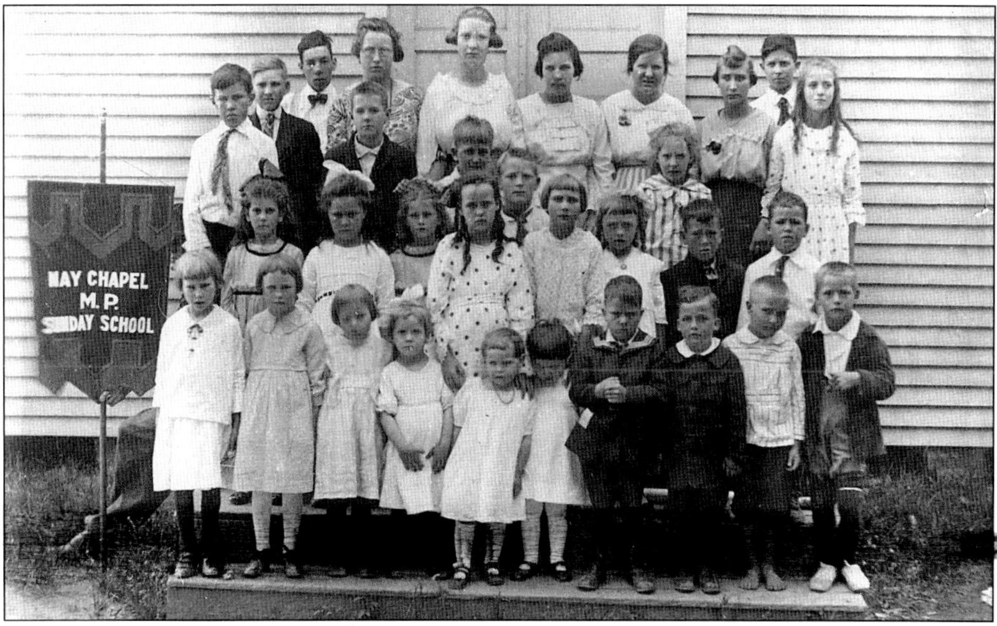


**NAY CHAPEL SUNDAY SCHOOL.** This early-20th-century photograph was taken of the children's Sunday school group at the Nay Chapel MP Church located atop the Coal & Coke Railroad tunnel in Union District. None of these children are identified. (Photo courtesy of UCHS, Sheila Tenney Thomason Collection.)

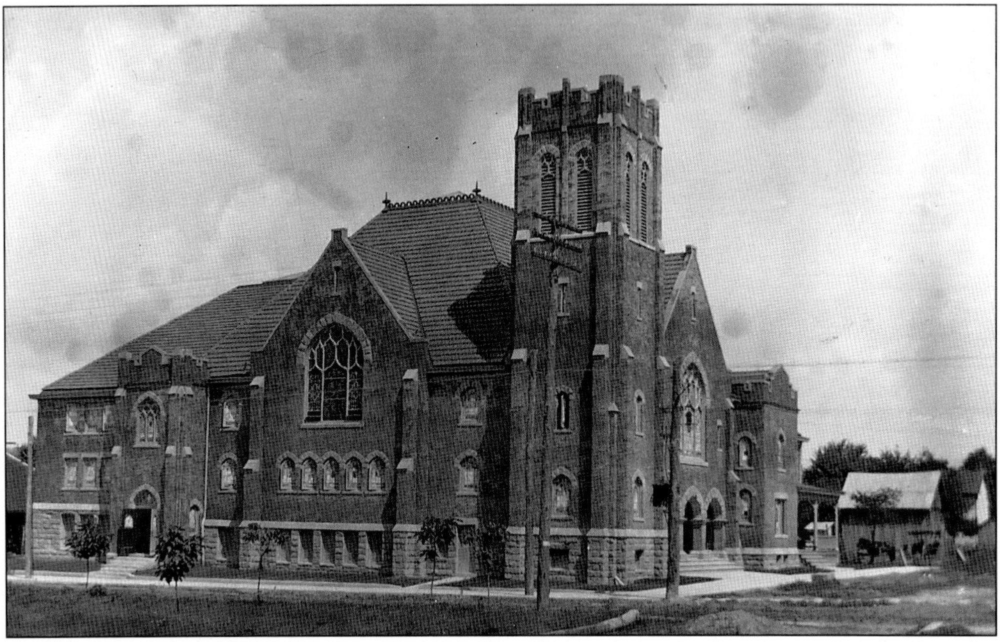

**FIRST UNITED METHODIST CHURCH, BUCKHANNON.** Pictured here in 1911 at its dedication is the fourth and present building used by this major Upshur County denomination. The congregation first gathered in the home of Abraham Carper Sr., and when the original log structure was built on a site "between Kanawha Street and the hill a little west of the College Avenue corner," it was named the "Carper Church." In 1850 the second building was constructed on the corner of Main and Florida Streets, and in 1883 the third building was dedicated at the location of today's Buckhannon City Hall and formerly the post office. By 1911, the congregation needed more space and built this commodious building on South Florida Street. (Photo courtesy of UCHS, Alan Sturm Collection.)

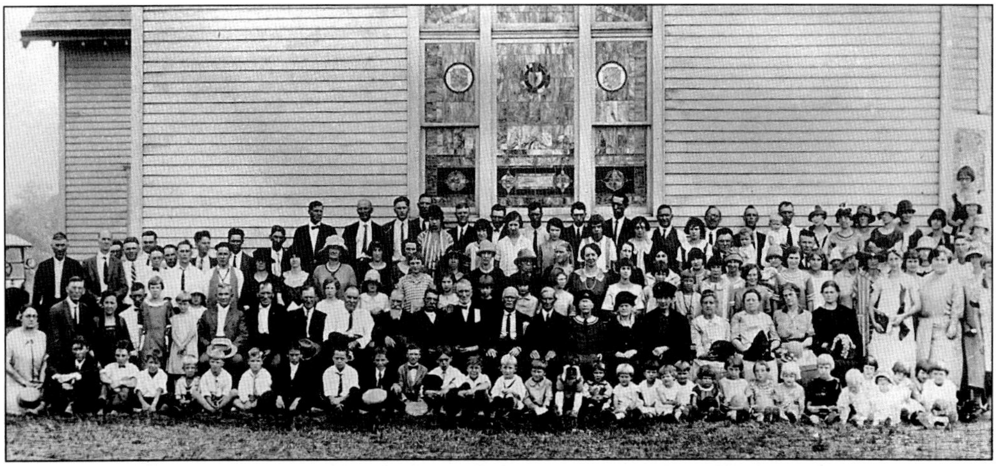

**FRENCHTON CHURCH GROUP.** Pictured here in the 1920s is the congregation of the Wesley Chapel Methodist Episcopal Church in Frenchton. This religious society was first organized in 1816 and their first log building was constructed in 1837, followed by a frame building in 1863. The name Wesley Chapel was given at that time, but sometimes the church was referred to as the Beechtown Church. In 1922, the new building, pictured here, was dedicated. (Photo courtesy of UCHS, Anna Lee Combs Collection.)

**BUCKHANNON PRESBYTERIAN CHURCH.** Established in 1849, the Buckhannon Church was first located on the corner of Kanawha and Lincoln Streets but was destroyed during the Civil War. The building pictured here was dedicated in 1879 and is located beside the fire station on Locust Street. The Buckhannon Presbyterians attempted to establish a college here in 1859 to be known as the "Baxter Institute," however, the Civil War prohibited the completion of the Meade Street/College Avenue building. The school was never established. (Photo courtesy of UCHS, Phyllis Miller Collection.)

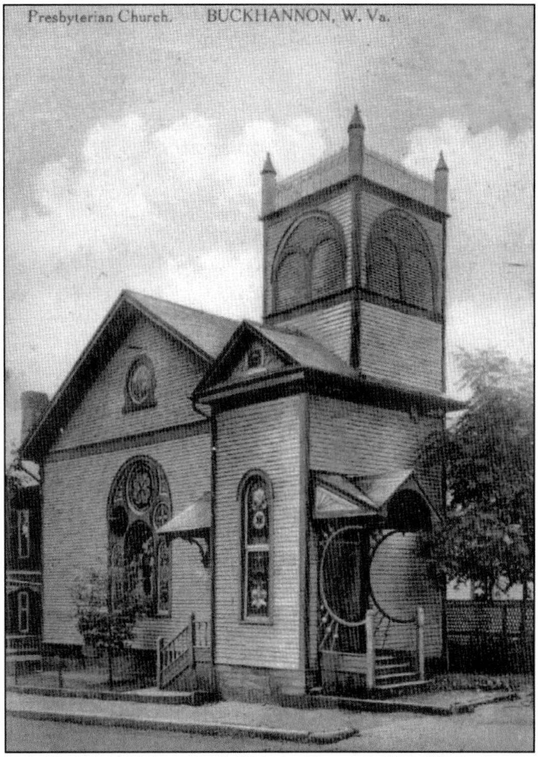


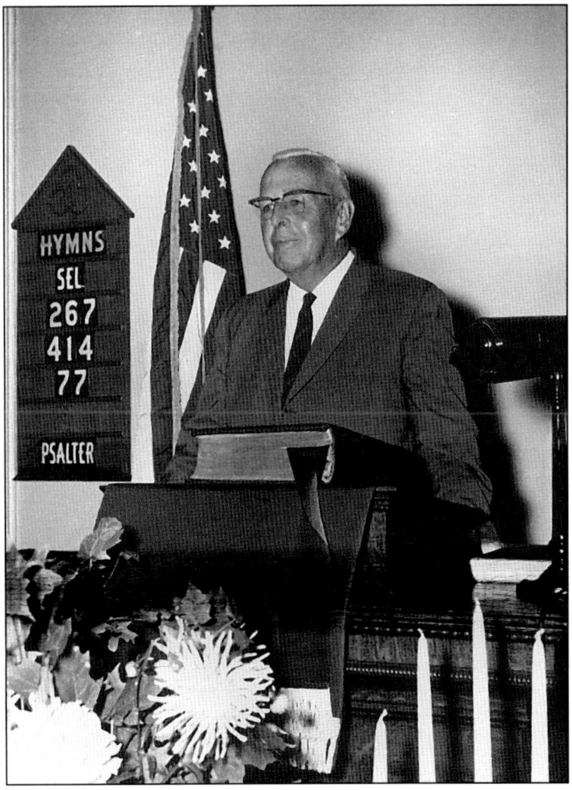


**FRENCH CREEK PRESBYTERIAN CHURCH.** Pictured here in 1969 is French Creek native son Dr. Maurice Brooks. The French Creek community was settled in the early 1800s by New Englanders, and in 1816 Rev. Asa Brooks organized the Presbyterian Church. The first building was constructed of logs in 1824, and the second one, built in 1851, was a frame structure. This building was accidentally burned during the Civil War when occupied by Federal troops. Future U.S. President, Rutherford B. Hayes, a Union lieutenant slept at least one night in that structure. The present building was constructed in 1866. The first Upshur County Temperance Society was organized at French Creek in 1828, and the first Bible Society was organized in 1829. (Photo courtesy of UCHS, Virginia Bly Hoover Collection.)

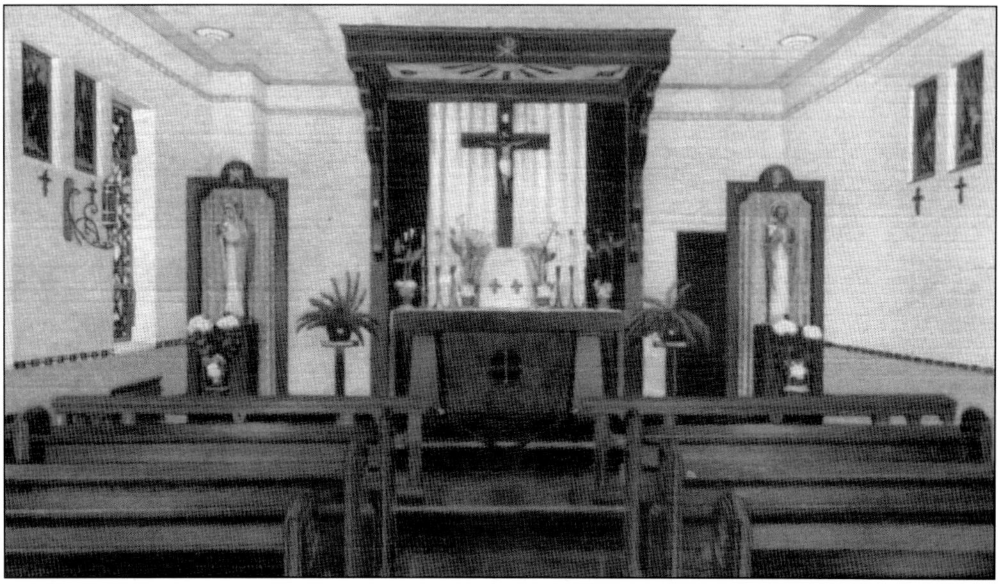

**CHAPEL AT ST. JOSEPH'S HOSPITAL.** Pictured in this 1930s postcard is the small hospital prayer chapel maintained by the Catholic Pallottine Missionary Sisters. The Catholic Church in Upshur County began *c.* 1861 in Union District with a group of Irish road builders. By 1875 the log building on the McDermott farm was replaced with a frame structure on the Fallon property and relocated in 1923 to the Vegan area. In Buckhannon, the first church building was located on Meade Street in 1895. After St. Joseph's Hospital opened in 1921, the Buckhannon church was relocated to Franklin Street in 1923. A Catholic parochial school was opened in connection with the church in 1922. The present building of the Holy Rosary Church on Main Street was built in 1959–1960. (Photo courtesy of UCHS, Noel W. Tenney Collection.)

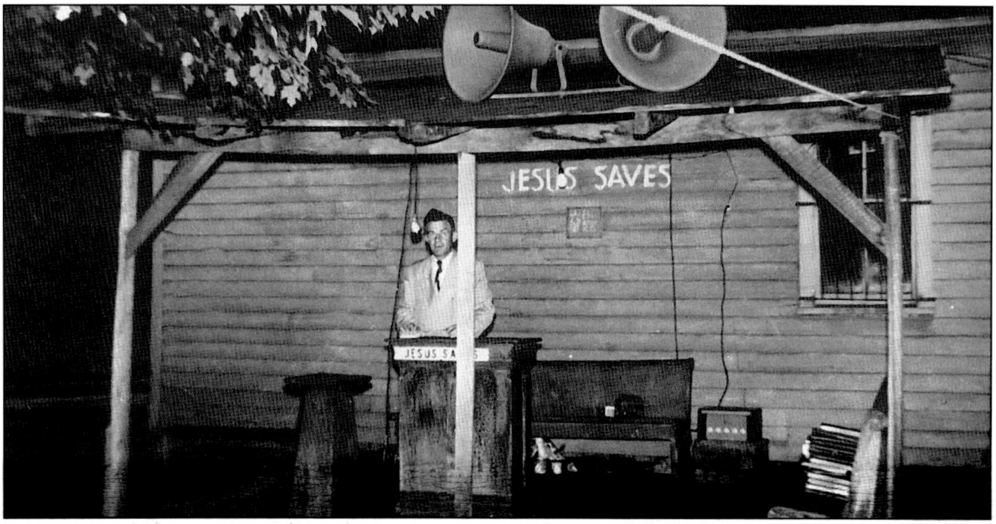


**CAMP MEETING.** This haunting 1957 night photograph shows Rev. Meade Gutshall preaching at a camp meeting in the Lantz community in Union District. Born in 1920, this young minister was an energetic and charismatic speaker, and hundreds of people attended his revivals and camp meeting services. Upshur County is rich in religious heritage and includes many denominations and ecclesiastical traditions. (Photo courtesy of UCHS, Lemoyne Wentz Wolfe Collection.)

# *Five*

# Schools and Education

*Schools began in the Buckhannon Valley with those established on Glady Fork in 1790 and on Radcliff's Run [near Skateland] in 1797. These were examples of "subscription" schools. Locations were as diverse as the formal building at Beechtown to the school held in "Wash Tenney's kitchen."*

*With the formation of West Virginia on June 20, 1863, one of the first acts of the state established "a system of free schools." At that time counties were divided into magisterial districts. Each community had a one-room school and the district had a school board responsible for maintaining the buildings and hiring teachers. The law established that there would be a school building for every four square miles, thus placing the buildings about two miles apart. It was also established that if students had to walk more than two miles, they were to be paid. By 1905, the A.B. Brooks map contained 117 district schools.*

*Institutions of higher education in Upshur County included Buckhannon Male and Female Academy, 1847–1866; French Creek Academy, 1871–1885; West Virginia Classical and Normal Academy, 1882–1897; West Virginia Wesleyan College, 1890–present; Indian Camp Normal, 1913–1918; and the Baxter Institute, which never really rose above its foundation.*

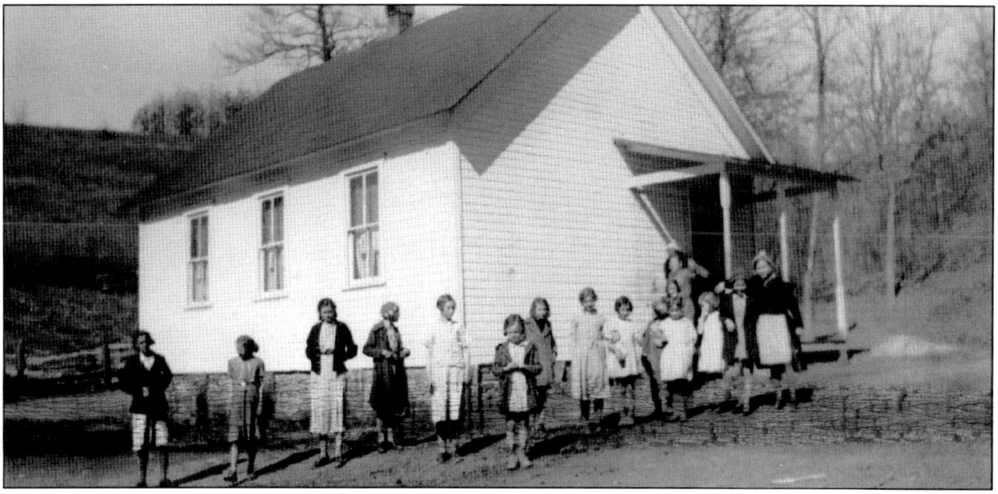

**Truby Run School.** Pictured here is the Washington District school with Beulah Koon as teacher in the 1930s. This is the typical style of end gable building that was used from the Civil War era until the 1920s in Upshur County for schools. The building still stands today. (Photo courtesy of UCHS, Noel W. Tenney Collection.)

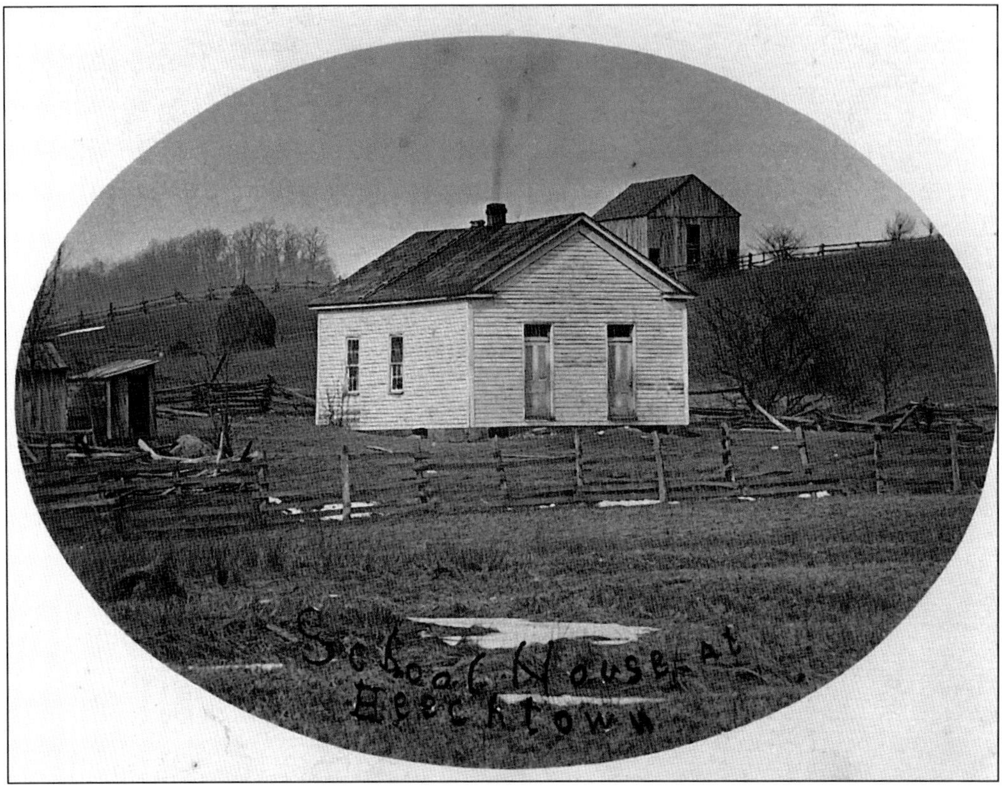


**Beechtown School.** Pictured above is one of the earliest Upshur County one-room schoolhouses; it is located near Frenchton in Banks District. (Photo courtesy of UCHS, Mary Alice Bragg Collection.)

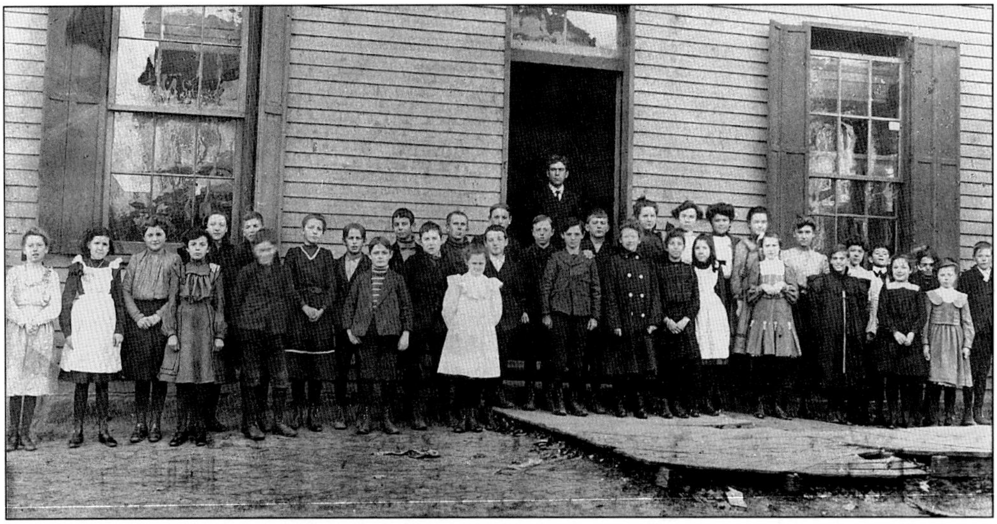

**East Main Street School Group.** This early-20th-century photograph contains unidentified students attending the first Buckhannon elementary school. The teacher was James Albert Grim. and by 1908, the building was no longer in use. At that time a new building was constructed next door. That building was in use until the 1990s and presently houses the Stockert Youth Center. (Photo courtesy of UCHS, Charles Waugaman Collection.)

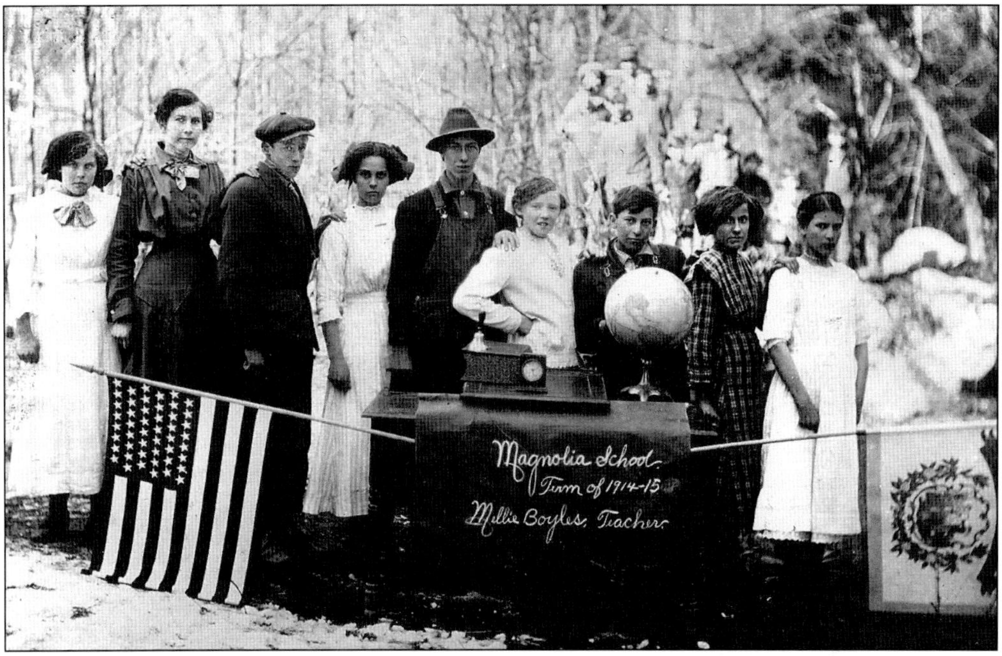


**MAGNOLIA SCHOOL GROUP.** This unidentified group of students at the Meade District school in 1914–1915 poses for the official class photograph. Other students in the background await their turn. Teacher Mellie Boyles appears second from the left. Often, the teacher was younger than the older students since teachers were hired with only an eighth-grade diploma and a teacher's certificate. (Photo courtesy of UCHS, Boyles Carter Collection.)

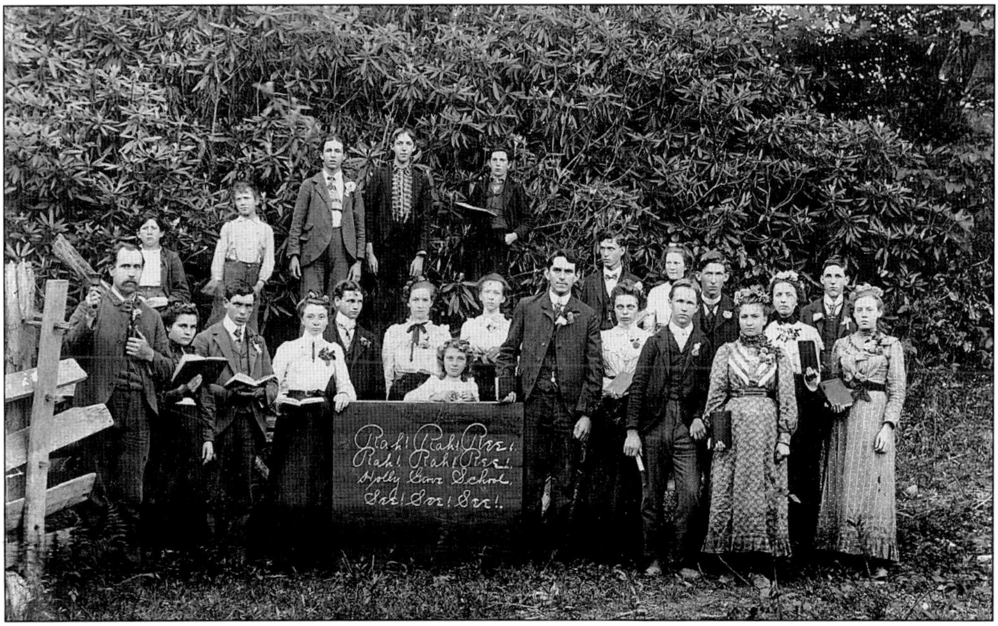


**HOLLY GROVE SCHOOL GROUP.** "Rah, Rah, Ree, Holly Grove School, See, See, See," is about all that is known concerning this c. 1900 Banks District school group. It would appear that the teacher is at the far left, holding the bell. Most likely this is a "last day of school" portrait since everyone is bedecked in flowers. (Photo courtesy of UCHS, Boyles Carter Collection.)

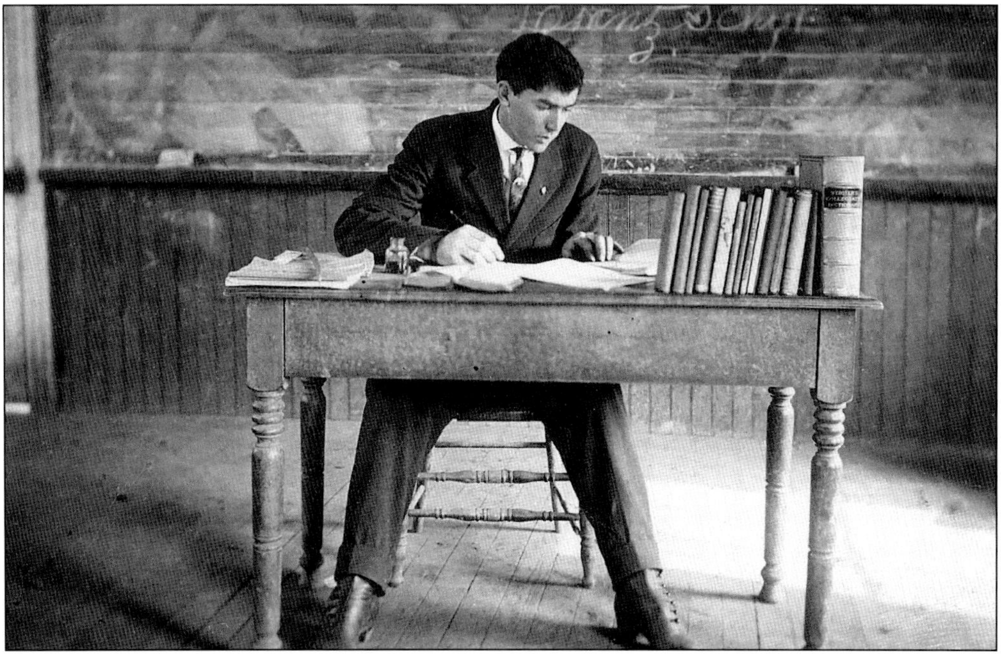

**Thomas Miles, Teacher.** Pictured here, in a rare interior school photograph, is Thomas Miles, a teacher at the Lorentz School in the early 20th century. Teachers of this era often completed a "Normal" teacher training program rather than having a college degree. (Photo courtesy of UCHS, Ralph Miles Collection.)

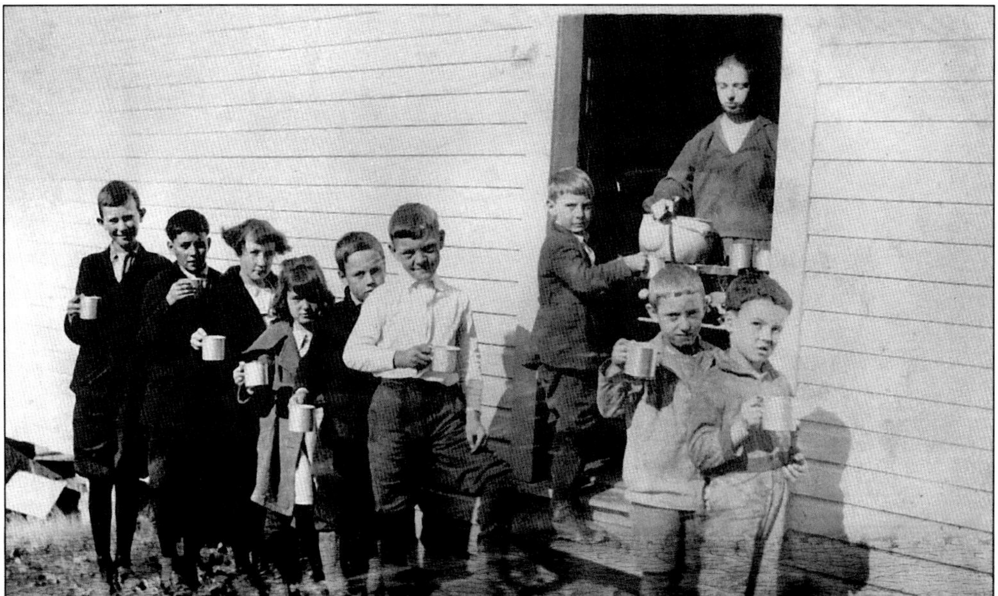

**Hot Lunch Program at Bridge Run School.** This 1922–1923 photograph depicts a very early hot lunch program put into operation by the teacher/cook Ireta Queen, pictured in the doorway. The students and teacher brought food and it was cooked on the small kerosene stove. Students here are unidentified except for Howard Queen, brother to the teacher, standing sixth from the left. (Photo courtesy of UCHS, Ireta Queen Randolph Collection.)

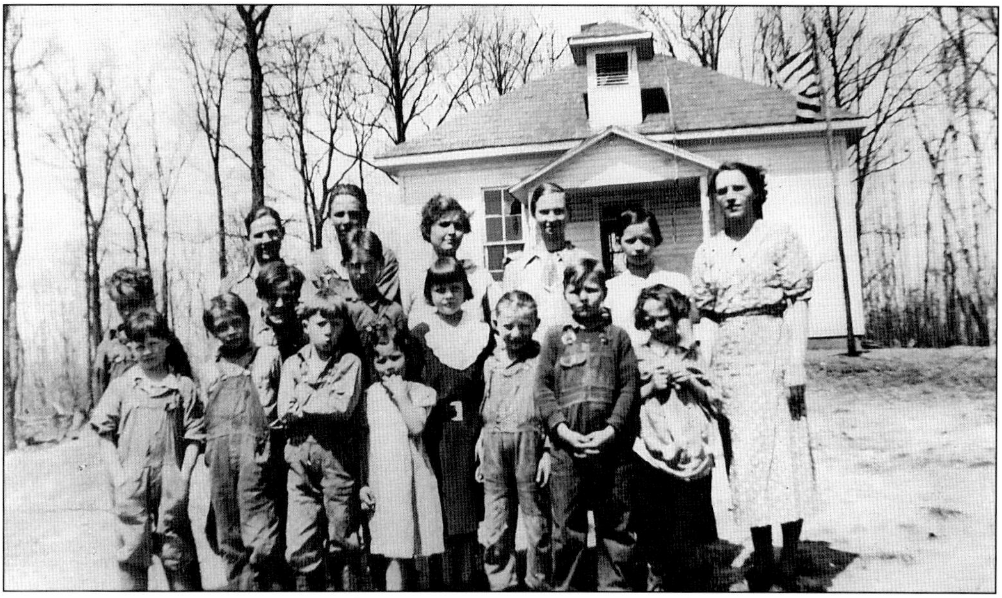

**UPPER TEN MILE SCHOOL.** Teacher Ruth Wamsley Taylor is pictured on the far right with these unidentified Washington District students, *c.* 1937. The pyramidal-roof style of one-room schoolhouses became popular around 1920 as a replacement to the simpler end gabled buildings like the one pictured below. (Photo courtesy of UCHS, Ruth Taylor Collection.)

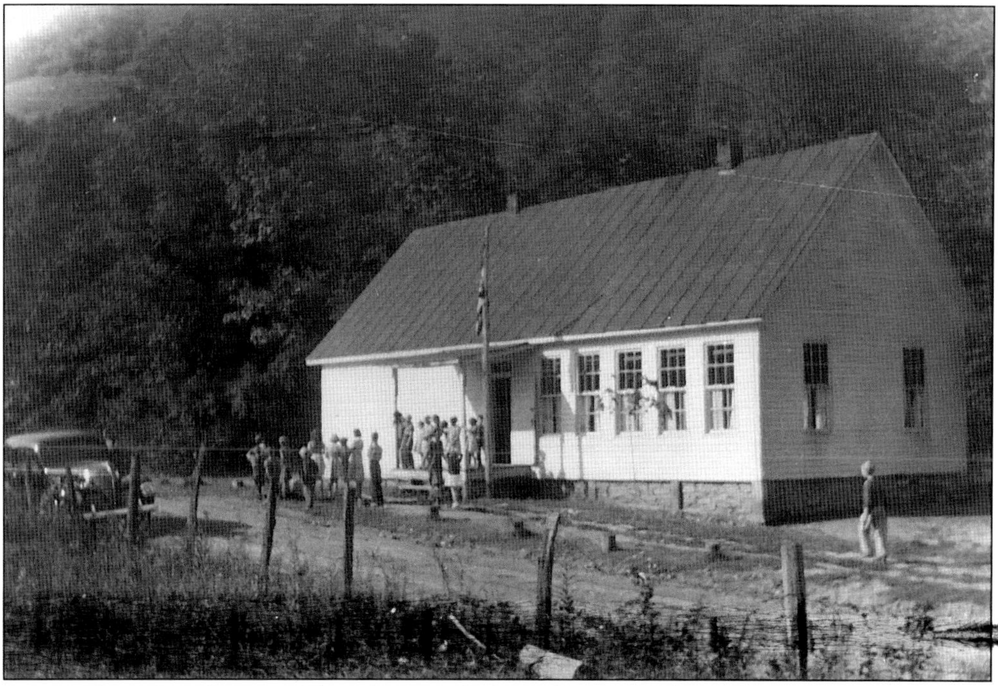

**LOWER TEN MILE SCHOOL.** This photograph from the 1930s shows the larger school located just about two miles from the one pictured at Upper Ten Mile. The law required that students not have to walk more than two miles to school, thus every community had its own. This Washington District building had been enlarged from one room to two because of the larger population. (Photo courtesy of UCHS, Avis Smallridge Collection.)

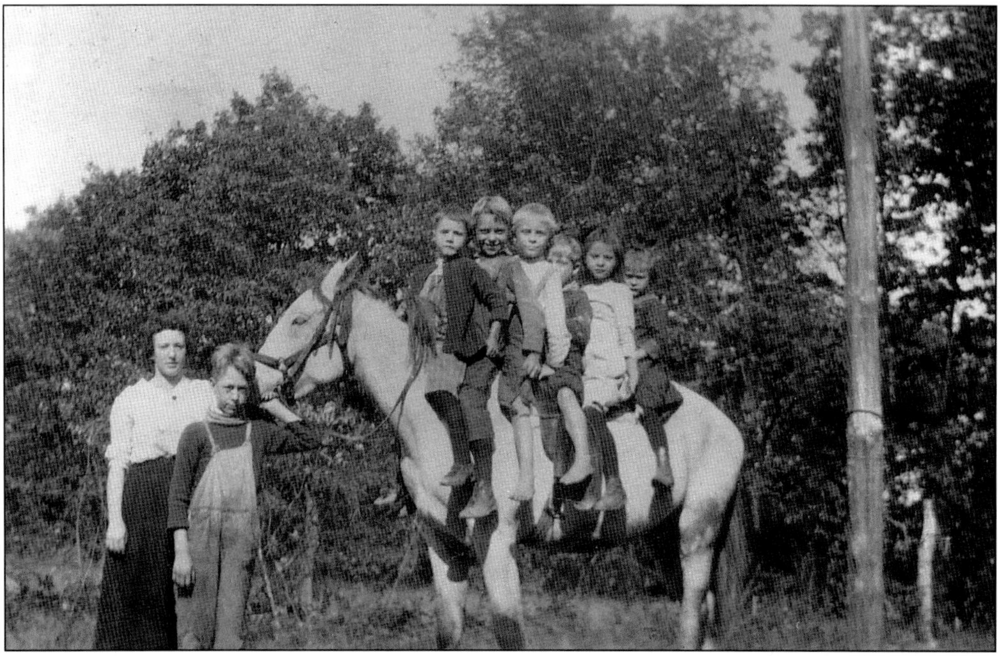

**A Horseback Ride at School.** This *c.* 1919 photograph depicts children sitting on their teacher's horse at the Kesling School before the time of school buses. Teacher Elsie G. Shreve at the far left, and Curtis Wentz is the front rider. The other students are unidentified. (Photo courtesy of UCHS, Lemoyne Wentz Wolfe Collection.)

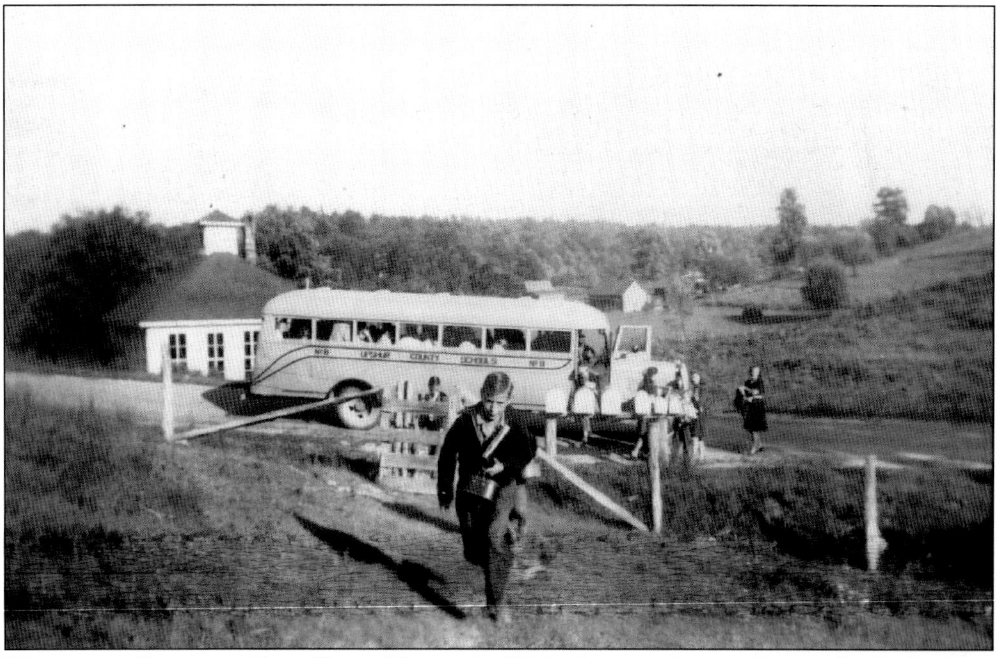

**Home from School in Flat Rock.** This early 1940s photograph was taken at the Bailey farm in Washington District. Pictured are Tom Bailey (running in front); Bill Bailey (going through the fence); and Juanita Koon (in front of the bus, in the dark dress). Bob Hanifan was the bus driver. (Photo courtesy of UCHS, Tom Bailey Collection.)

**AFRICAN-AMERICAN VICTORIA SCHOOL GRADUATION PROGRAM.** In the early part of the 20th century, following the move of the African-American school from Franklin Street, a new building was located on Victoria Street (approximately where the board of education warehouse is now located). With the 1913 arrival of Principal C.W. Warfield, a full high school, four-year college preparatory course was initiated. This building burned in 1925, and the Upshur County Board of Education erected a new brick structure to house the first through twelfth grade black school on Baxter Street. This was now the center of the African-American community; there was also a black church located nearby. (Document courtesy of UCHS, permanent collection.)

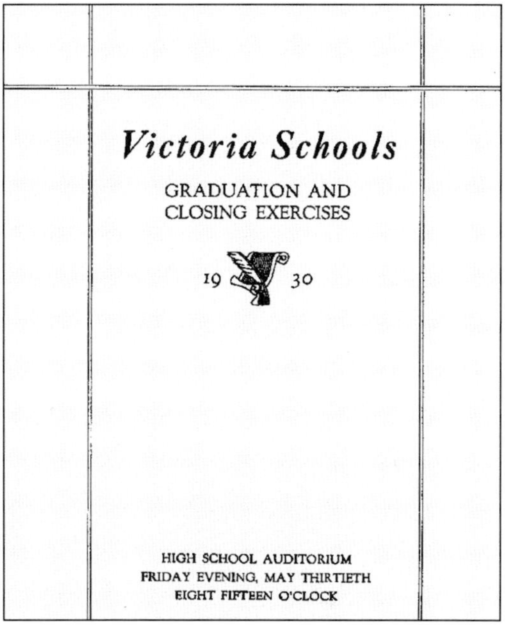
Victoria Schools

GRADUATION AND CLOSING EXERCISES

19 30

HIGH SCHOOL AUDITORIUM
FRIDAY EVENING, MAY THIRTIETH
EIGHT FIFTEEN O'CLOCK

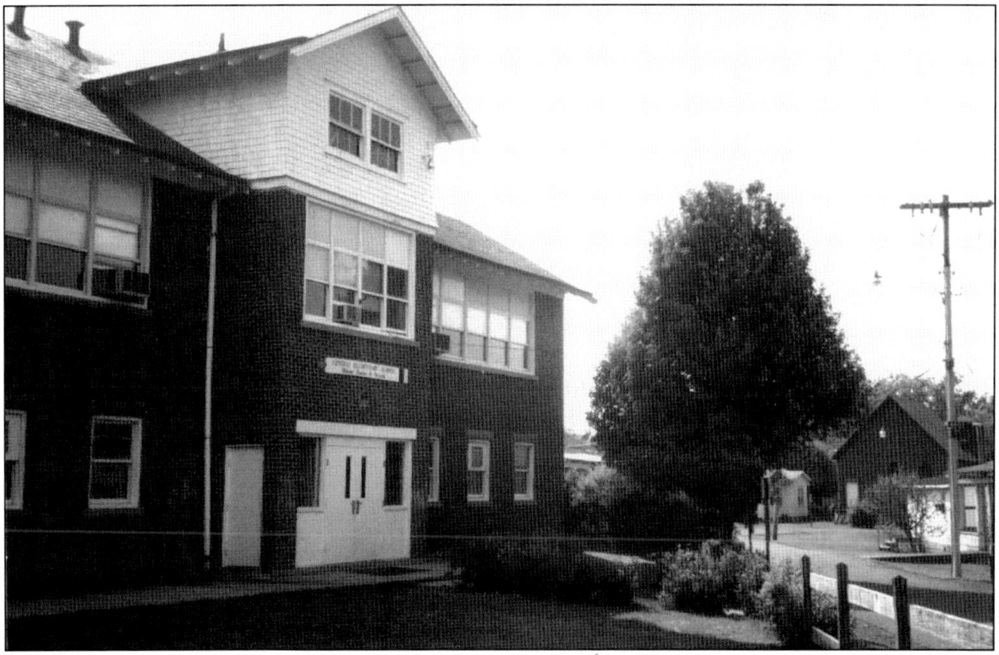

**VICTORIA SCHOOL.** The Victoria School continued until 1949, by which time Buckhannon's African-American community had dwindled drastically. The few remaining high school students were transported to the Kelly Miller School in Clarksburg, and a small wooden building was constructed beside the black church on Latham Street for the remaining elementary students. As pictured here, the old Victoria School became Central Elementary School in the fall of 1949. African-American students continued to use their own small building until the 1950s when they were finally integrated into the regular schools. Few today know of the rich black heritage of Buckhannon's own Victoria School. (Photo courtesy of UCHS, permanent collection.)

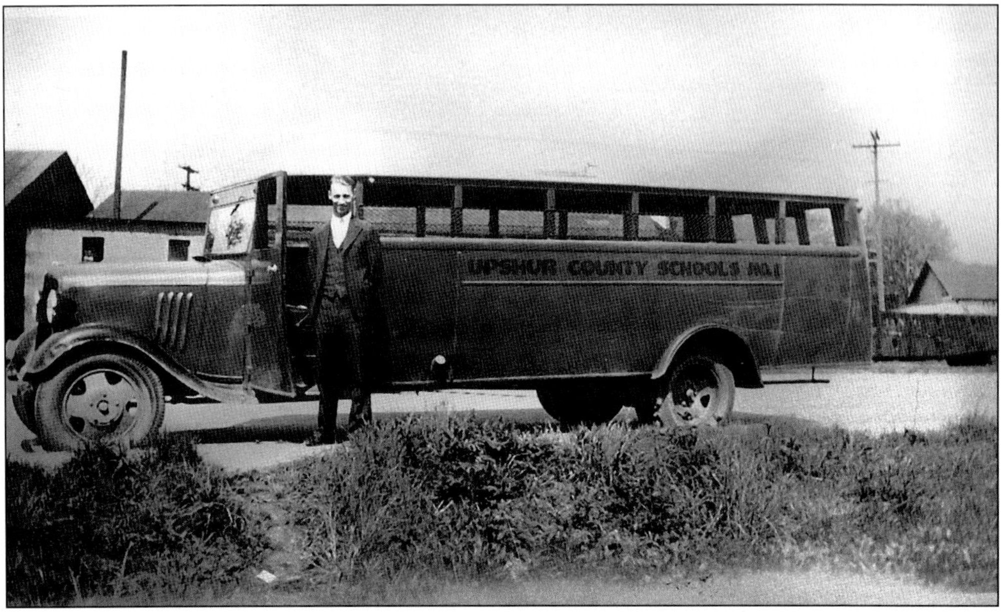


**UPSHUR COUNTY SCHOOL BUS #1.** Upshur County schools began operating free school bus service to students in the 1930s, and "Old Number 1" is pictured here with the first county school bus driver, Madison Carr, in 1937. (Photo courtesy of UCHS, Madison Carr Collection.)

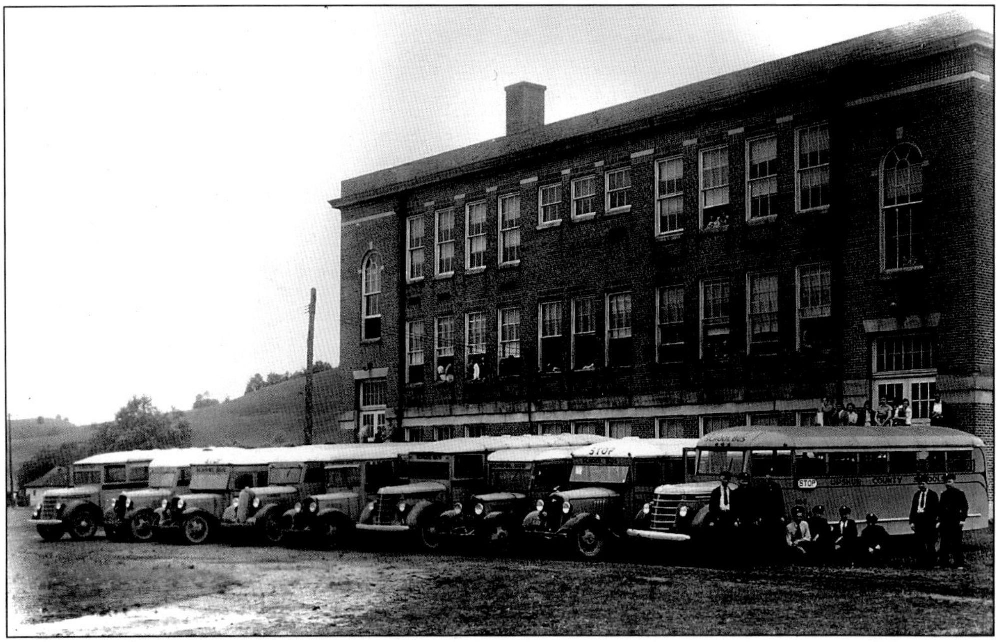

**THE SCHOOL BUS FLEET, 1937.** In 1933, West Virginia initiated the "county system" abolishing district boards of education. School consolidation began slowly at that time as did the providing of school bus transportation. Pictured here in 1937, in front of the Upshur County High School, is the entire fleet of school buses for the county. At that time there were still 98 one-room schools throughout the county. (Photo courtesy of UCHS, Madison Carr Collection.)

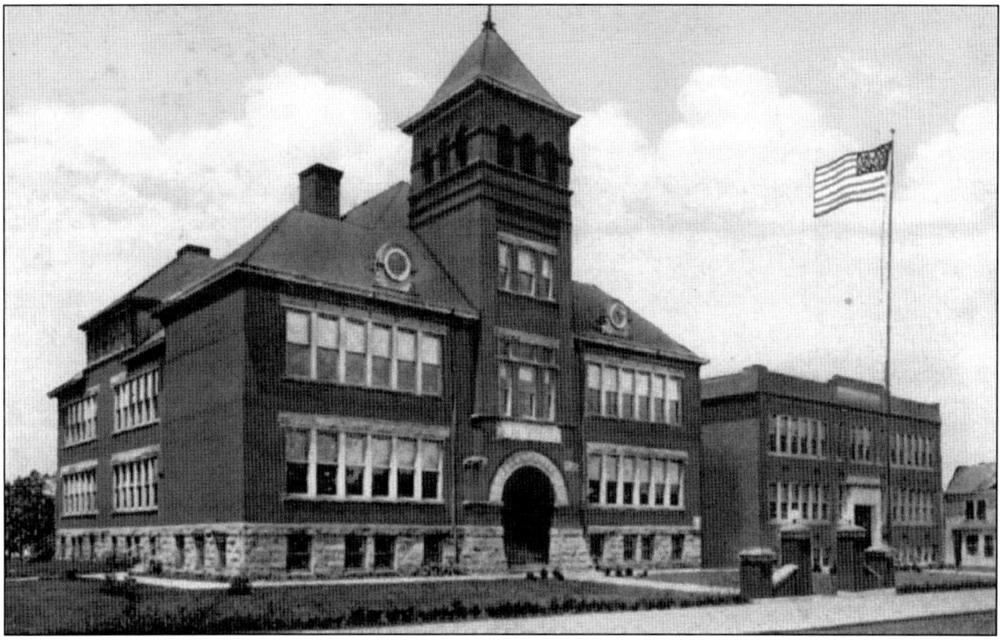

**BUCKHANNON HIGH SCHOOL.** Buckhannon High School had its beginnings in the old East Main Street School building in 1886. In 1908, a modern brick building was constructed on College Avenue, pictured here in this postcard. (Photo courtesy of UCHS, Phyllis Miller Collection.)

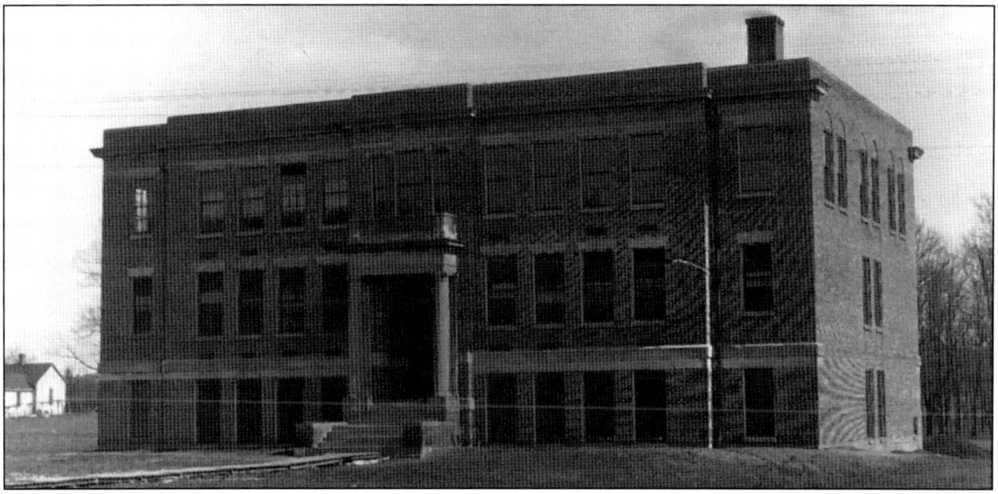

**UPSHUR COUNTY HIGH SCHOOL.** This Hode Clark photograph depicts the newly constructed Upshur County High School, 1923–1924, in Tennerton. This school was created to serve primarily rural county students. This school and Buckhannon High School functioned separately until the county system of 1933. At that time the schools were joined under the name Buckhannon-Upshur High School, City Division and Tennerton Division, yet with town and country students still separated. In 1959, with additions to the Tennerton building, the high school was consolidated into one center and the Junior High School was created on College Avenue in the old building. In 1976 a new high school building was opened three miles south of Tennerton, and in 1991 the old College Avenue building was demolished. (Photo courtesy of UCHS, Alan Sturm Collection.)

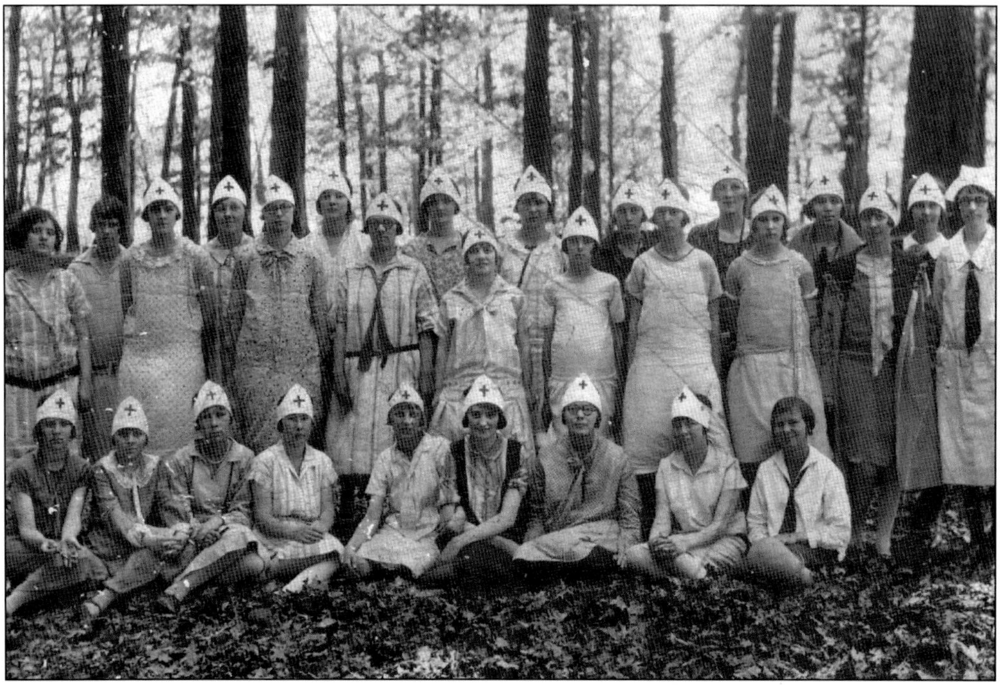

**Upshur County High School Nursing Class.** In this 1920s photograph, the nursing students are unidentified except for Leila Tenney, seventh from the left on the front row. The county high school had various vocational courses such as agriculture and nursing. This photograph was taken in the Jackson Grove at the back of the school. (Photo courtesy of UCHS, Leila Tenney Ours Collection.)

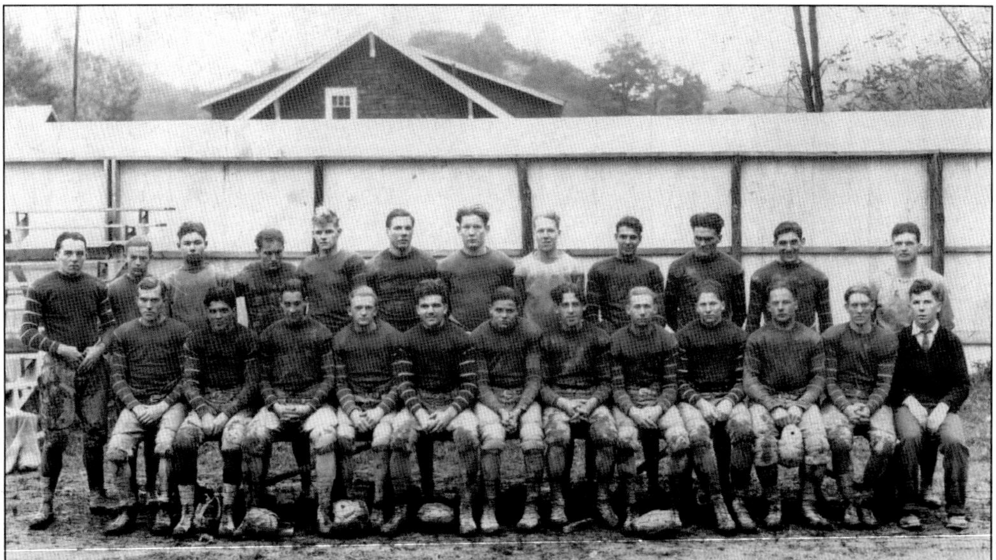

**Upshur County High School Football Team.** This mid-1920s photograph depicts the beginnings of the football program at the new county high school. The only athletes identified are Newton Anderson (far left) and Mayford Ours (center rear). (Photo courtesy of UCHS, Richard Anderson Collection.)

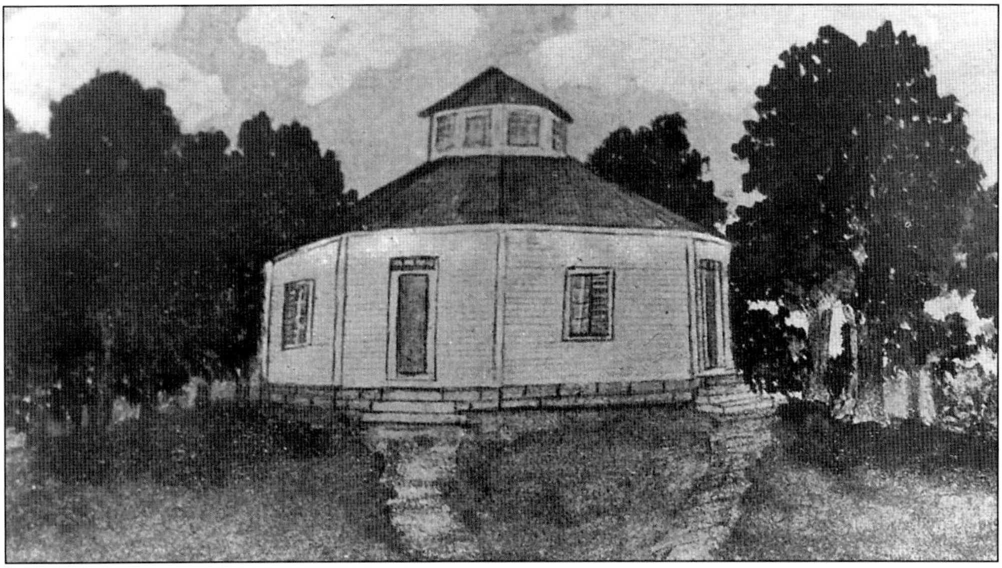

**French Creek Institute.** Pictured in this Hode Clark photograph of an early drawing is the "Academy" at French Creek. The people of that settlement brought with them their New England "piety, love of education, thrifty ways, hatred of slavery, temperance, frugality, willingness to work hard, and love of neighbor." In 1871 the French Creek Institute (the "Academy") was established "to be a male and female academy to train up teachers and promote education generally." The first principal was Rev. Loyal Young and others included Myra Brooks, J. Loomis Gould, and R.A. Armstrong. This school continued until 1885. (Photo courtesy of UCHS, Alan Sturm Collection.)

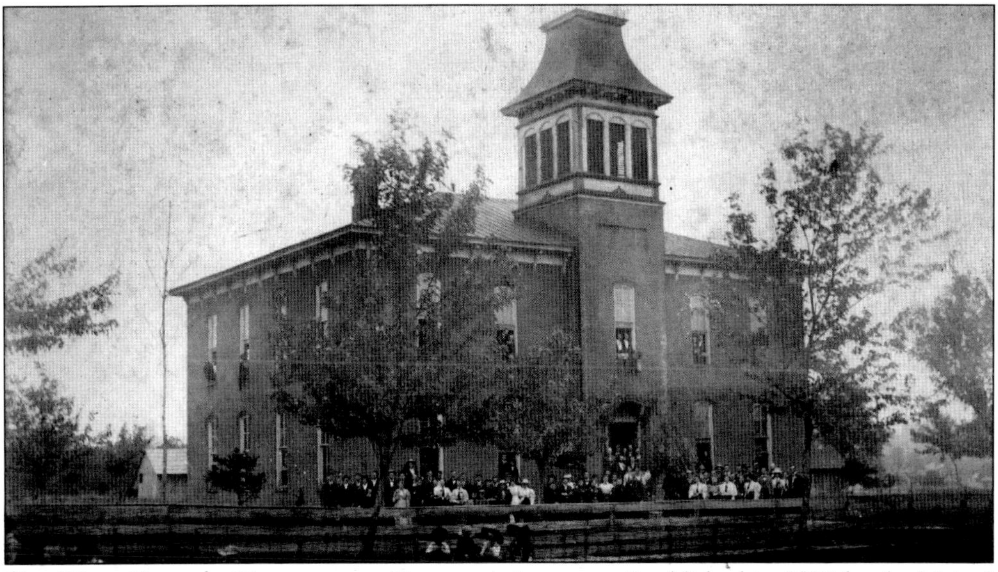

**The West Virginia Normal and Classical Academy.** Established in 1882 by the United Brethren in Christ, this institution was on College Avenue, the present site of the Academy Primary School. College Avenue was named for this institution. A building of 10 rooms housed classical and philosophical courses equivalent to a junior college program as well as a teacher's course, or "normal" training. The institution was renamed Union College and then moved to Mason County in 1897. (Photo courtesy of UCHS, Charles Wereley Collection.)

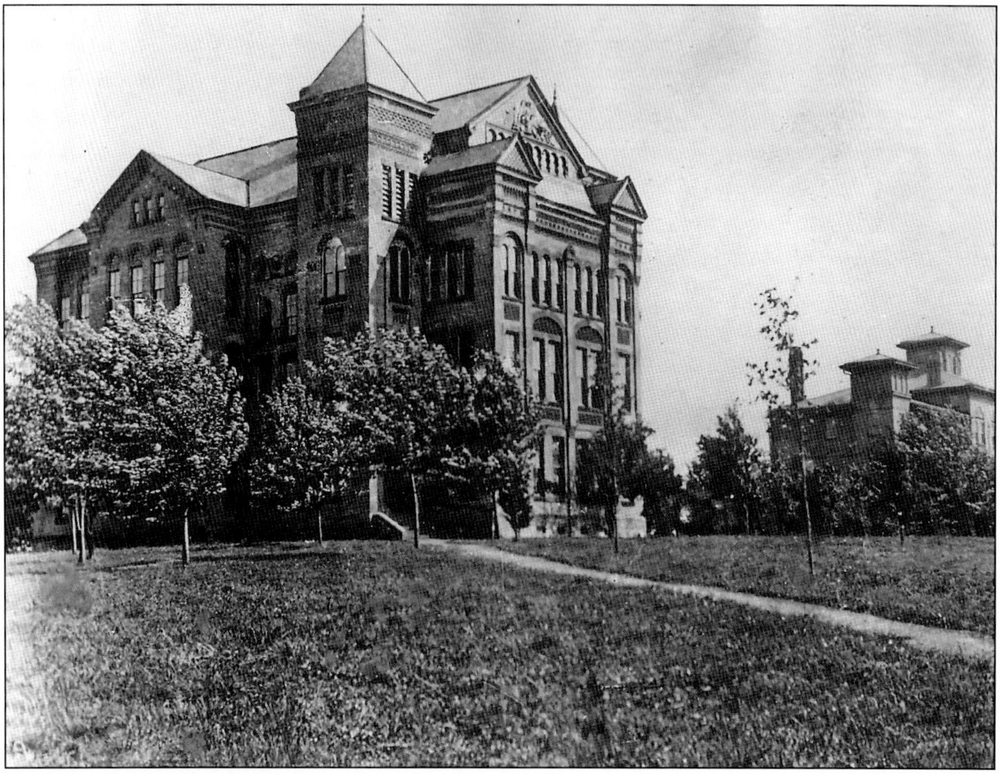

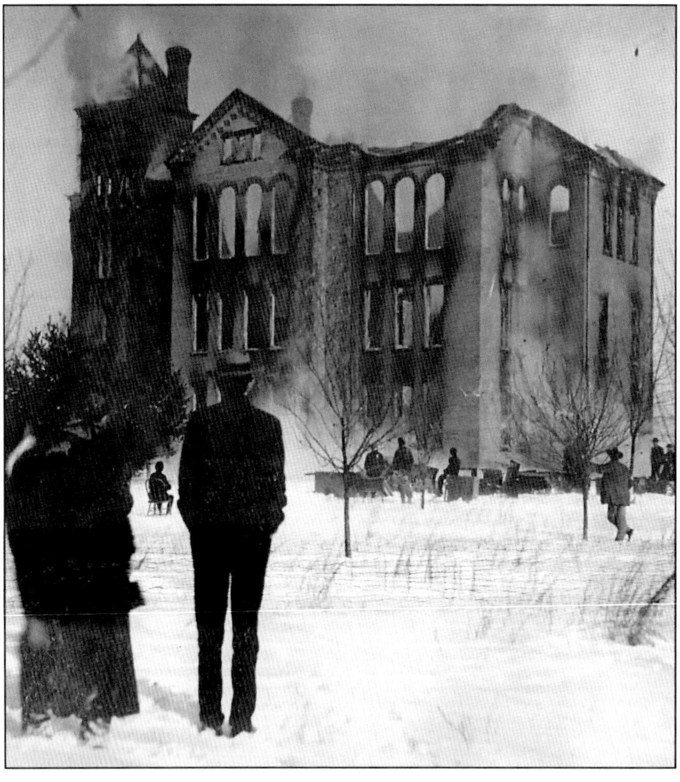

**West Virginia Conference Seminary and Fire.** Picture above is the original building of the now large campus known as West Virginia Wesleyan College. Established in 1890 as the West Virginia Conference Seminary, a college class schedule was added in 1903 and the institution name changed to Wesleyan University of West Virginia in 1904. Following a major fire that destroyed the seminary building on February 5, 1905, the board of trustees unanimously voted to change the school name to West Virginia Wesleyan College on June 5, 1906. (Photos courtesy of UCHS, permanent collection.)

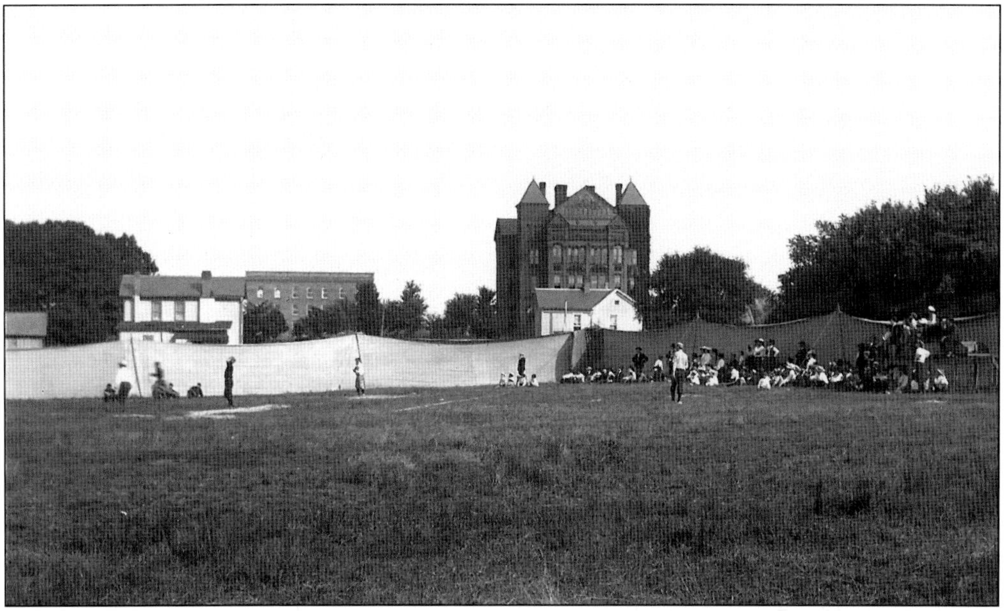

**Seminary Sports.** This photograph, taken between 1902 and 1905, depicts a sports event in front of what is now West Virginia Wesleyan College. The old seminary building is in the background. (Photo courtesy of UCHS, Noel W. Tenney Collection.)

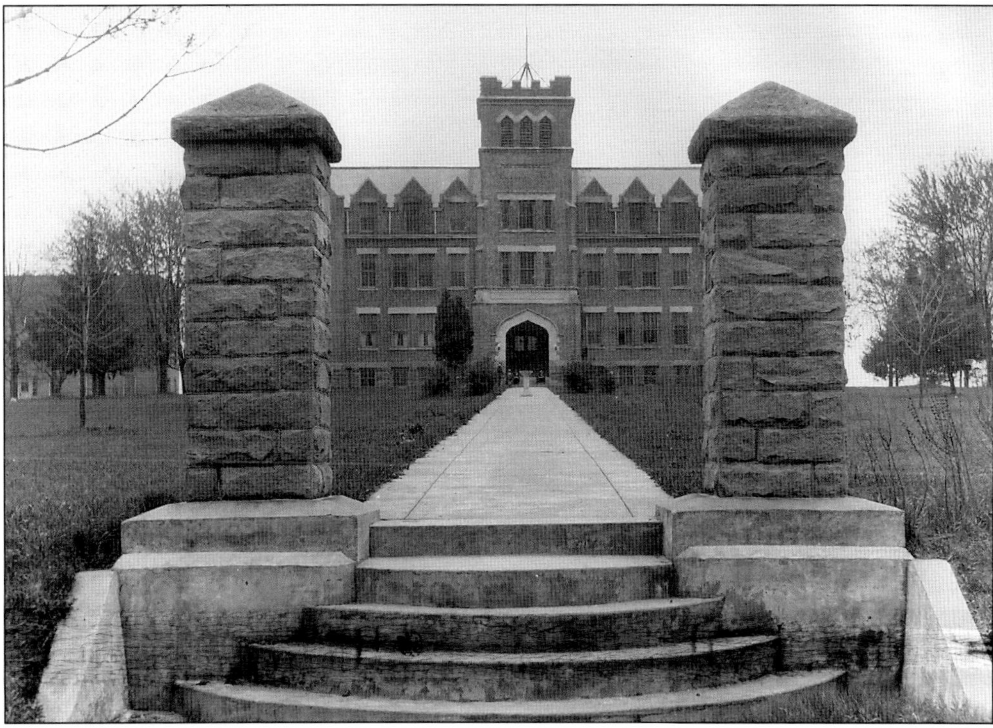

**West Virginia Wesleyan College Administration Building.** This early-20th-century Hode Clark photograph shows the structure that replaced the burned seminary building. This building was quickly constructed and occupied by the following year. The "Harvey Harmer" gateposts were constructed in 1908. (Photo courtesy of UCHS, Alan Sturm Collection.)

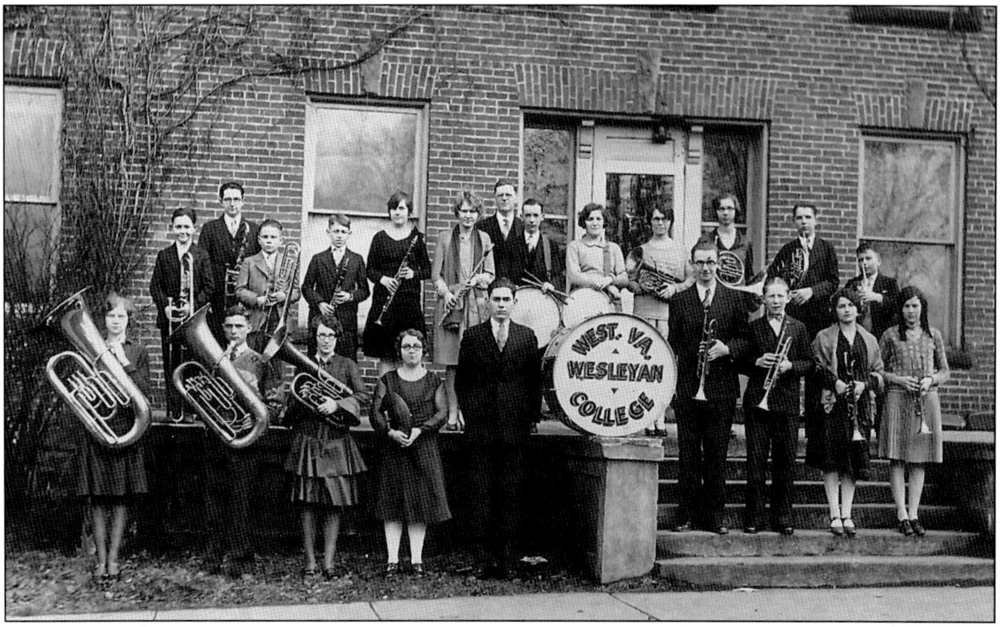


**WEST VIRGINIA WESLEYAN BAND.** Pictured here is the beginning of the WV Wesleyan College band. According to the *Murmurmontis*, the school's yearbook, the group was organized in 1936–1937 and primarily played for sports activities. Individual members are not identified. (Photo courtesy of UCHS, Juanita Reger Collection.)

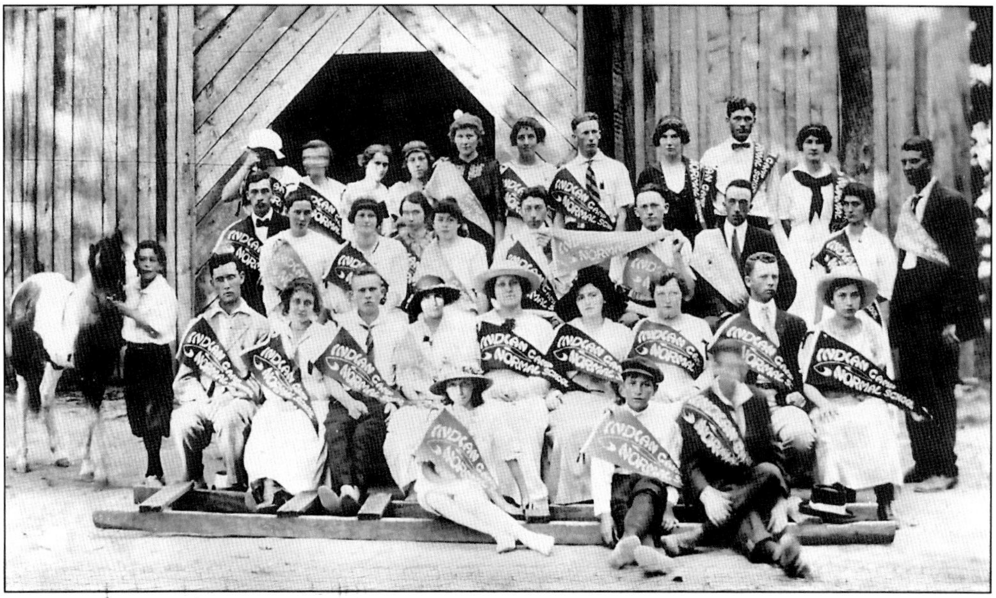

**INDIAN CAMP NORMAL SCHOOL.** In a cooperative effort between the United Brethren Church and Indian Camp community people, a teacher training school was established, and in 1913 a wooden structure was built. The first classes were held in the spring of 1914 under the direction of Professor J.H. Ashworth and E.C. Brooks. The school closed in 1918 because of World War I and did not reopen. The building still stands today and is used as a community center. Directly below the building is the famous Indian Camp Rock. (Photo courtesy of UCHS, Brian Huffman Collection.)

## *Six*

# Times of Crisis and Conflict

*Upshur County has always been prone to perennial flooding, and several "hundred year" or "once in a lifetime" floods have occurred throughout the county, causing great damage and some loss of life. The 1918 flood, along with those of the 1930s and the "big one" in 1985, have provided us with several images of devastation. Flooding, along with some severe snowstorms and fires have been the source of most of the county's natural and manmade disasters.*

*In the face of crisis and need, Upshur County has always stepped forward quickly to assist with and fulfill the needs of the community, state, and nation when called upon. Whether it be natural disaster or wartime conflict, at home or abroad, citizens of this county have always given of their time, resources, and lives in times of need.*

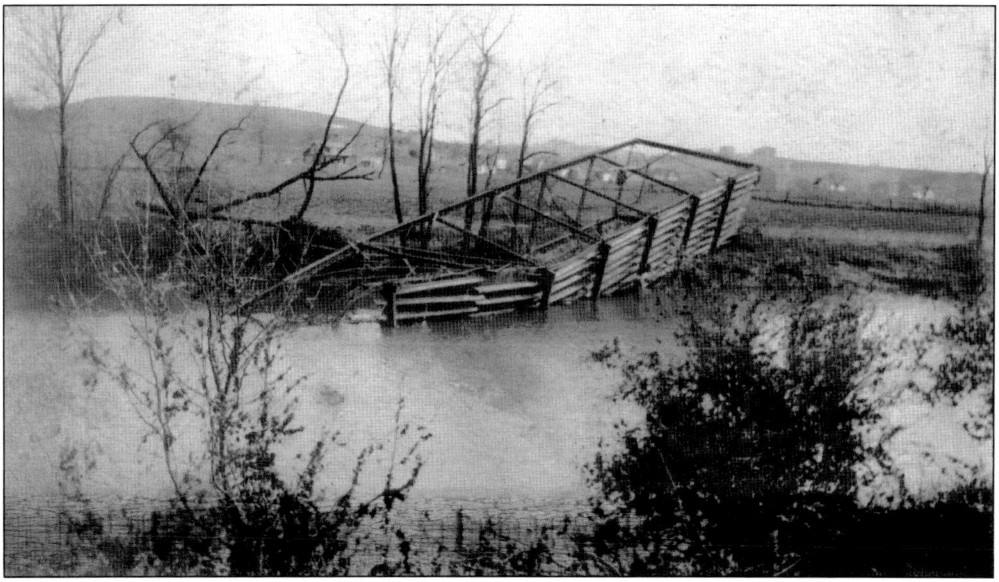

**Poe Bridge Takes A Ride.** This real photo postcard, taken just after the flood of March 13, 1918, shows the South Buckhannon Poe Bridge where it ran aground in the big bend of the Buckhannon River behind West Virginia Wesleyan College. The bridge had cost $2,071 to build in 1894 and the reassembling price was $2,848.60. This Marion Street landmark was demolished in the 1990s. (Photo courtesy of UCHS, Neil Brake Collection.)

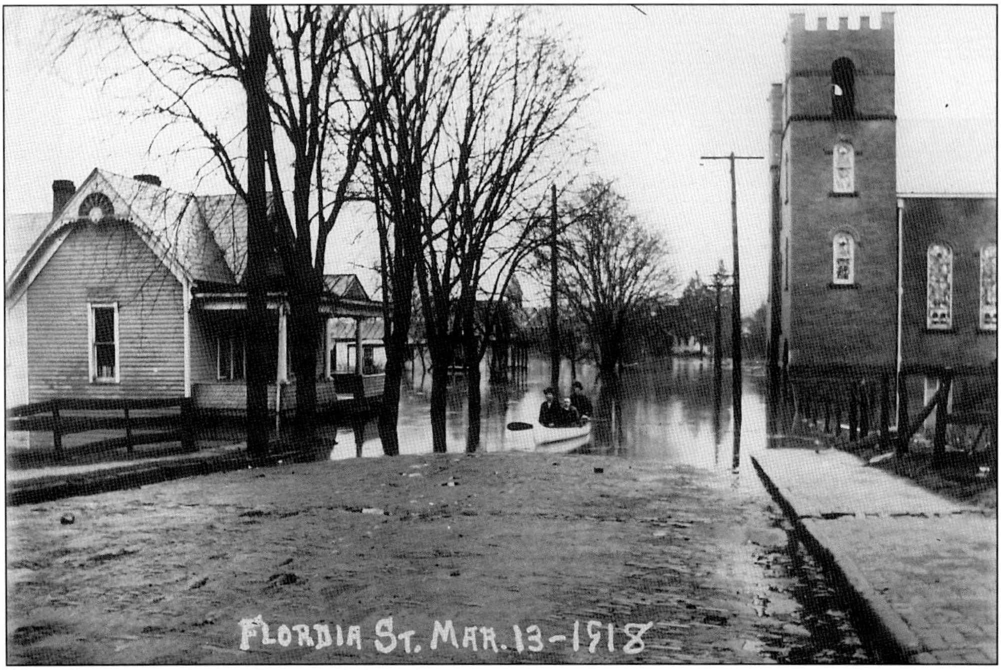


**FLOOD OF 1918.** These two photographs depict the high waters of March 13, 1918. Flooding has been a continual problem in the town of Buckhannon and surrounding areas. Pictured at the top is the area of Florida Street with the old EUB church building on the right. The bottom photograph shows the lower end of what is now Kanawha Street with the A.P. Russell business on the left, the B&O depot in the center, and the T.B. Drummond building on the right. (Photos courtesy of UCHS, Howard Hiner Collection.)

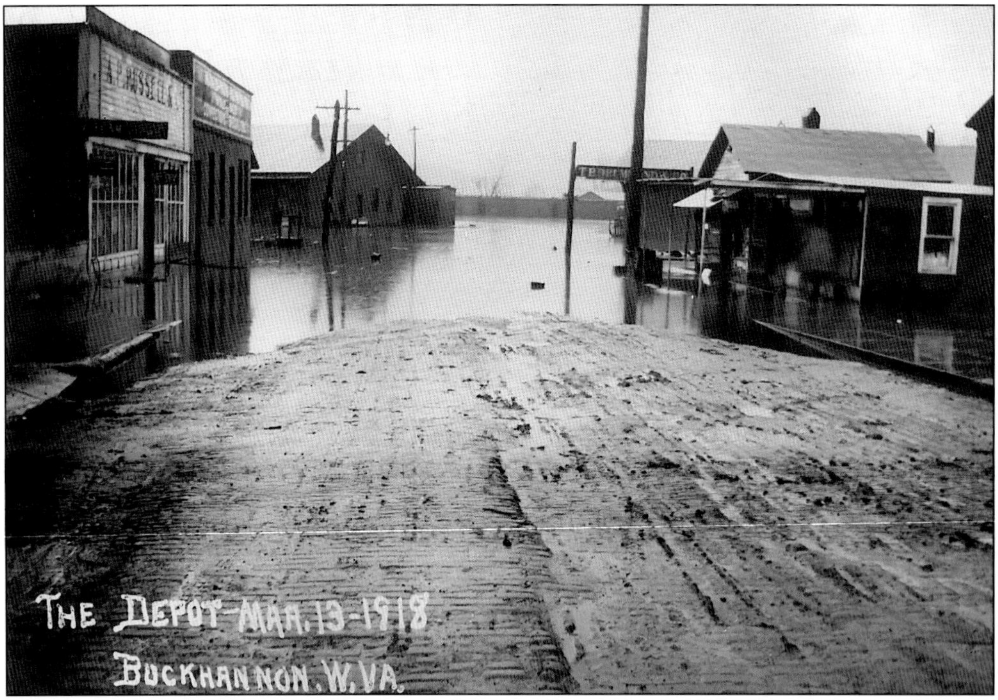

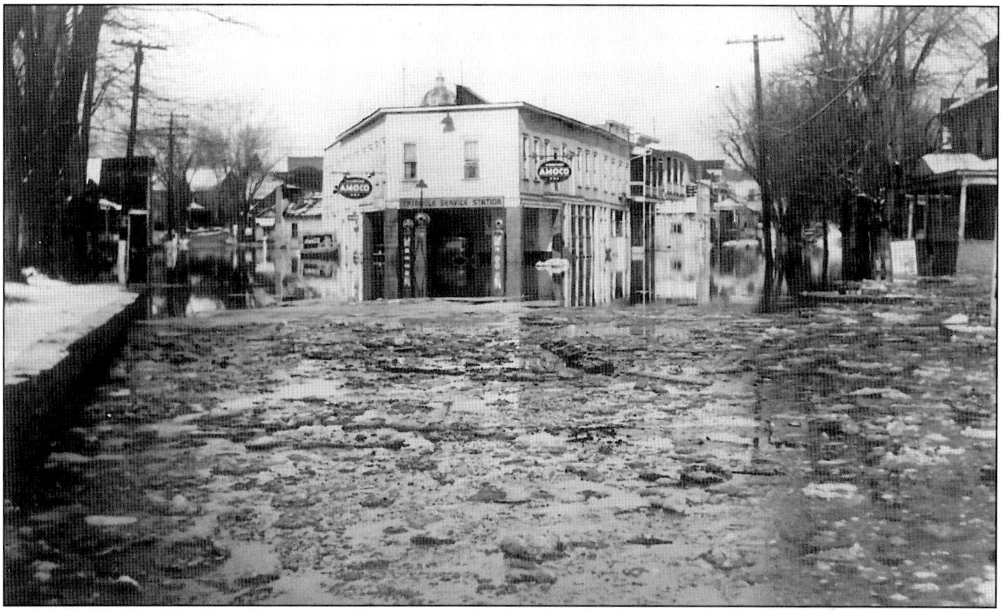

**FLOOD AT THE TRIANGLE.** One of the first Buckhannon Street areas to perpetually flood is the infamous Triangle area. With every downpour, water from the overflowing Fink's Run spreads quickly across this area. The top photograph, from the 1940s, shows the Triangle Service Station with not only flood damage but the post-flood freeze and ice. The bottom photograph, taken in 1967, shows the same scene with lots of water on road. (Photos courtesy of UCHS, Henry Marple and WV Wesleyan Collections.)

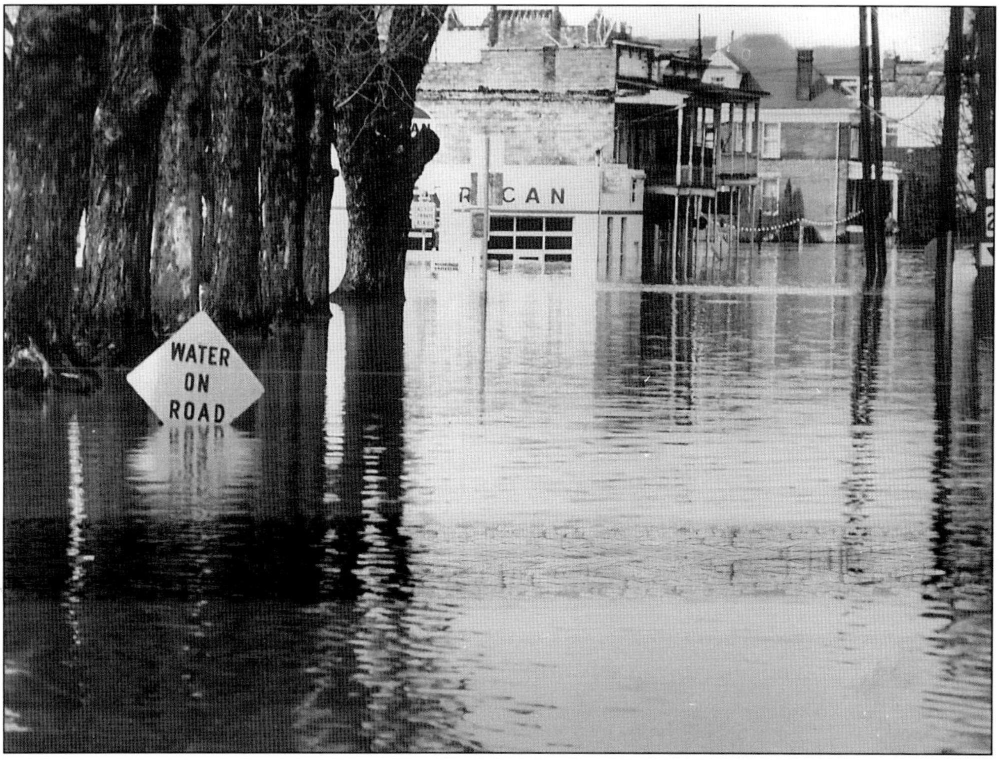

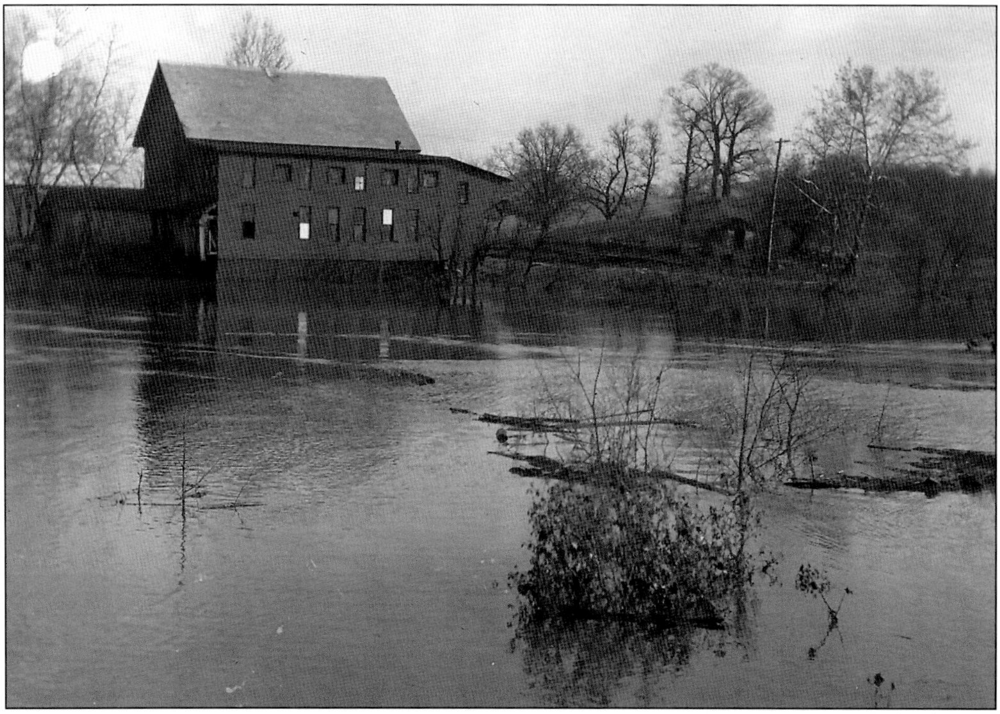

**Daniel D.T. Farnsworth Grist Mill.** Built *c.* 1860 along the Buckhannon River near the manmade mill race on Island Avenue, this gristmill operated for many years, primarily as a flour mill. A sawmill was also operated nearby and was situated over the millrace itself. Daniel D.T. Farnsworth was a prominent Buckhannon business person as well as the second governor of West Virginia, albeit, only for a few days. (Photo courtesy of UCHS, Alan Sturm Collection.)

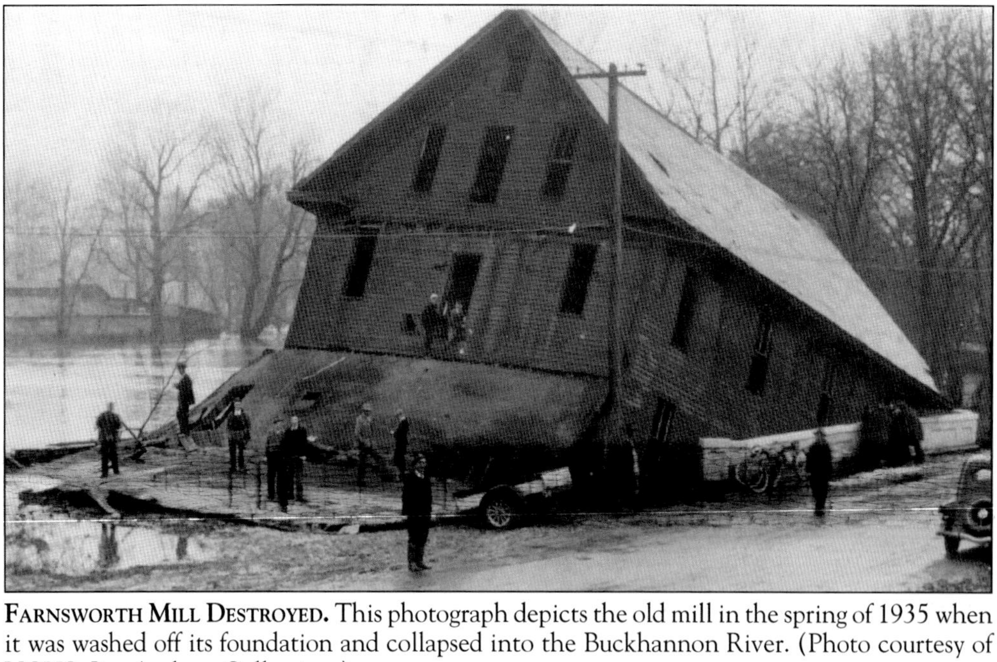

**Farnsworth Mill Destroyed.** This photograph depicts the old mill in the spring of 1935 when it was washed off its foundation and collapsed into the Buckhannon River. (Photo courtesy of UCHS, Jim Amlung Collection.)

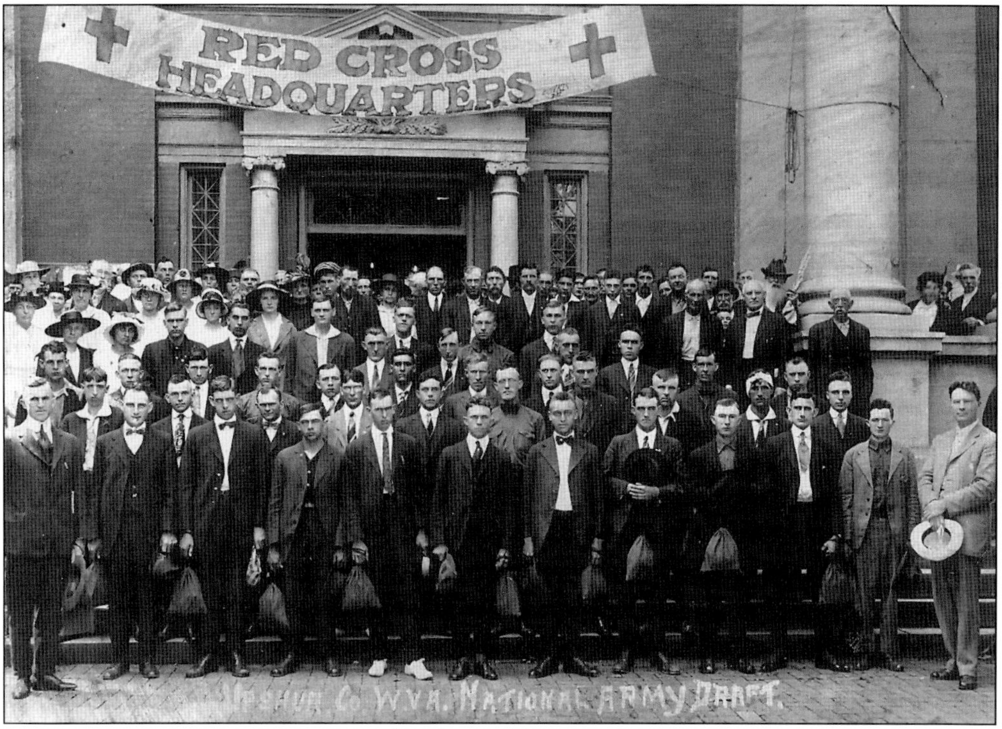


**World War I Draft Day.** Pictured in front of the courthouse on April 27, 1918 are Upshur County draftees answering the "clarion call" for service in the U.S. military. During the previous year, Upshur County citizens had answered the call by organizing the "Arm and Farm Association" in order that "each and everyone be able to contribute our 'mite' to the man at the front." (Photo courtesy of UCHS, George Lanham Collection.)

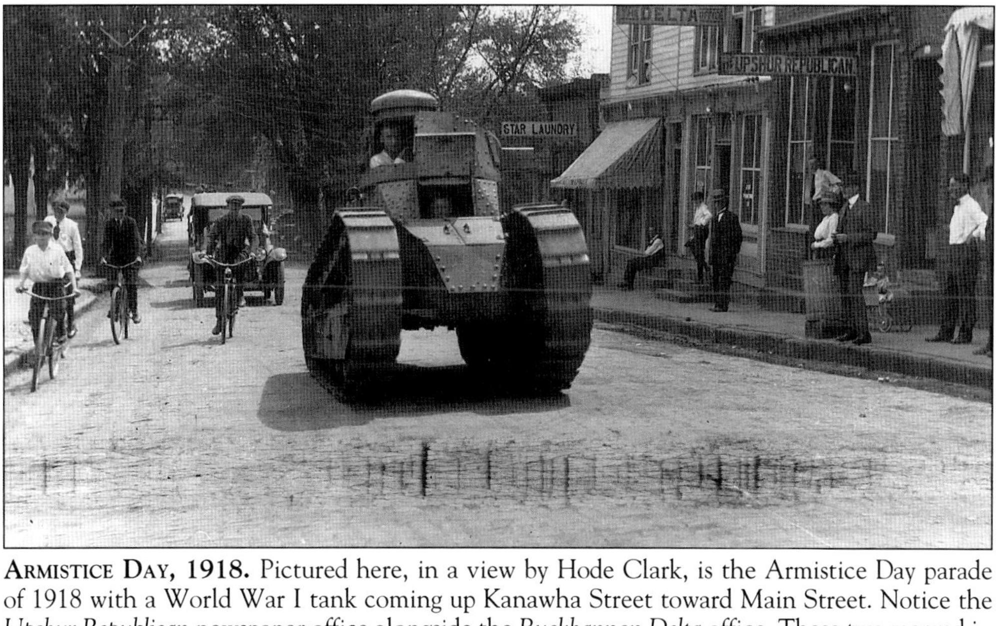


**Armistice Day, 1918.** Pictured here, in a view by Hode Clark, is the Armistice Day parade of 1918 with a World War I tank coming up Kanawha Street toward Main Street. Notice the *Upshur Republican* newspaper office alongside the *Buckhannon Delta* office. These two merged in 1929 to form the *Republican Delta.* (Photo courtesy of UCHS, "Tuck" Farnsworth Collection.)

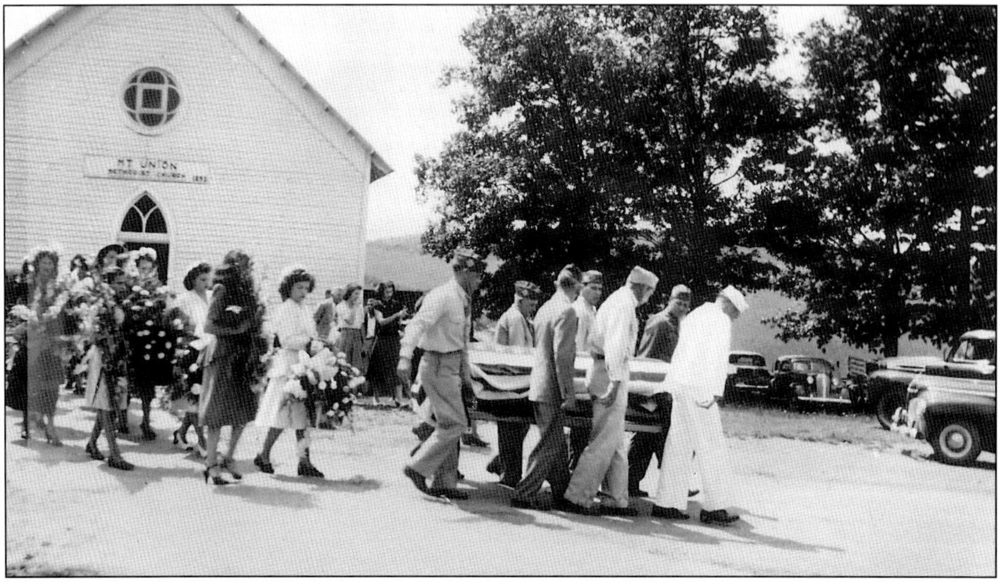


**WORLD WAR II BURIALS.** As late as 1952, World War II military casualties were being returned for local burial. The one above took place at the Mt. Union Church cemetery in Washington District and the one below was at the Abbott Methodist Church cemetery in Meade District. (Photos courtesy of UCHS, Sheila Tenney Thomason Collection.)

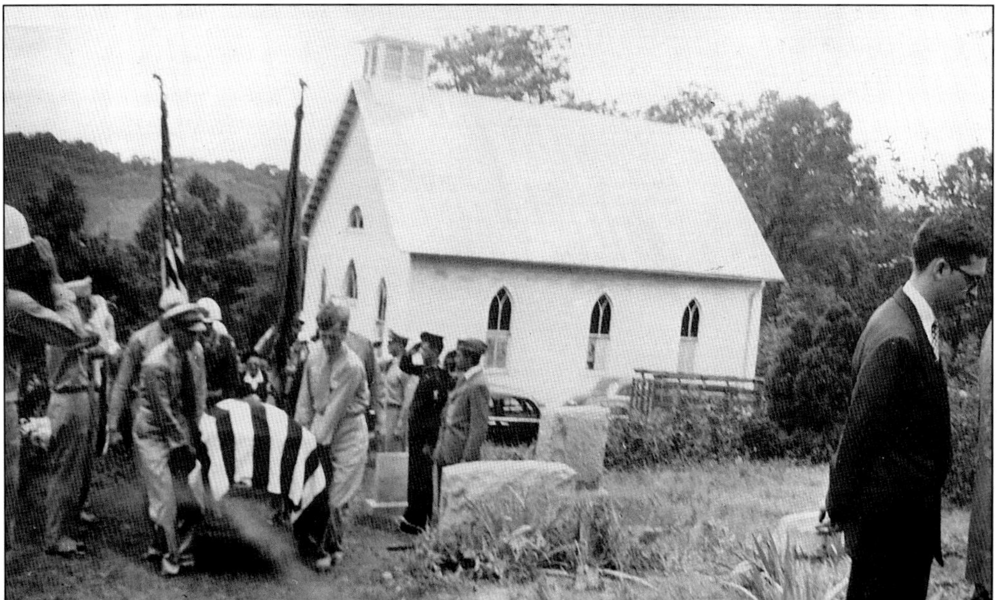

# *Seven*

# Organizations and Events

*Returning veterans of the Civil War formed the Grand Army of the Republic (GAR), while community bands were formed all over Upshur County to play for patriotic and social gatherings. This area has seen many fraternal and social clubs and organizations come and go; yet, many are still in existence today after a long and rich local history. Even though the Boy and Girl Scouts have been organized here for nearly a century, it was really the 4-H program that involved the greatest number of young people with its various programs, camps, and events. The pre–4-H "Corn Club" was formed in French Creek in 1914 along with the "Canning" and "Potato and Chicken" clubs. By 1942, 4-H was so well established that a youth camp was created at Selbyville.*

*In 1936, the first Strawberry Festival was established in Upshur County, and in 2001 the 60th anniversary was celebrated. (Though there were no festivals during the World War II years.) Pageantry, royalty, parades, and more parades are all a part of this annual celebration.*

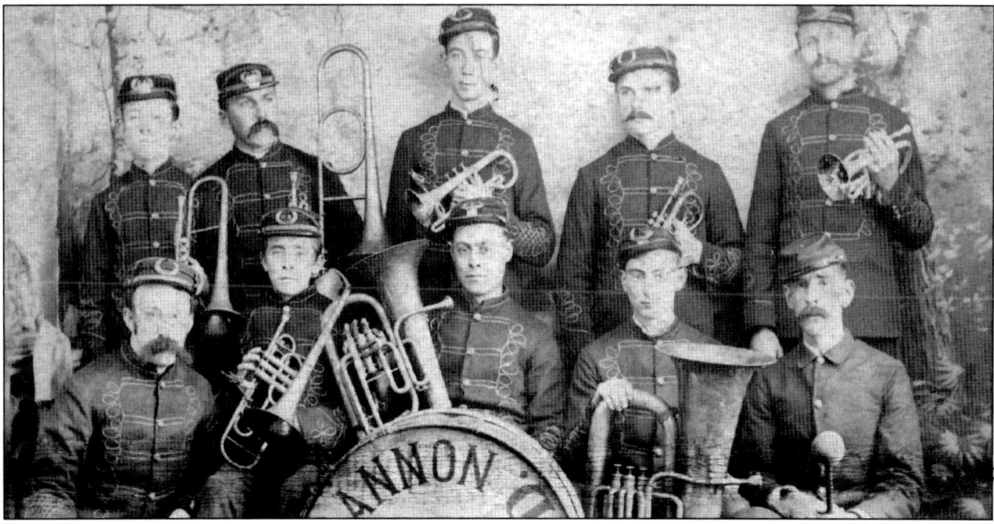


**Buckhannon Band.** This classic P.D. Foreman 1890s photograph shows members of the early Buckhannon Band who are identified, from left to right, as (front row) Bud Drennington, Hugh Skinner, Phil Rollins, George Mathers, and Bob Martin; (back row) Guy Skinner, Bob Neff, unidentified, Ernest Kummer, and Maj. G.A. Smith (band leader). (Photo courtesy of UCHS, Jack Byers Collection.)

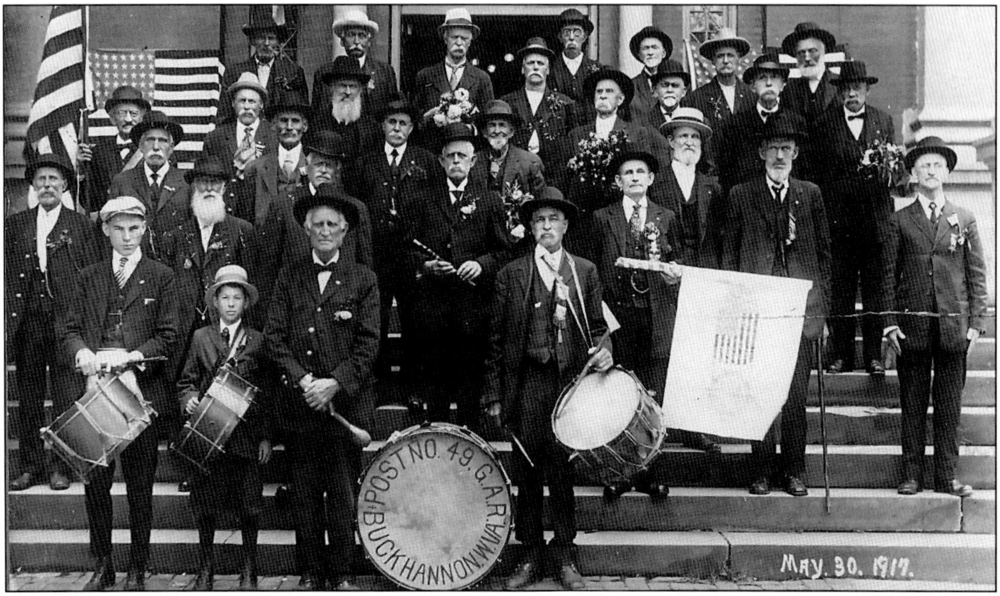


**GRAND ARMY OF THE REPUBLIC.** This 1917 Memorial Day celebration depicts one of the last rallies of the Buckahnnon GAR Post No. 49. Pictured, from left to right, are (front row) two unidentified people, Miner C. Lemons, and Spencer Phillips; (second row) James T. Richards, Ashley Wilfong, Dr. J.J. Morgan, Boyers Morgan, unidentified, Jonathan Hathaway, and Ben Malone; (third row) George W. Shipman, Foster Hinkle, L.B. Chidester, ? Martin, and ? Woodford; (fourth row) Tom Neff, unidentified, Cyrus Hinkle, Dave Morgan, A.F. Simpson, Daniel Chidester, and George Been; (fifth row) two unidentified people, Col. W.G.L. Totten, unidentified, Elam Dooley, Hiram Pyles, and two more unidentified individuals. (Photos courtesy of UCHS, Connie Bailey Collection.)

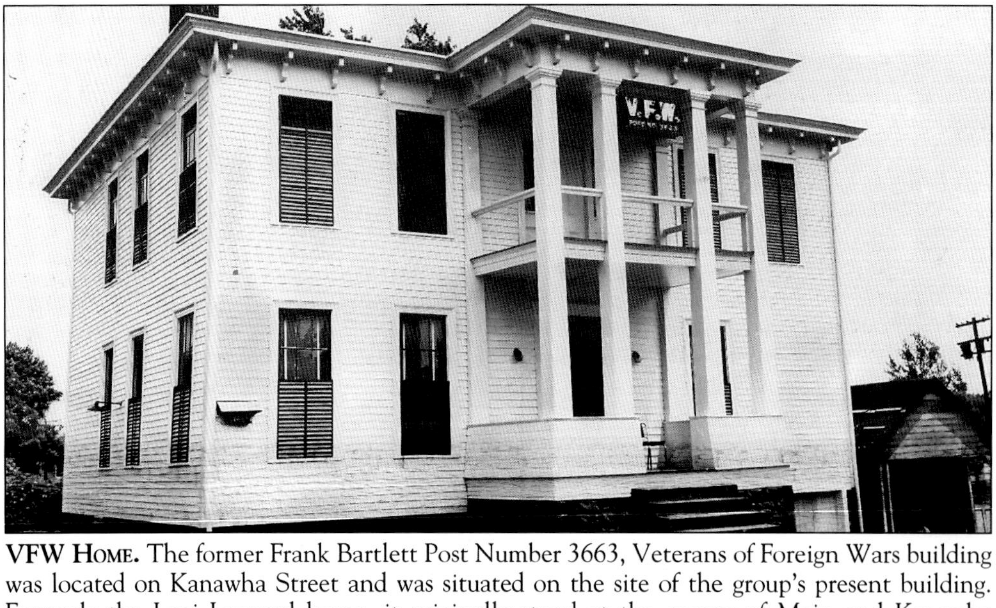


**VFW HOME.** The former Frank Bartlett Post Number 3663, Veterans of Foreign Wars building was located on Kanawha Street and was situated on the site of the group's present building. Formerly the Levi Leonard home, it originally stood at the corner of Main and Kanawha Streets, facing Main Street. It was demolished in the 1970s. (Photos courtesy of UCHS, Howard Hiner Collection.)

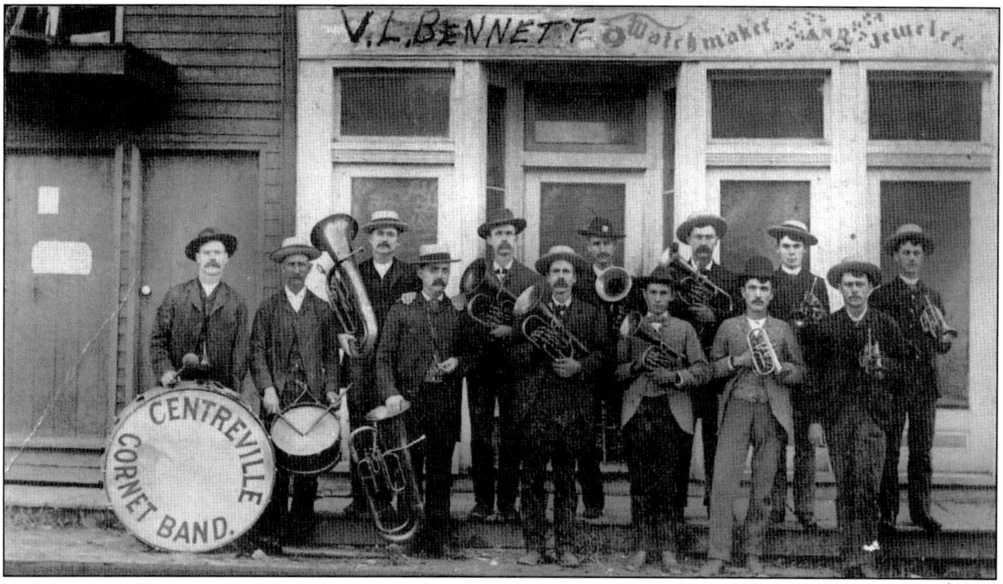


**CENTERVILLE CORNET BAND.** Pictured in this June 1887 photograph taken in Centerville (now Rock Cave) are members of the band organized in 1886 and discontinued in 1889. The members, from left to right, are T.M. Cheveront, Miner C. Lemmons, Stoug Flint, John T. Boyd, Eugene Brown, Enoch Andrew, John McAvoy, Marshall T. Smith, Robert C. Boggs, Charles C. Ferrell, William T. Curry, Vernon L. Bennett, and Al W. Rice. Instruments were $6.50 for each brass cornet; $14 for the baritone cornet; $23 for the large bass cornet; $5.50 for the snare drum; and $15 for the bass drum. (Photo courtesy of UCHS, permanent collection.)

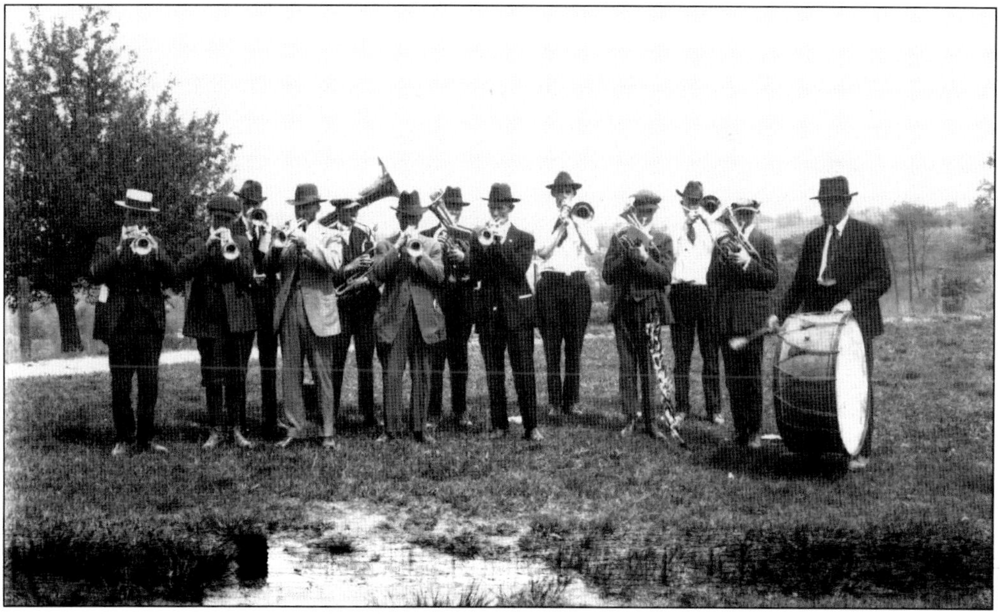

**FRENCH CREEK BAND.** Depicted in this *c.* 1920 photograph is the Meade District, French Creek community band. Although individual members cannot be identified in this photograph, the band included Frank Knight, Russell Phillips, Ross Mearns, Harold Smallridge, Doctor Van Tromp, Parley Rexroad, John Armstrong, Lyell Colerider, and others. (Photo courtesy of UCHS, Noel W. Tenney Collection.)

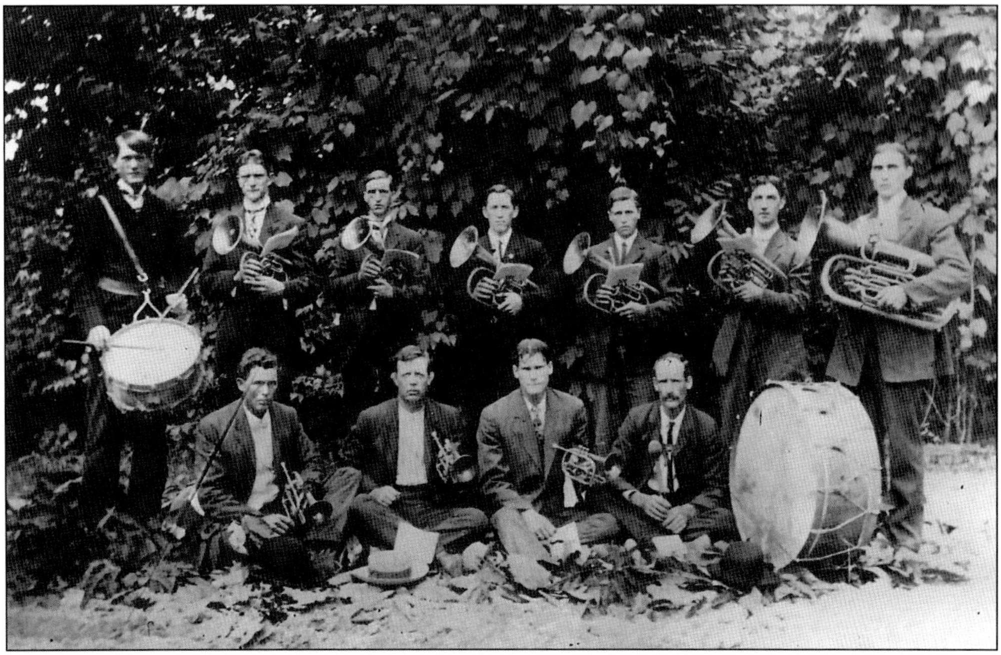

**The 1908 Union–Kedron–Sand Run Band.** This 1908 photograph of the brass band was taken by James Arthur Simmons. Pictured, from left to right, are (front row) Floyd Montgomery, Bill Tallman, Fred Tenney, and Opha Tenney; (back row) Homer Tenney, Dr. J.L. Montgomery, Marcellus "Fats" Montgomery, Joe Hornbeck, Ed Hornbeck, Burton Hornbeck, and Porter Tenney. Local brass and string bands were quite popular during this time throughout Upshur County. (Photo courtesy of UCHS, Sheila Tenney Thomason Collection.)

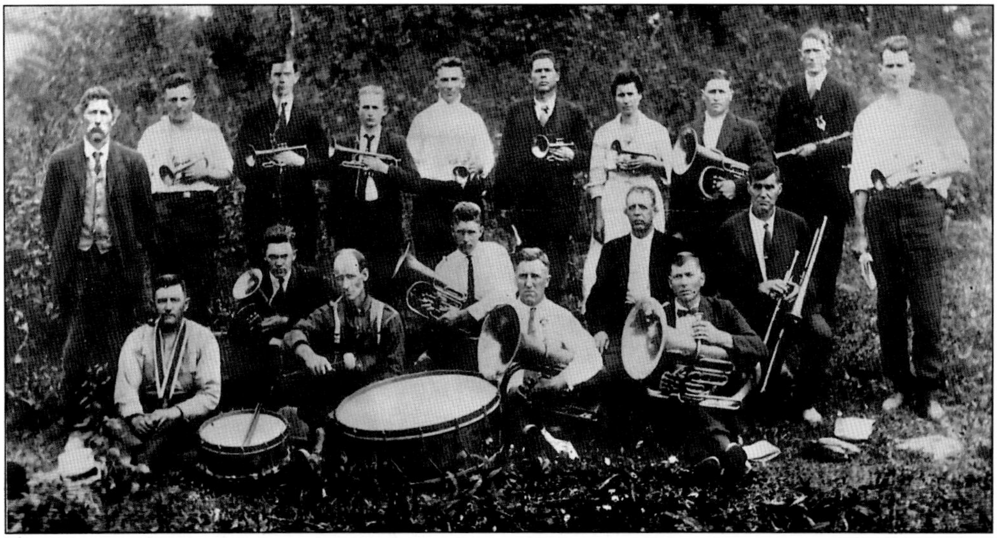

**The 1920 Union–Kedron–Sand Run Band.** Band members in this 1920 James Arthur Simmons photograph are, from left to right, (front row) Warrick Osburn, Earl Opha Tenney, Sam Montgomery, Jim Montgomery, Bill Tallman, Coleman Hinkle, and "Dutch" R.H. Baughman; (back row) Gearl Osburn, ? Warrick, Basil Grove, Carl Hornbeck, Ralph Wamsley, Floyd Montgomery, Viola Montgomery (wife of Floyd), Ed Hornbeck, Homer Tenney, and Fred Tenney. (Photos courtesy of UCHS, Sheila Tenney Thomason Collection.)

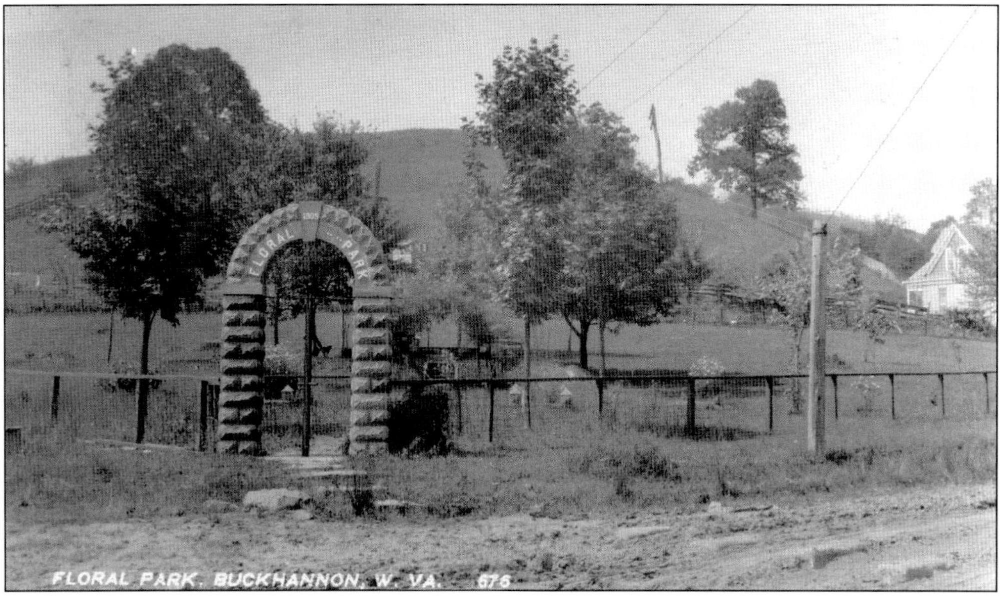


**Floral Park.** Taken October 28th, 1911, this real photo postcard shows the small triangular park between Kanawha, Marion, and Barbour Streets. This had been the site of a Civil War battle, locally called the "Battle of Water Tank Hill," in August 1862. The Garden Club was formed in the early 1930s and renamed the Fred Brooks Garden Club after Mr. Brook's death in 1933. Today the arch has been recreated and the park is known as the Fred Brooks Park. (Photo courtesy of UCHS, Phyllis Miller Collection.)

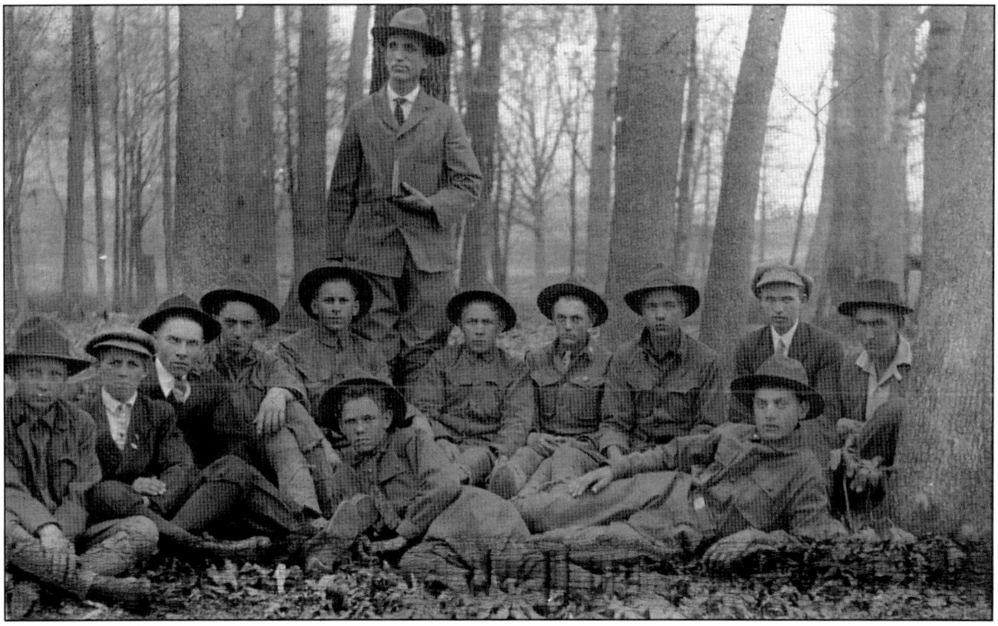

**Frenchton Boy Scouts.** This real photo postcard was taken *c.* 1914 and shows, from left to right, the following boys of the troop: (front row) Hall Talbott and Ralph Wilson; (middle row) Lowe Armstrong, Hartsel Smith, Earl Talbott, Rex Harper, Arlie Smith, Monter Harper, Keith Simons, Dorsey Farnsworth, George Hyre, and Ross Phillips; (back row) Scoutmaster Parley Cutright. (Photo courtesy of UCHS, Doris Orsburn Collection.)

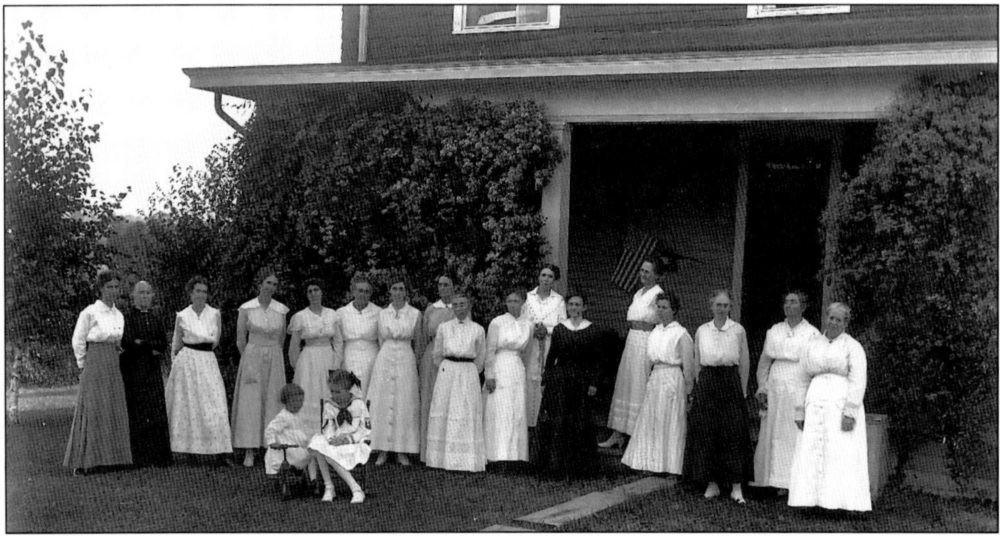

**FRENCH CREEK FARM WOMEN'S CLUB.** This 1918–1919 Fred Brooks photograph depicts one of the first West Virginia University Extension Service's Farm Women's Clubs in Upshur County. None of the children on the front row are identified, but those on the back row are, from left to right, Georgia Phillips Thomas, Josephine Brooks, Blanche VanTromp, Nora Phillips, Rita Lemons Page, Nell Vance Brooks, Amanda Phillips, Lora Brooks, Mary Phillips Wingrove, Mabel Brooks Vance, Grace Lance Young, Grace Brooks, Elise Bunten Page, Maude Colerider Talbott, Juanita Phillips Jones, and ? Brooks. (Photo courtesy of UCHS, Fred Brooks Collection.)

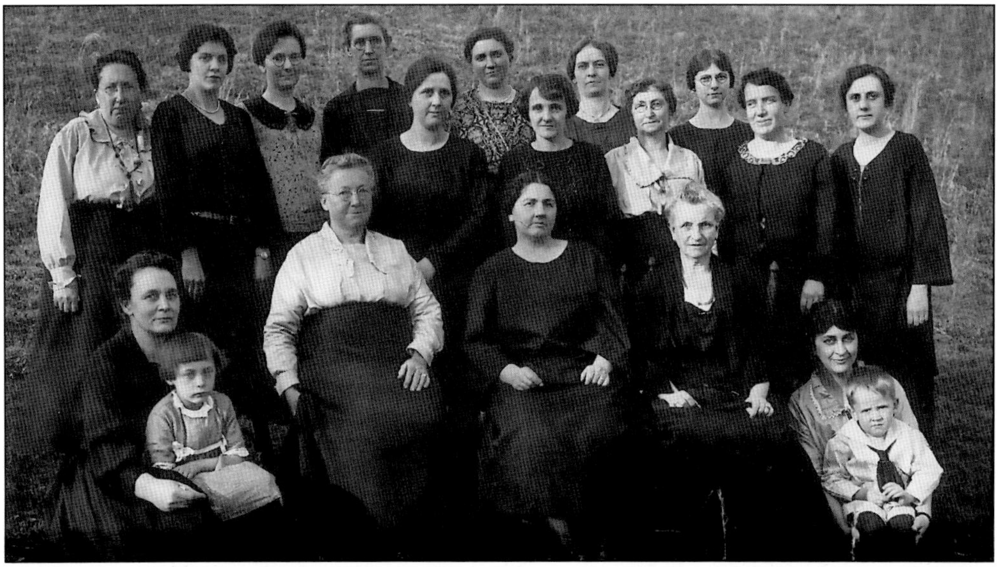

**LORENTZ FARM WOMEN'S CLUB.** Fred Brooks took this photograph in 1923 at Lorentz. Pictured, from left to right, are (front row, seated) Bird Allman; Betty, daughter of Bird Allman; Matty Betts; Ersa Borum; Mrs. J.M. Allman; Mary McMorrow Brown, Upshur County's first home demonstration agent; and David Cartwright; (back row) Mrs. John Collins, Freda Miles, Iva Queen, Isa Lorentz, Grace Cartwright, Nora Casto, Lessie Casto, Vertenice Grose, Etta Miles, Elva Hinkle, Lucie Queen, and Ruth Marple. (Photo courtesy of UCHS, Fred Brooks Collection.)

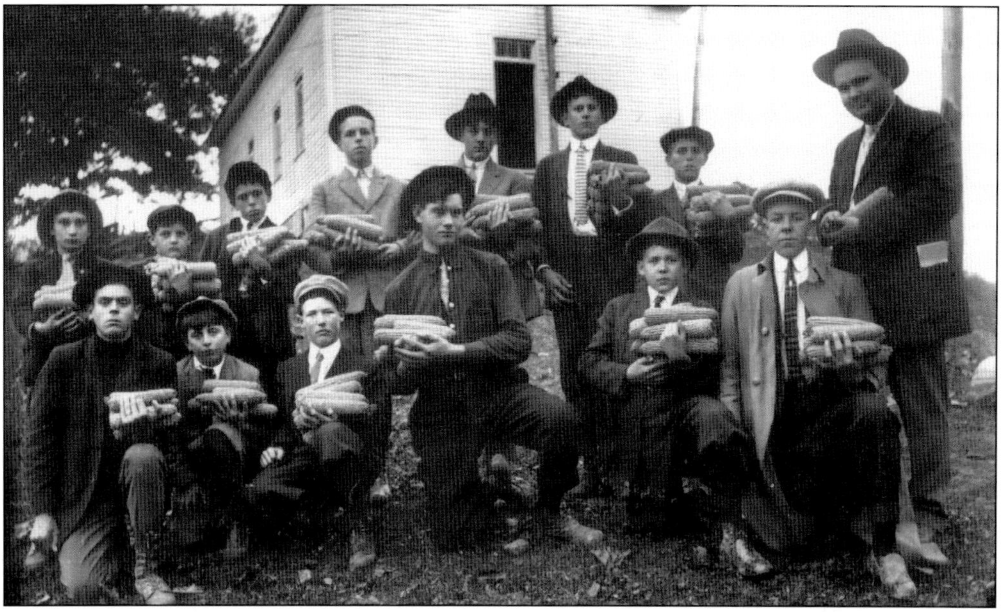

**Corn Club at French Creek.** The beginnings of the 4-H program in Upshur County is captured in this October 1914 photograph. Known then as the "Corn" or "Canning" as well as the "Potato and Chicken" clubs, these boys are holding ears of corn as their symbol. Pictured, from left to right, are (front row) Orr Phillips, Wirt Jones, Hugh Casto, Walter Phillips, Basil Page, and Lawrence See; (back row) Walter Swecker, Dent Irvin, Layman Phillips, Maurice Brooks, Keith Simons, Arlie Smith, Hartsel Smith, and state 4-H agent William H. Kendricks. (Photo courtesy of UCHS, Brooks Casto Collection.)

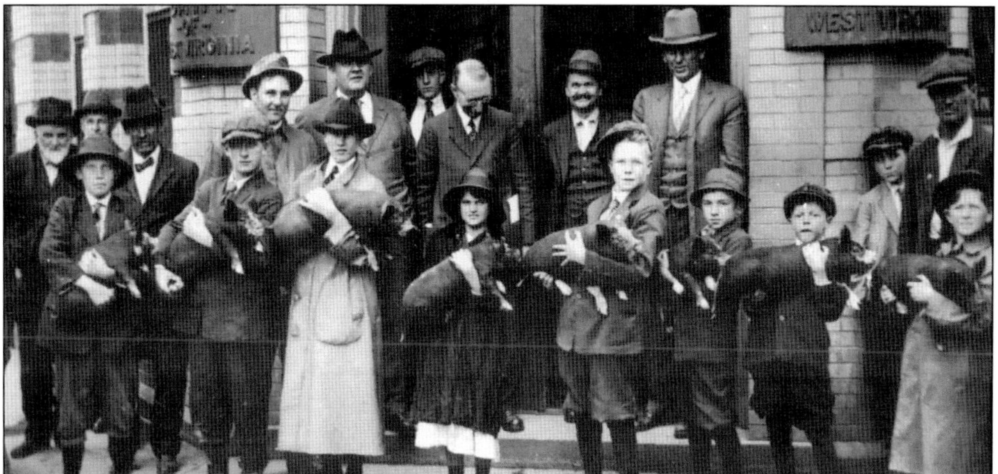

**Pig Distribution.** Depicted in this May 10, 1919 photograph, which was taken in front of the People's Bank on the corner of Main and Kanawha Streets, is the distribution of the second allotment of purebred Berkshire pigs given through the Farm Bureau and the People's Bank. Children receiving the pigs, from left to right, are as follows: Kermit Wilson, Arden Morrison, Brooks Casto, Clara Woomer, Scott Mearns, Paul Thomas, Gail Marsh, and Robert Smith. County Agent J. Earl Romine and C.B. "Uncle Charlie" Wilson are also listed. (Photo courtesy of UCHS, Brooks Casto Collection.)

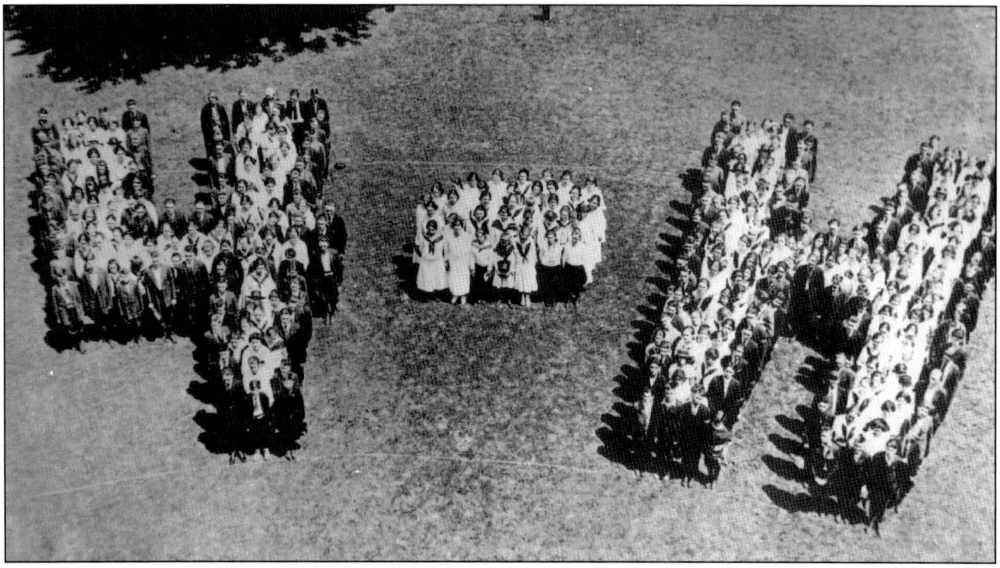

**THE 4-H CLUBS.** The 4-H boys and girls program began early in southern West Virginia and then spread statewide. By 1914, Upshur County had various clubs that would become the more organized 4-H program. Upshur Countians are included in this 1921 4-H photograph of West Virginia prize winners taken at West Virginia University in Morgantown. (Photo courtesy of UCHS, Brooks Casto Collection.)

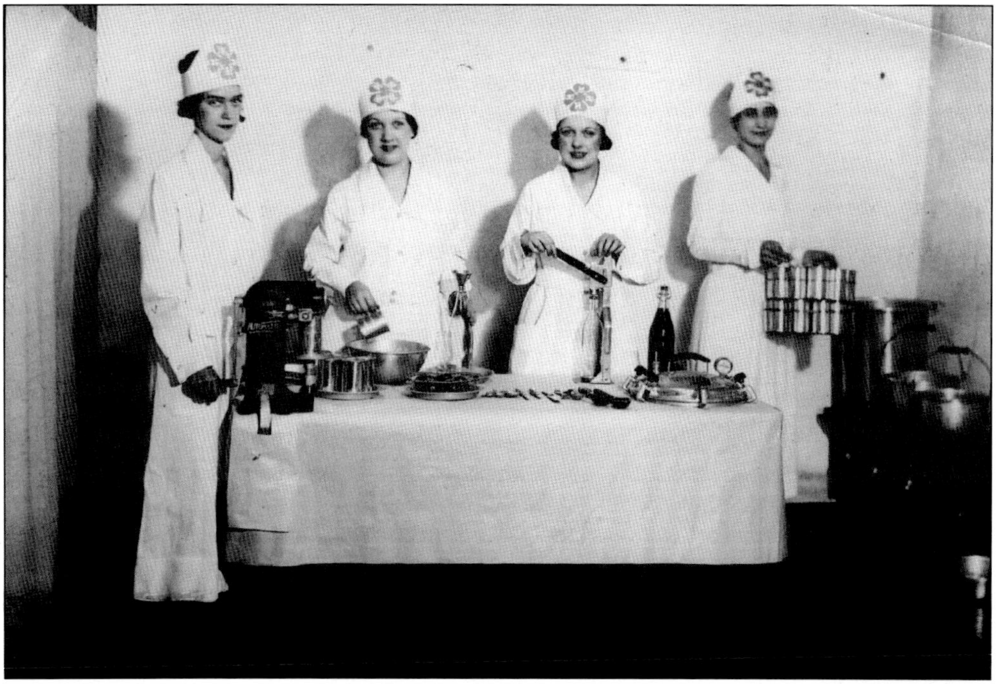

**SOME 4-H LADIES CANNING.** This 1933 photograph shows, from left to right, Ruth and Gladys Stump, Madge Kidd, and Kathryn Casto demonstrating various methods of preserving food by canning. The 4-H program was primarily a rural agricultural concept which sought to enhance "head, hand, heart, and health" needs for children. (Photo courtesy of UCHS, Brooks Casto Collection.)

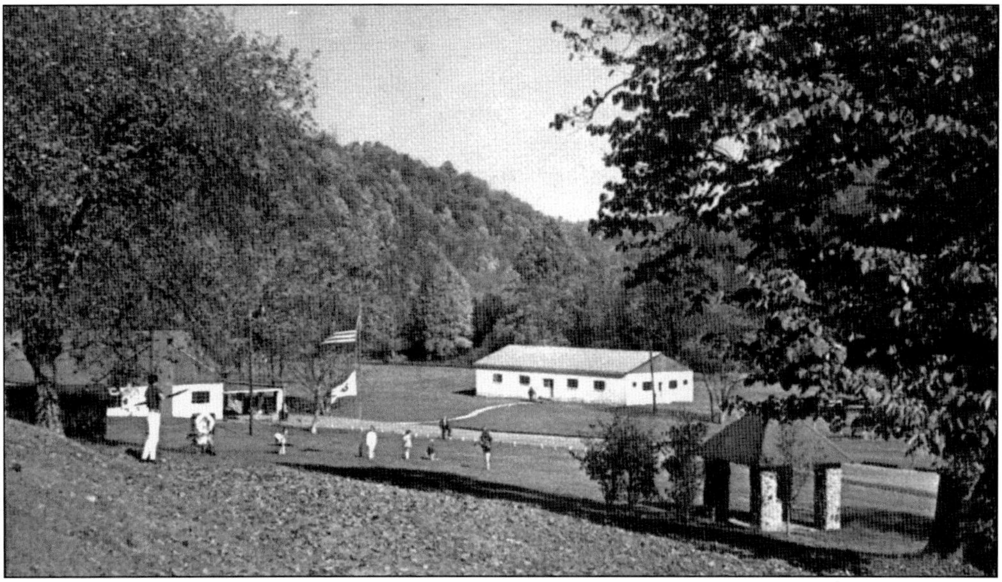

**The 4-H Camp at Selbyville.** After holding 4-H camps at various Upshur County locations, including West Virginia Wesleyan College and Indian Camp, the Cooperative Extension Service and the Upshur County Farm Bureau arranged for the purchase of the old Buckhannon Chemical facility at Selbyville on which to develop a 4-H/Youth Camp. This was done in 1942 and the cost of the property was $6,000. When this photograph was taken in the late 1960s by Dr. Harold Almond, the camp had developed many new buildings; it continues to function today as a youth camp and conference center. (Photo courtesy of UCHS, purchased collection.)

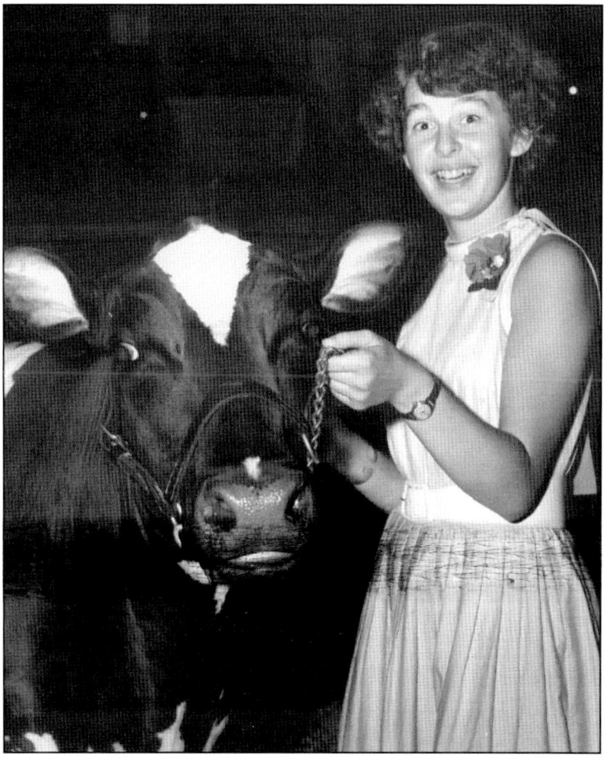

**The 4-H Grand Champion.** This 1950s 4-H dairy project and its enthusiastic owner depict the spirit of the program's training and agricultural base. Unfortunately, the young lady and her winning champion are unidentified. (Photo courtesy of UCHS, Brooks Casto Collection.)

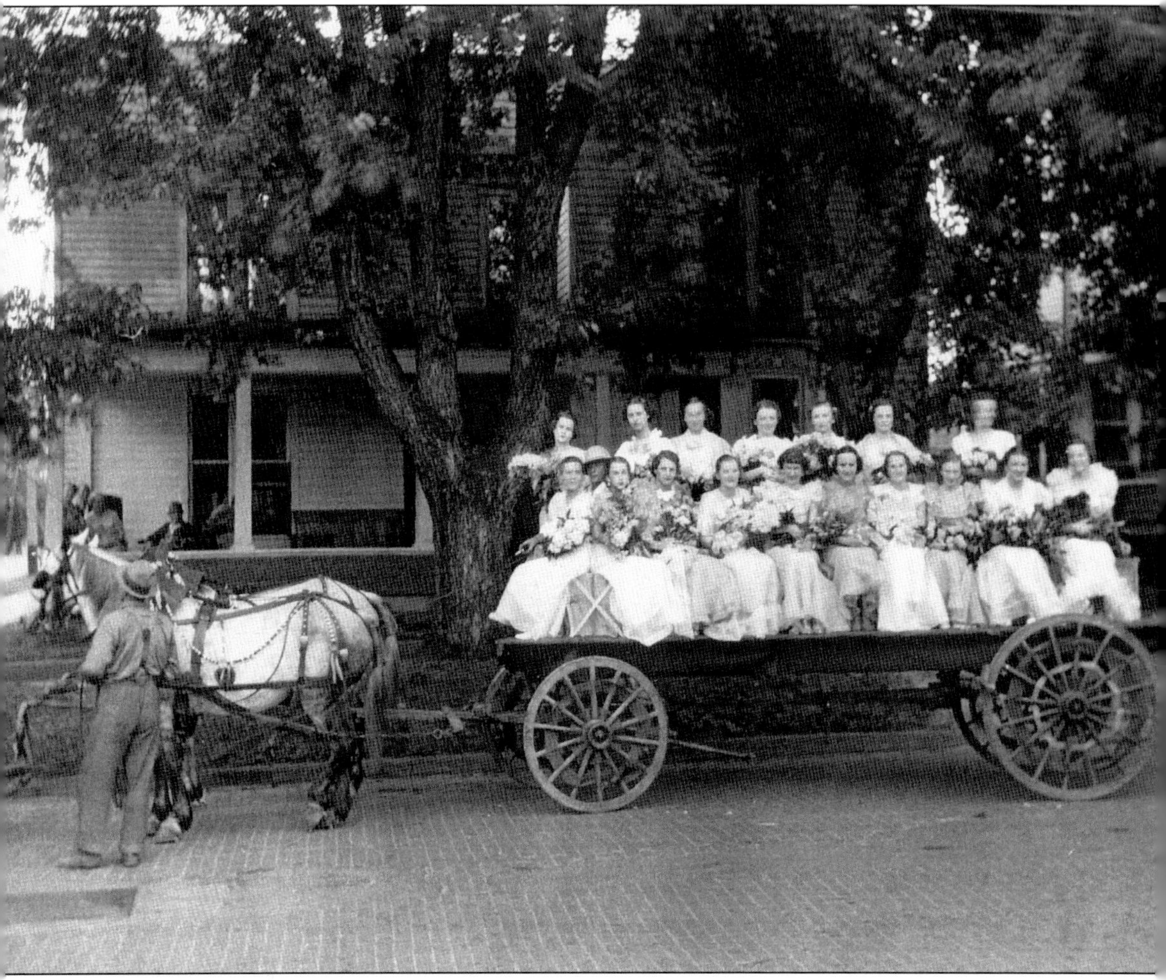

**West Virginia Strawberry Festival.** In May 1936 a small group of individuals interested in economic development met at a Lions Club gathering in the old Valley Hotel to discuss ways of increasing the production of strawberries. Just three weeks later the first West Virginia Strawberry Festival was held with a king and queen, horse-drawn floats, and lots of berries. During the World War II–era the festival was discontinued for five years. Horse-drawn floats, like the one pictured here, were discontinued after the first year because a princess fell and was injured. The festival marked its 60th anniversary in 2001. (Photo courtesy of UCHS, Home Hardware Collection.)

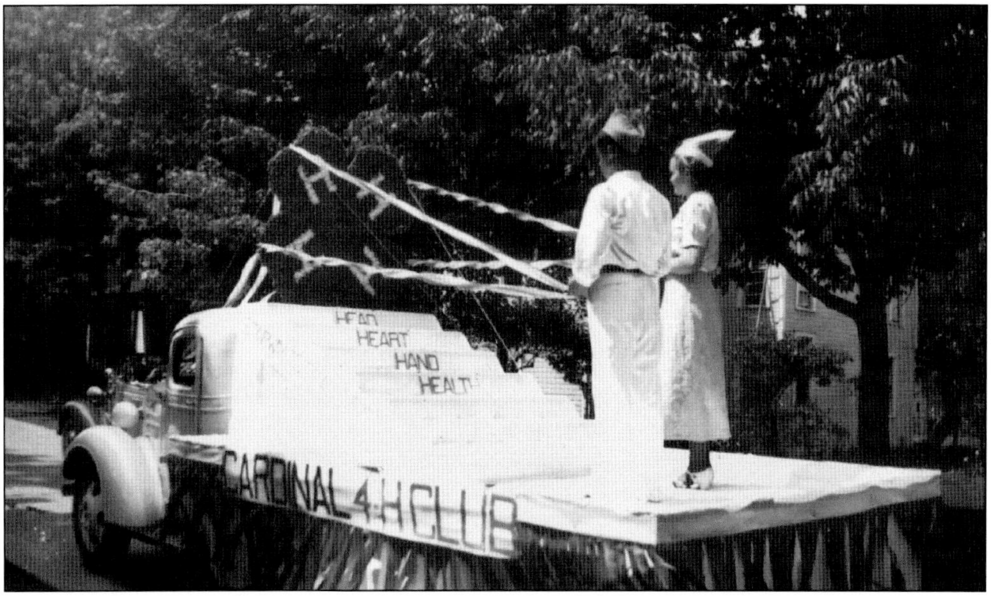


**A 4-H FLOAT.** This 1937 photograph shows Carrol Ford, left, and Martha Coyner, right, riding the "Cardinal 4-H Club" float in the second Strawberry Festival. The four H's represent Head, Heart, Hand, and Health. (Photo courtesy of UCHS, Brooks Casto Collection.)

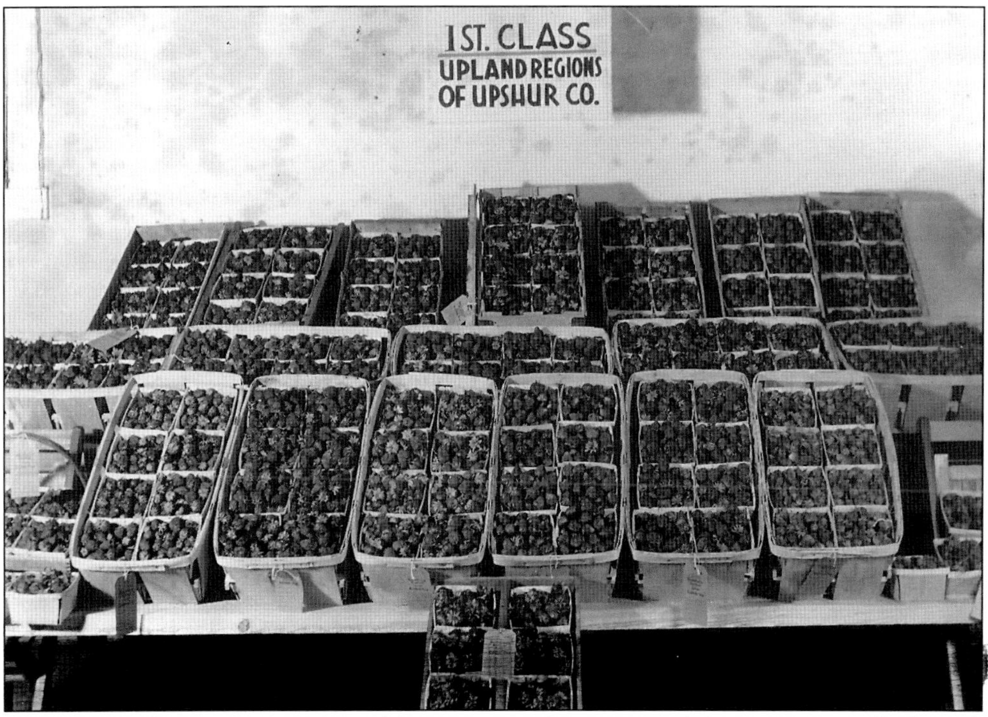


**STRAWBERRY COMPETITION.** Pictured here are strawberries on exhibit at a very early festival. During the early years of the West Virginia Strawberry Festival, great emphasis was placed on cultivating large fields for strawberry production. Thousands of gallons of Upshur berries were sold in Pittsburgh for ice cream making. (Photo courtesy of UCHS, Home Hardware Collection.)

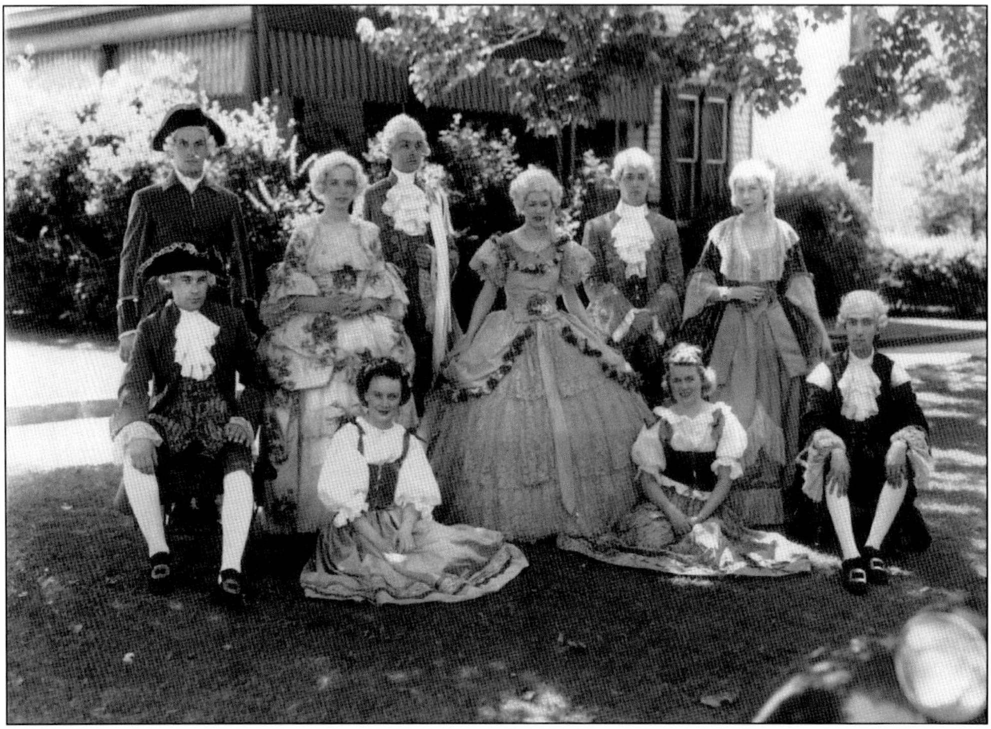

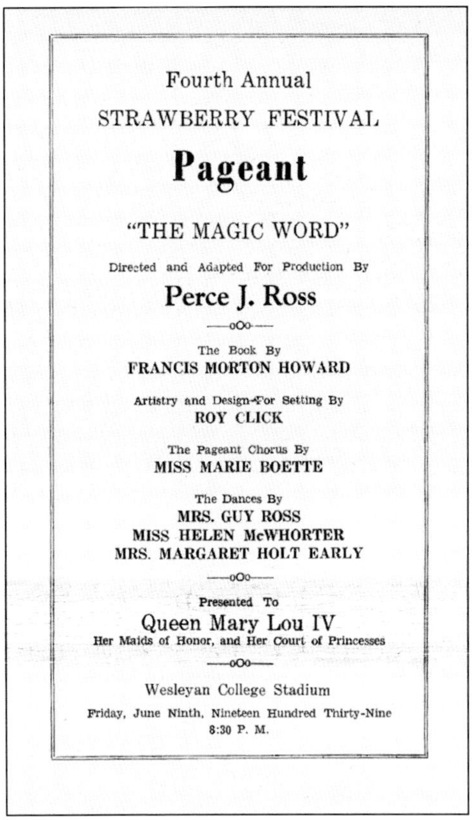

Fourth Annual
STRAWBERRY FESTIVAL

**Pageant**

"THE MAGIC WORD"

Directed and Adapted For Production By

**Perce J. Ross**

—oOo—

The Book By
**FRANCIS MORTON HOWARD**

Artistry and Design-For Setting By
**ROY CLICK**

The Pageant Chorus By
**MISS MARIE BOETTE**

The Dances By
**MRS. GUY ROSS**
**MISS HELEN McWHORTER**
**MRS. MARGARET HOLT EARLY**

—oOo—

**Presented To**
Queen Mary Lou IV
**Her Maids of Honor, and Her Court of Princesses**

—oOo—

Wesleyan College Stadium
Friday, June Ninth, Nineteen Hundred Thirty-Nine
8:30 P. M.

**STRAWBERRY FESTIVAL PAGEANT, 1939.** The highlight of the early festivals was the pageants or plays. The 1939 program and cast pictured here featured the production of *The Magic Word* under the direction of the well-remembered Perce J. Ross. Marie Boette, chorus director, was at that time the director of choral music at West Virginia Wesleyan College. The program lists H.C. Farnsworth, Cora Mae Stout, Peg Watson, Betty Williams, Eugene Stewart, Betty Rae Shumaker, Junior Hinkle, Guy Douglas Jr., Flossie Lineberger, and Donald Davis as the cast; however, the only individual to be accurately identified in the photograph is the well-known "Tuck" Farnsworth, pictured in the center back row. (Document and photo courtesy of UCHS, Farnsworth Estate Collection.)

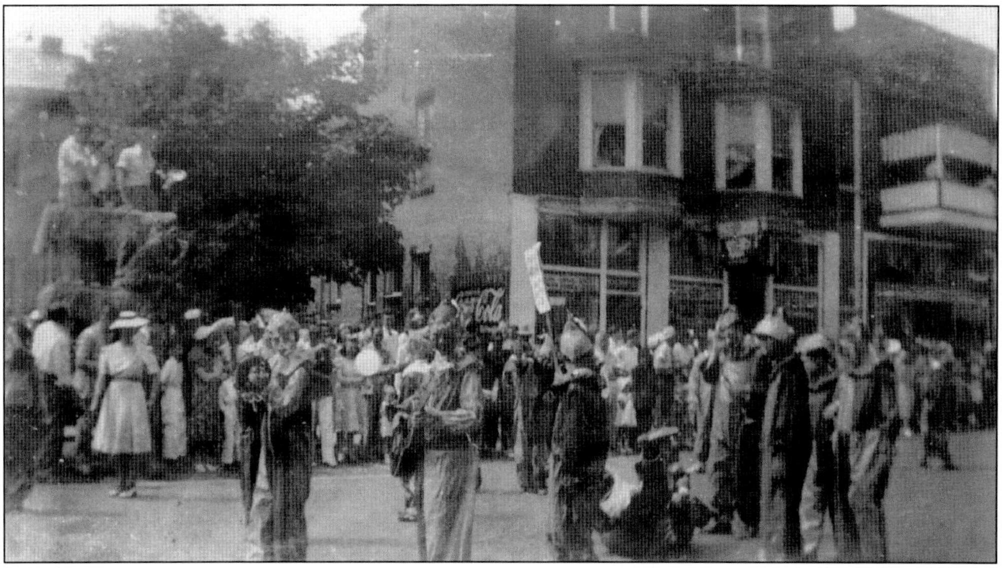

**CHILDREN'S PARADE, 1940.** An important aspect of the early Strawberry Festivals were the youth parades. This photograph, depicting the theme "The Circus" with children in clown costumes, was taken in front of the present-day Bookstore on Main Street. This parade was held early Thursday morning each year during the festival. Students from all over the county took part with many teachers serving on the parade committee. (Photo courtesy of UCHS, Tom Bailey Collection.)

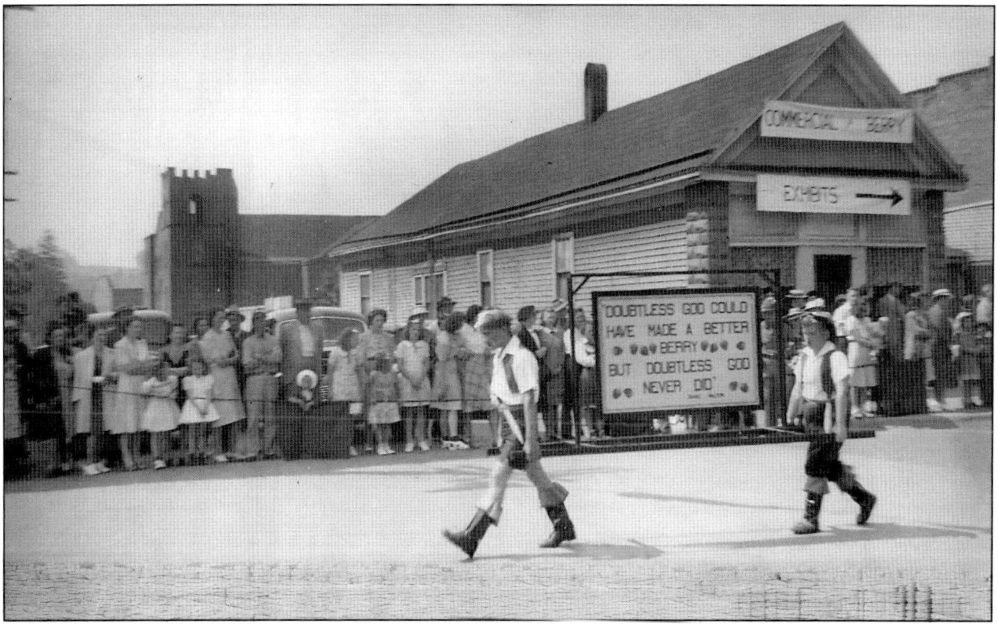


**CHILDREN'S PARADE, 1941.** The theme of the 1941 parade was "Our Golden Treasure: The Life and Growth of the Strawberry." Once again, children from throughout the county participated in the Children's Parade on Thursday morning. Pictured here are two unidentified boys carrying a sign, near the corner of South Florida and Main Streets, which reads, "Doubtless God could have made a better berry, but doubtless God never did"—Isaac Walton. (Photo courtesy of UCHS, Bekki Lewis Leigh Collection.)

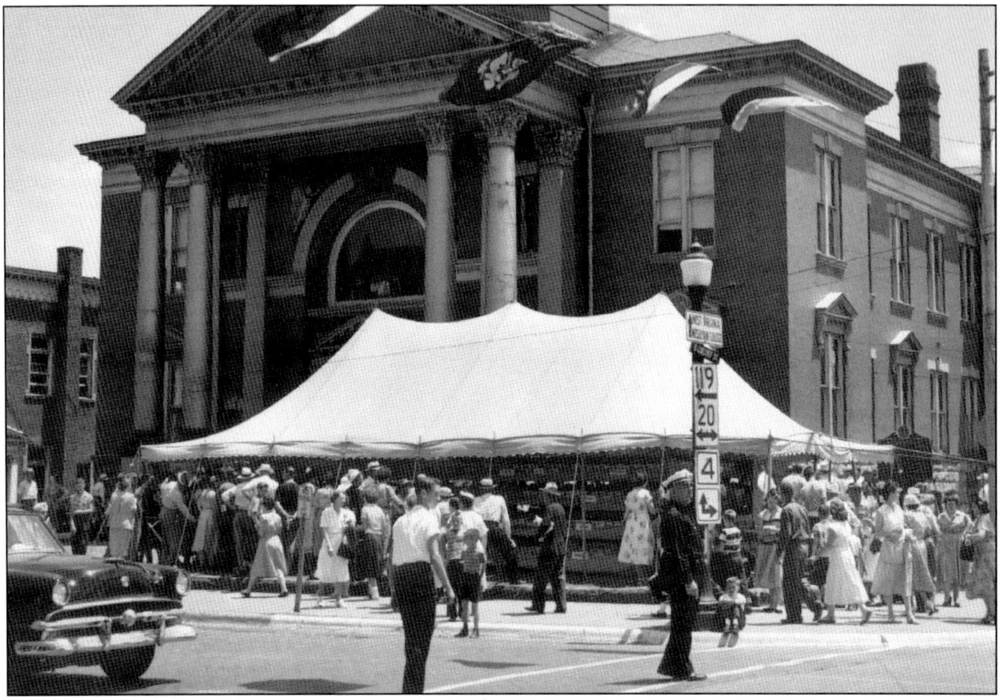

**STRAWBERRY EXHIBIT.** This 1955 Strawberry Festival exhibit in front of the courthouse reflects the greater emphasis on the production of berries than perhaps more recent festivals. About this time, Dr. Harold Almond, a local doctor, initiated the "sweetest berry" judging that was done by 12-year-old children whose taste buds were at the height of sensitivity. The courthouse appears to be in a state of needed repair notably on the columns and the dome base. (Photo courtesy of UCHS, Brooks Casto Collection.)

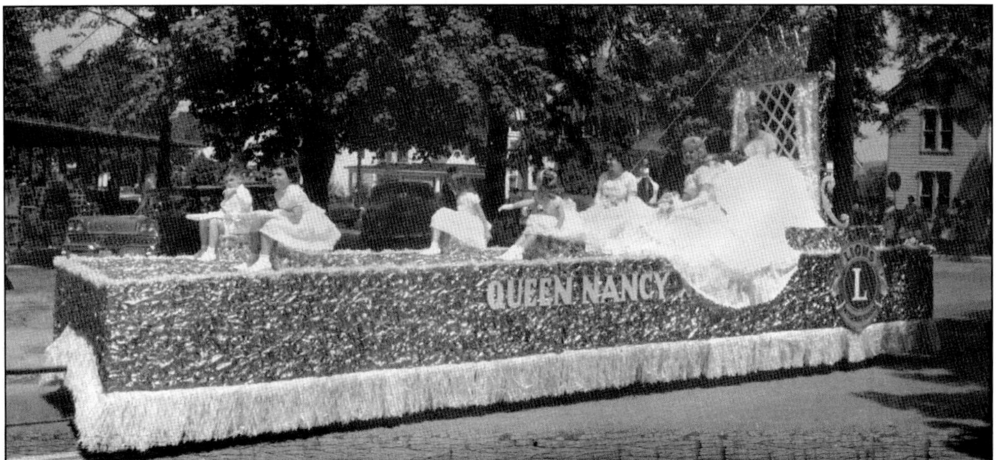


**STRAWBERRY FESTIVAL QUEEN NANCY, 1960.** At the core of the festival was, of course, the royal court and its pageantry. Pictured here in the 19th festival year is Queen Nancy Grace Conwell of Harrison County with maids Suzanne John of Lewis County and Sandra Hickman of Doddridge County. The court children are unidentified. Looking carefully at the background of the photograph, one can see that the new addition to the Academy Grade School is being built. (Photo courtesy of UCHS, Delf A. Narona Estate.)

# *Eight*

# Businesses and Services

*From the time that the Goff brothers first established a general merchandise business in Buckhannon or Jacob Lorentz hauled his merchandise over the mountains on pack horses, businesses have come and gone in Upshur County. Practically every community had its own grist and saw mills, general stores, blacksmith shops, and any other business that the community wanted or could afford. In Buckhannon hotels, mills, general stores, department stores, photography studios and galleries, grocery stores, theaters, and an opera house have all been a part of the landscape, historically and contemporarily.*

*Dairies were a major part of the rural agricultural economy. Undertakers were needed in town and the country as well. Taxi and bus services came later in the 20th century, as did the need and possibility of insurance and hospitals. Electricity, city water, and telephone service came with the progress of the 20th century. Pictured in this chapter are examples of these many business and service endeavors.*

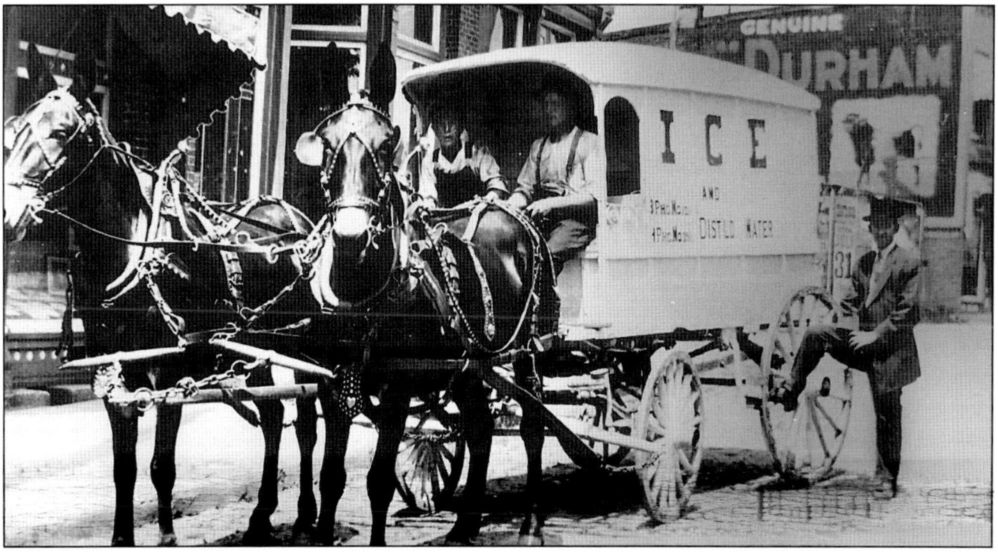


**John Smith, Iceman.** This photograph of John Smith and his helper with their ice wagon was taken in the early 20th century by Hode Clark just in front of Clark's studio on West Main Street. Smith continued to deliver ice through the 1930s. The old Upshur Building is in the immediate background, and the "Genuine Durham" building is still present today opposite the courthouse corner. (Photo courtesy of UCHS, Howard Hiner Collection.)

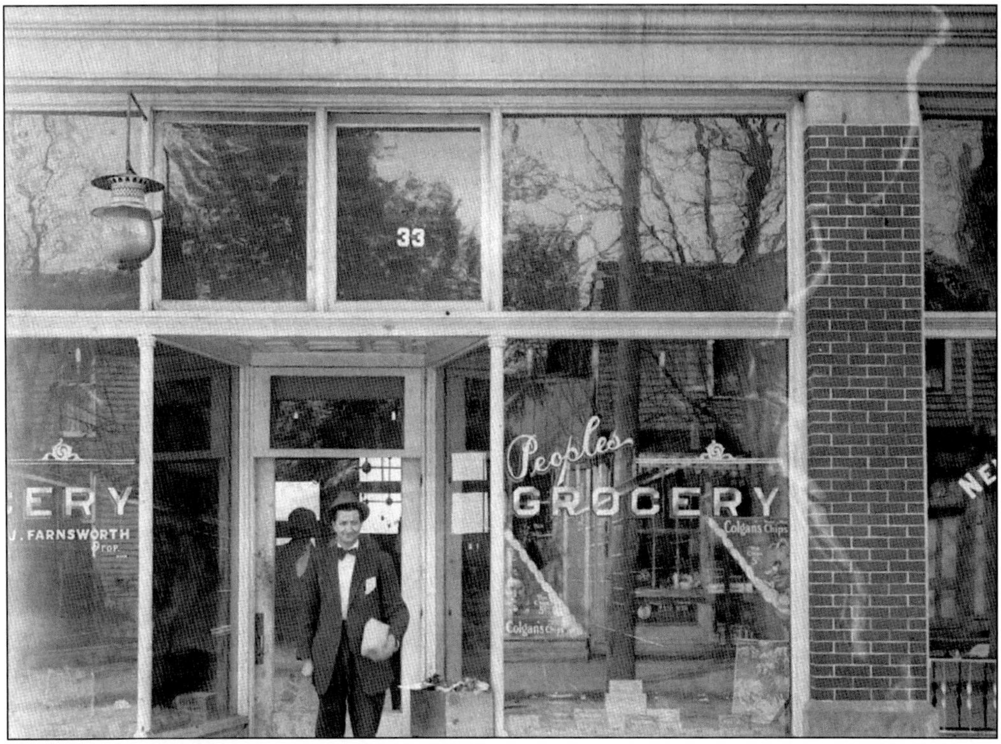


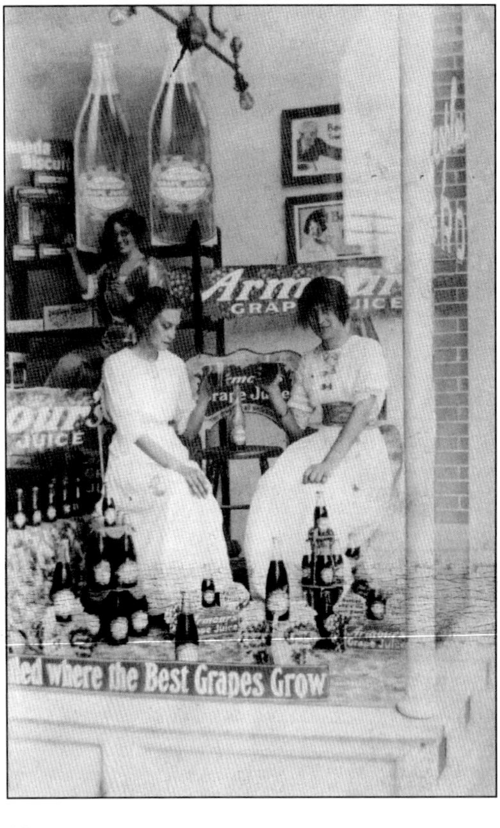


**PEOPLES GROCERY, 33 EAST MAIN STREET.** Pictured in the 1910–1919 photograph above is William J. "Dude" Farnsworth in front of his place of business, located in the Stockert Building. The People's Grocery was a landmark on this corner until it closed in 1973. From the time of Dude's death in 1919, the business was operated by the beloved Horace "Tuck" Farnsworth; his wife, Lucille Murray; and sister Elizabeth Farnsworth. The real photo postcard of the "live" window display at left shows Elizabeth (left) with an unidentified woman, *c.* 1919. The New Arlington Hotel was to the right. (Photo courtesy of UCHS, Farnsworth Estate Collection.)

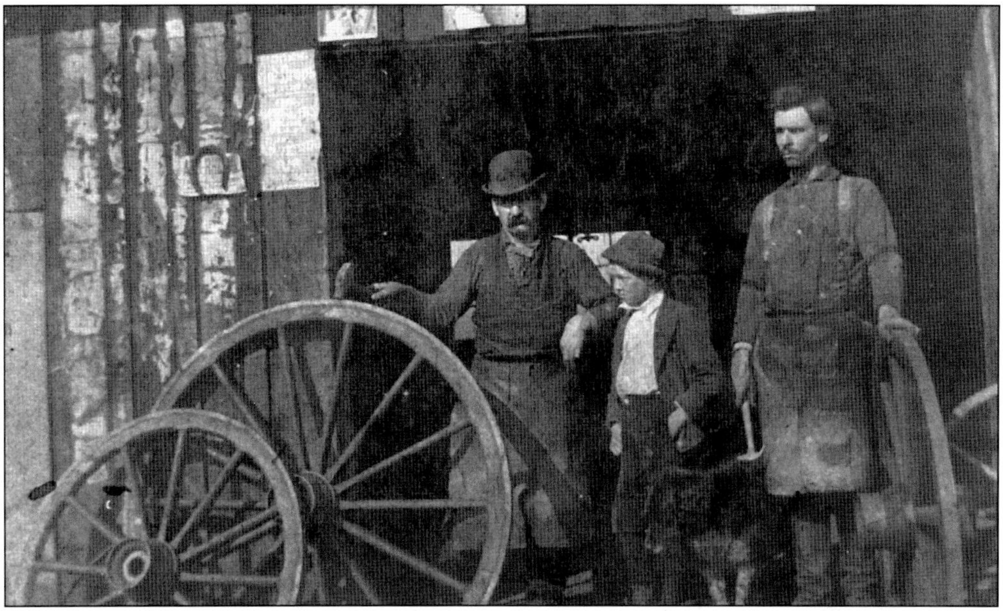

**ROCK CAVE BLACKSMITH SHOP.** Pictured c. 1910, from left to right, are John Vincent, owner; son Hubert; and Cooper Smith in front of Mr. Vincent's blacksmith in Rock Cave. (Photo courtesy of UCHS, Beulah Riffle Collection.)

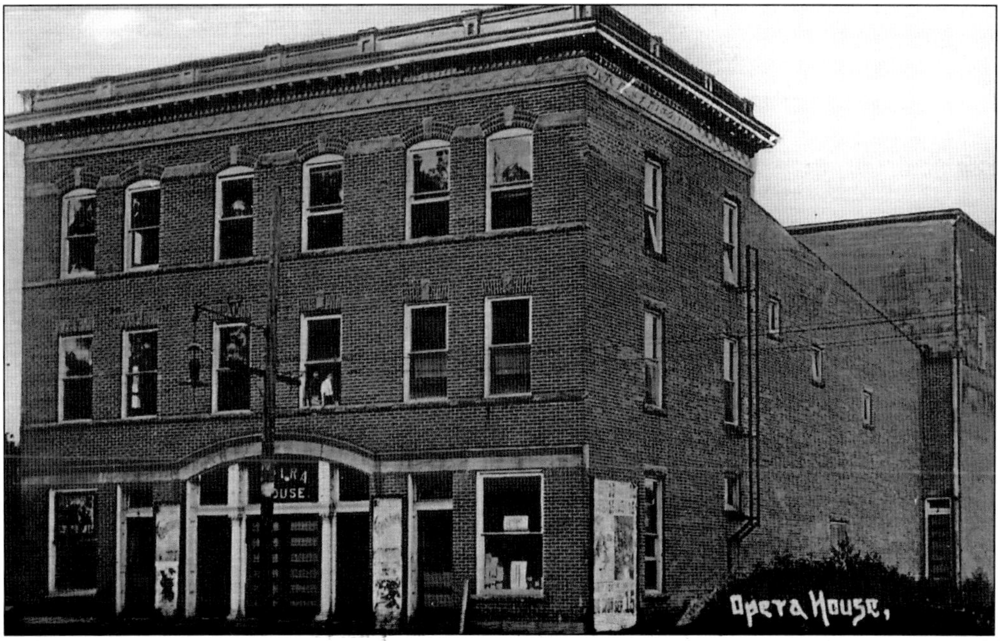


**BUCKHANNON OPERA HOUSE.** Buckhannon's New Opera House, located on North Kanawha Street, opened in 1903. Designed by Upshur County's leading architect, Draper C. Hughes, it cost $16,000 to build and seated 800 people. The stage was 30 by 52 feet and was illuminated with 150 incandescent lights. Over the years the structure served as town hall, a stage for live shows, and a motion picture theater. By 1950, with the establishment of the Kanawha and the Colonial theaters, the last film had been shown here, and on September 14, 1960, the building was destroyed by fire. (Photo courtesy of UCHS, Robert Grose Collection.)

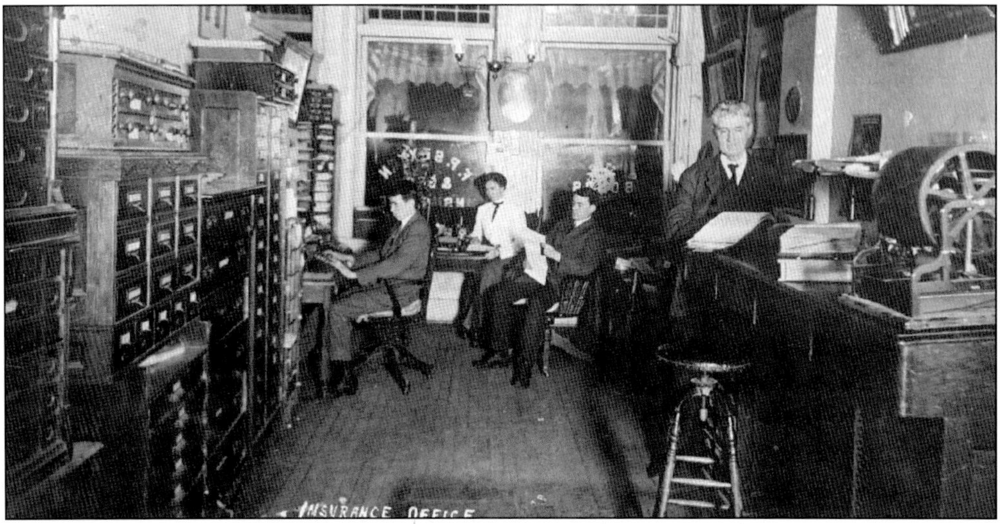

**SEXTON BROTHERS INSURANCE OFFICE.** This *c.* 1912 real photo postcard depicts the office of F.P. and Karl B. Sexton, insurance salesmen. The business was established in 1891 by F.P. with Karl B. joining in 1906. The exact identification of the individuals pictured here is not available. The Sextons' was the first insurance agency established in Upshur County and their motto was "Insurance that Insures." (Photo courtesy of UCHS, Anna Lee Combs Collection.)

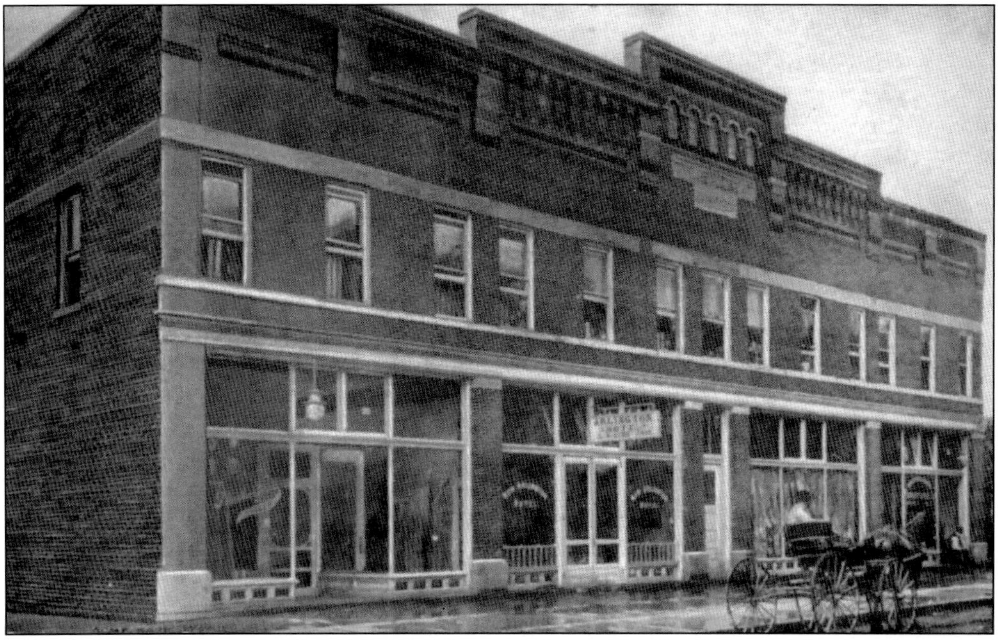

**NEW ARLINGTON HOTEL.** This 1908–1910 image shows the Stockert Building on East Main Street in Buckhannon. Built in 1908, it housed three businesses at the time of this photograph. In the left room was Shackleford's Grocery (to become People's Grocery in 1910); the two middle rooms held the New Arlington Hotel with L.W. Zinn, proprietor; and the far right room was the Whitescarver Furniture and Undertaking Store (to become Whitescarvers Undertakers, which relocated to various places before ending on Kanawha Street). Home Hardware has occupied most of this building since opening in 1947. (Photo courtesy of UCHS, Phyllis Miller Collection.)

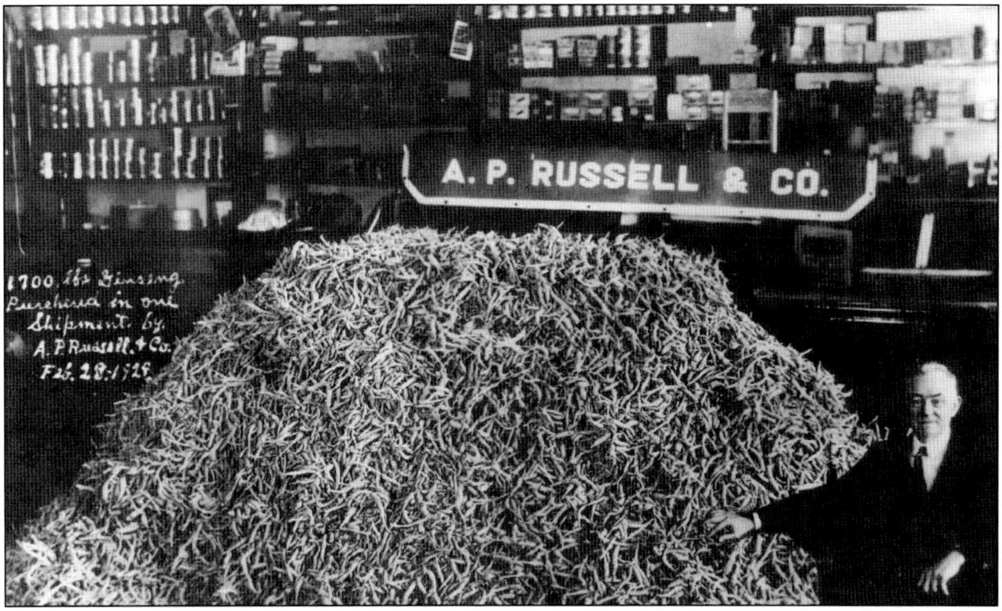


**A.P. Russell and Company, Ginseng.** Pictured here on February 28, 1929 is Asbury Patrick Russell with the famous photograph of "1700 lbs.of ginseng purchased in one shipment by A.P. Russell & Company." This building was where Kyle Reger, a nephew of Mr. Russell, later had his building supply business. (Photo courtesy of UCHS, Milford Reger Collection.)

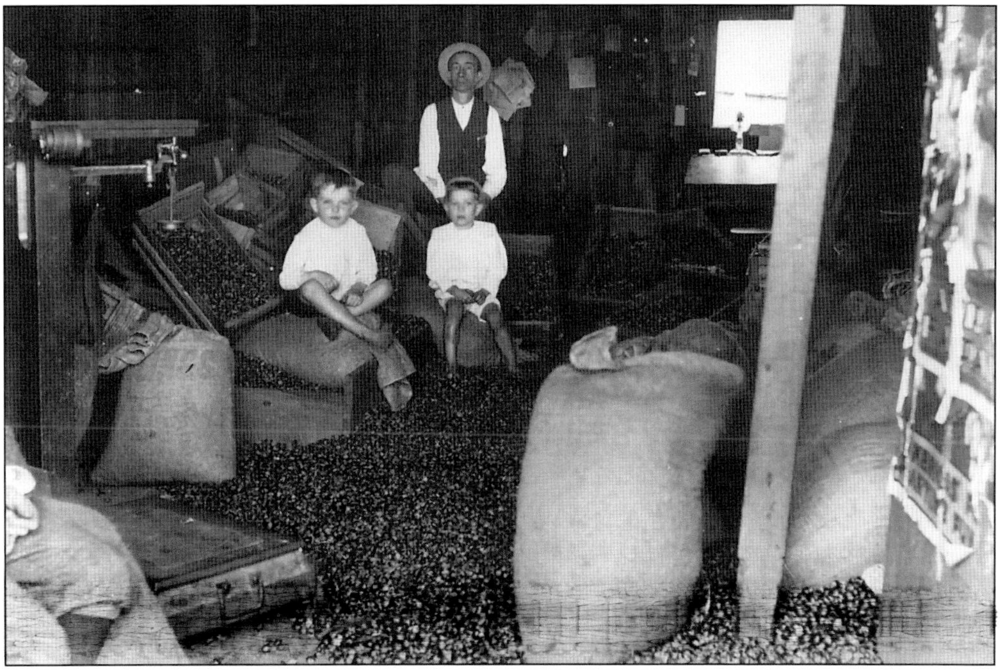

**A.P. Russell and Company, Chestnuts.** Pictured in this Hode Clark *c.* 1905 photograph, from left to right, are (front row) Raymond "Shoppy" Clark, son of the photographer; and Howard Farnsworth; (back row) T. O. Farnsworth, Howard's father. Mr. Russell bought and sold in bulk as seen here. Farmers hauled chestnuts by the wagonload before the blight caused the near extinction of this tree species.(Photo courtesy of UCHS, Howard Hiner Collection.)

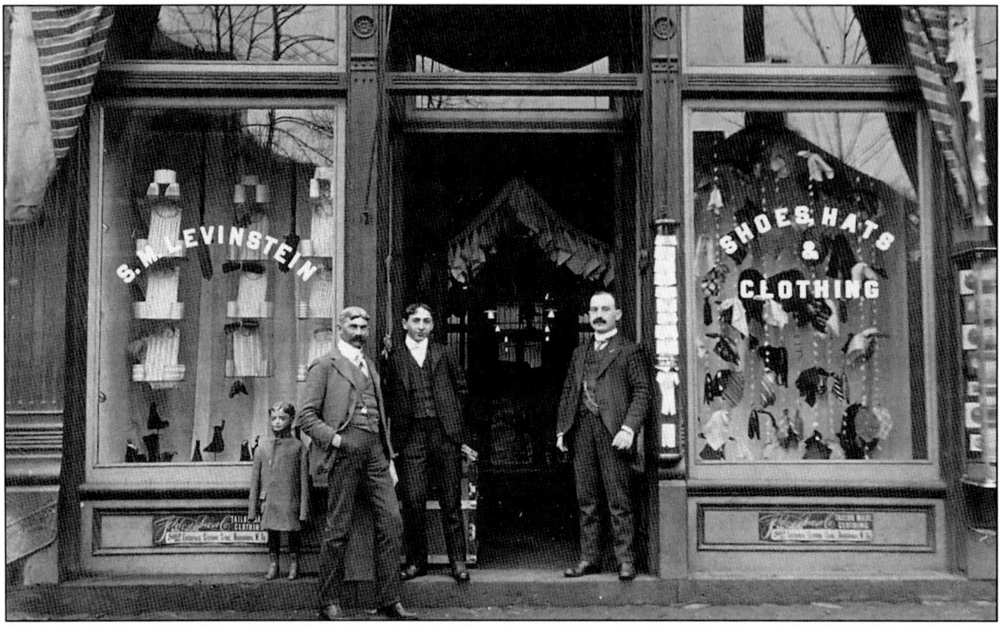


**LEVINSTEIN'S DEPARTMENT STORE.** Pictured here is the Simon Levinstein Clothing Store, c. 1900. Mr. Levinstein arrived in the Buckhannon Valley from Baltimore as a 15-year-old Russian-Jewish peddler. In 1898 he open his first place of business, moving into the T.J. Farnsworth building, pictured here, in 1900. In 1912 he moved his business to the corner of Kanawha and Main Streets, where the law offices of Burton Hunter are presently located. The three men here are unidentified. The business lasted until the mid-1940s. (Photo courtesy of UCHS, Tom Stockert Estate Collection.)

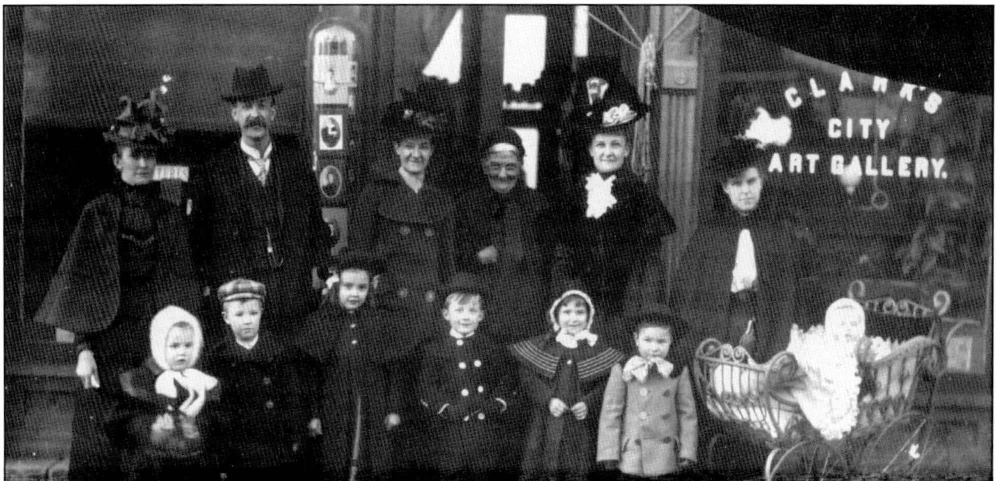


**CLARK'S CITY ART GALLERY.** Horace R. Hode Clark established his photography business in the late 1890s and became the most prolific of all Upshur County photographers. His images recorded all aspects of life in Buckhannon and Uphsur County, from business interiors to residence and church buildings to family groups and portraits. These people are all unidentified. Clark's studio was located at 59 West Main Street beside the old Upshur Building and was purchased by Howard Hiner in the 1950s. This image was made from one of several glass negatives salvaged by Mr. Hiner. (Photo courtesy of UCHS, Permanent Collection.)

**Murphy's 5¢ & 10¢.** This five-and-dime store, pictured c. 1930, was located in the T.J. Farnsworth building across from the courthouse. The business was soon moved further up Main Street and expanded in 1937. It remained there until it closed in the late 1990s; today, the Main Street Antique Mall occupies the space. (Photo courtesy of UCHS, Howard Hiner Collection.)

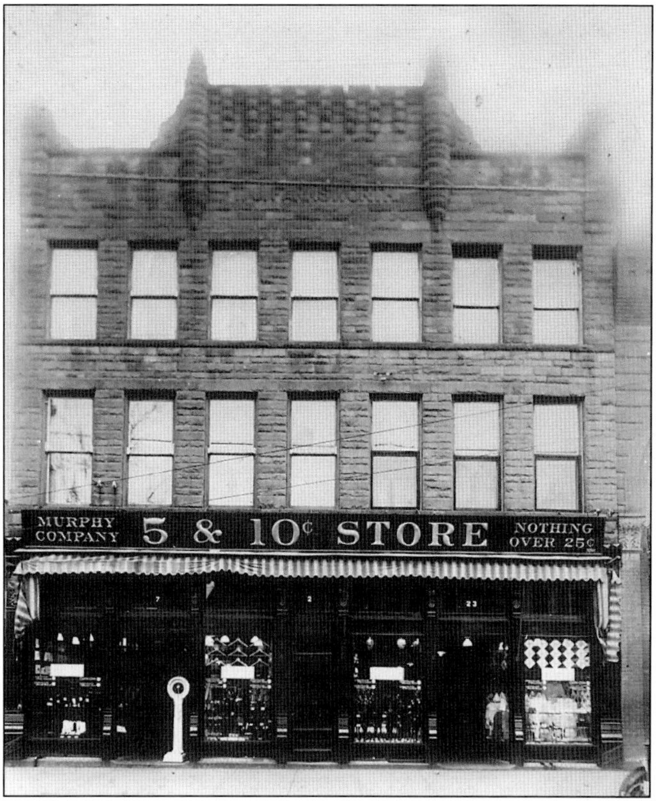


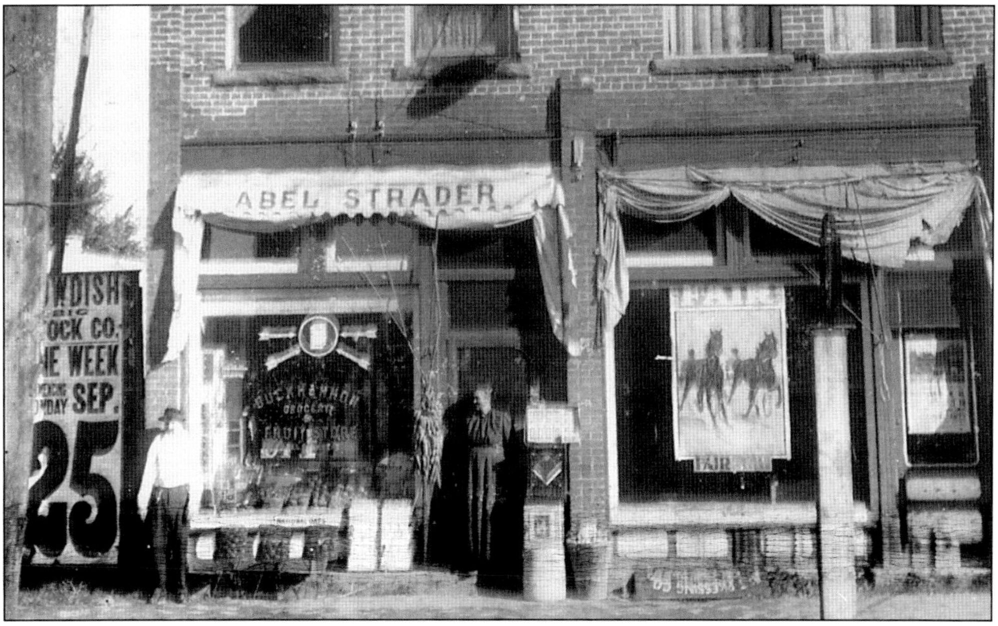


**Abel Strader Business.** This Buckhannon Grocery and Fruit Store photograph, taken in 1905, depicts one of the many small businesses on Main Street, Buckhannon. Abel Strader and his wife are pictured in front of their place of business. (Photo courtesy of UCHS, Noel W. Tenney Collection.)

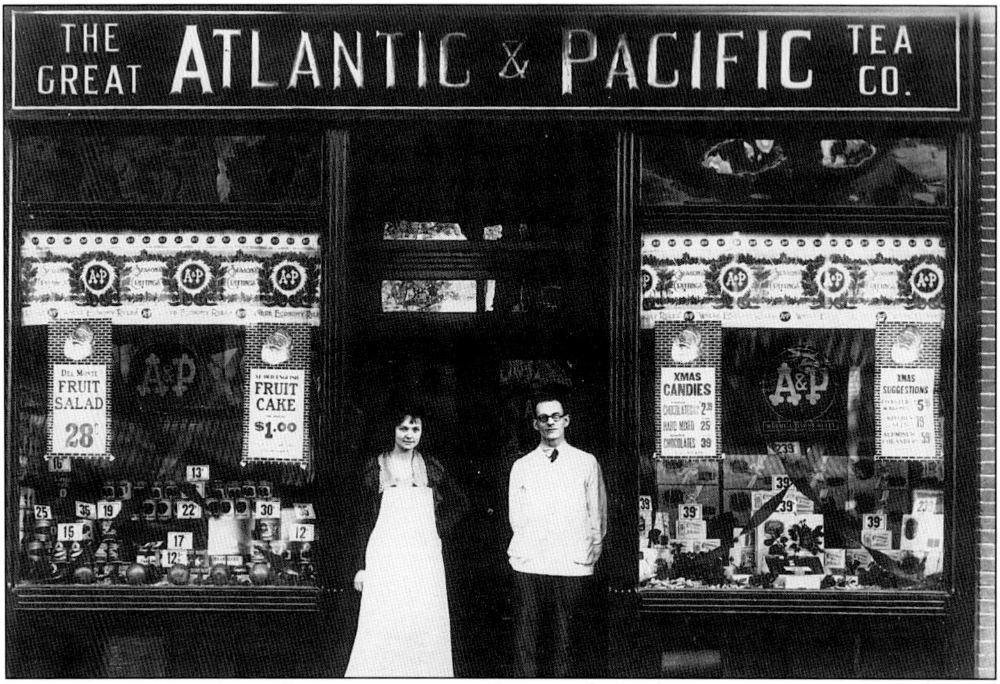


**ATLANTIC AND PACIFIC STORE.** The first A&P store opened on Main Street, Buckhannon in 1925. Pictured here are two unidentified clerks at the 15 East Main Street location (present location of the Bookstore) with the store windows all decked out for Christmas sales in the 1930s. In 1940 the two A&P stores on Main Street were consolidated into the new building on Spring Street. (Photo courtesy of UCHS, Howard Hiner Collection.)

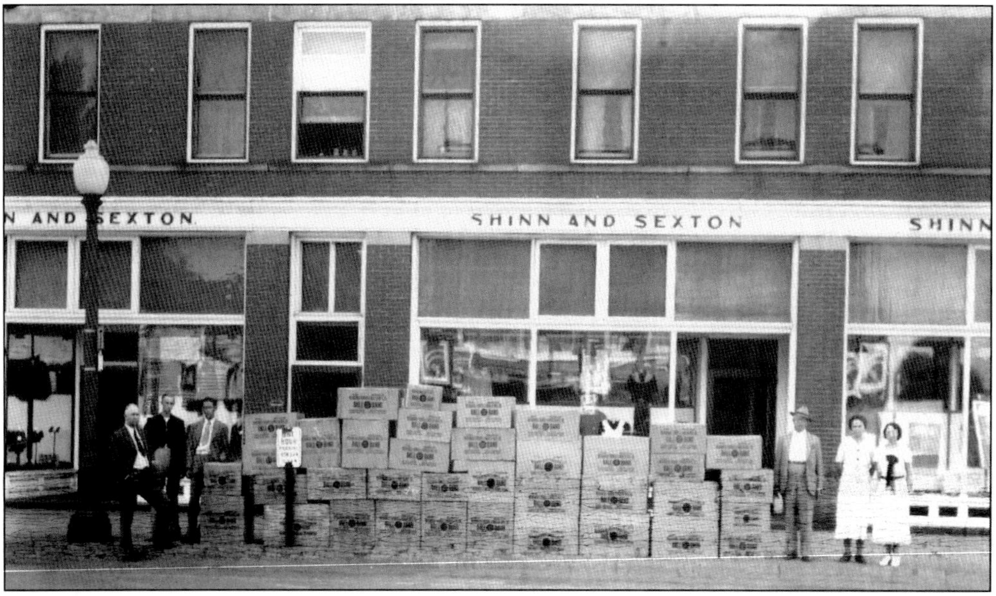


**SHINN AND SEXTON.** Following the closing of the New Arlington Hotel in 1916, the Shinn and Sexton Department Store became the next occupant of the Stockert Building on East Main Street. Pictured here is the unidentified staff of that business receiving a large shipment of Ball footwear in the 1930s or early 1940s. (Photo courtesy of UCHS, permanent collection.)

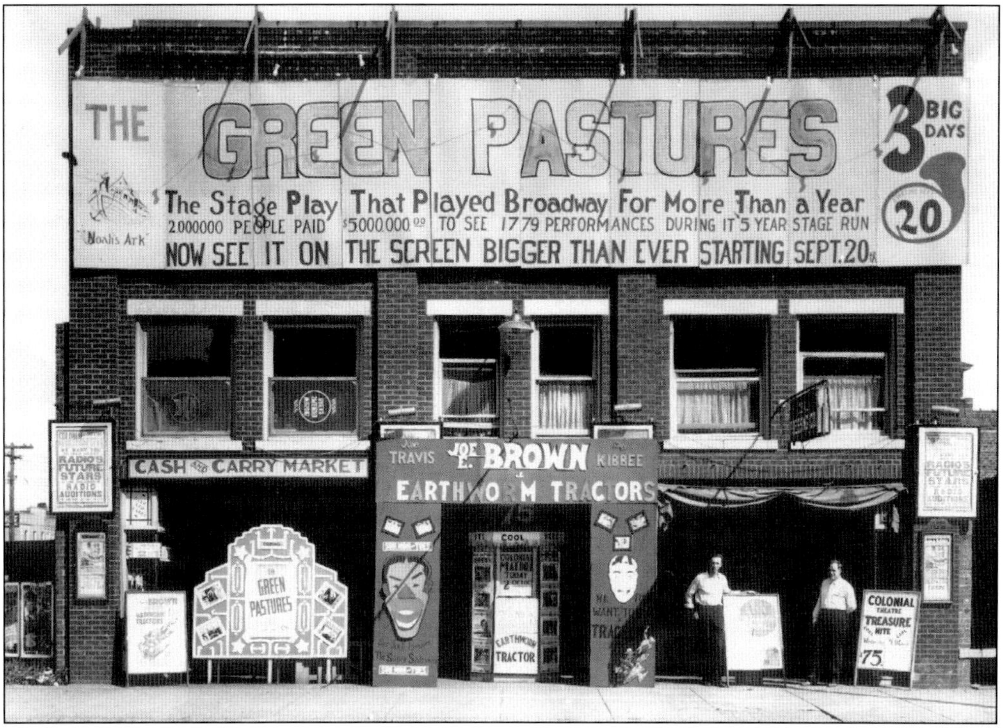


**THE GREEN PASTURES.** This 1937 photograph of the Colonial Theatre shows the preparations for *The Green Pastures* extravaganza. Garland West opened his theater in 1929 and operated a cleaning and pressing shop there also. Pictured, from left to right, are Enoch Watson, projectionist, and West. This business was located on East Main Street directly across from Home Hardware. (Photo courtesy of UCHS, permanent collection.)

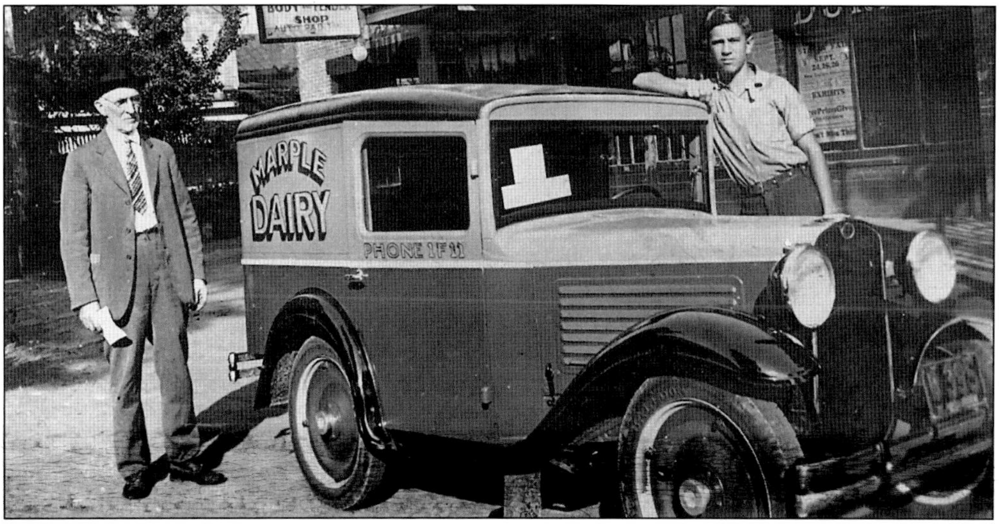


**MARPLE DAIRY.** Frank Marple, left, and his son Henry Marple are shown with their small delivery van in the 1930s. The Marple Dairy was situated on Weston Road near Lorentz. Small farm dairies were scattered throughout Upshur County, and many will remember such names as Brown's, Phillips Maple Lawn, St. Clairs, Upshur, and the Home Dairy of West Virginia on College Avenue. (Photo courtesy of UCHS, Henry Marple Collection.)

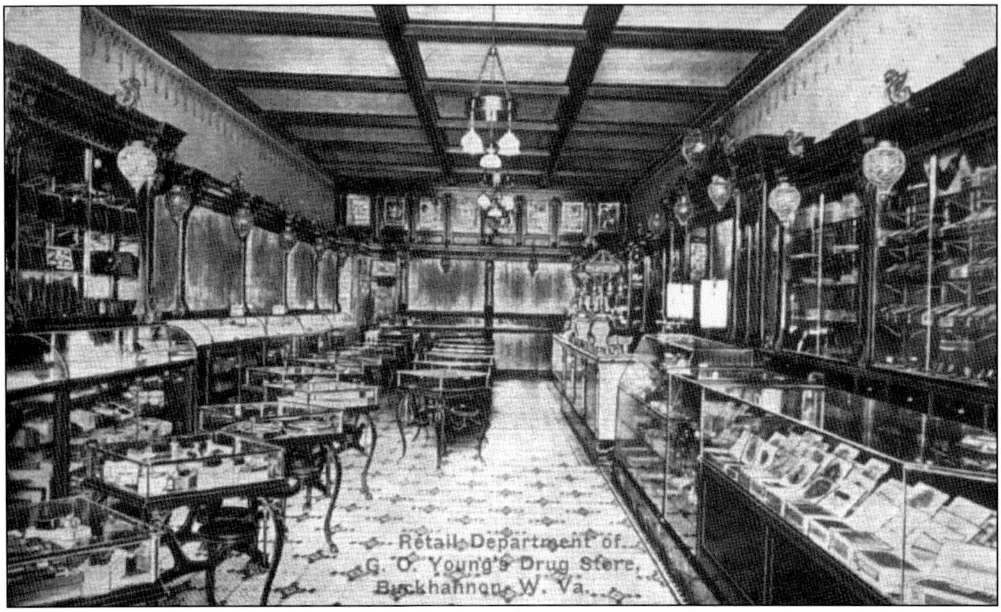


**G.O. Young Drug Store.** This postcard view of the interior of the famous Young's Drug Store shows the elegance that was created in 1911 when the building opened. The 17 ice cream tables alone could seat 68 people at once. Young was in business until the mid-1940s when he sold to it to Edward Baxa. A few years later it became Miller's Pharmacy, which operates there today. (Photo courtesy of UCHS, Phyllis Miller Collection.)

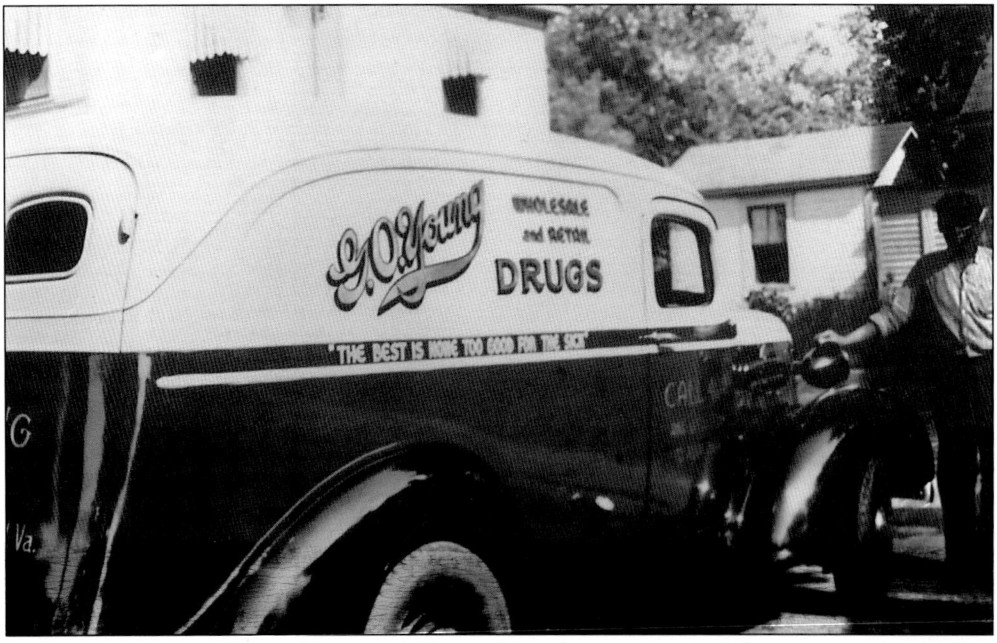


**G.O. Young Drug Store Delivery.** Home delivery was a sign of the times, as pictured in this 1931 delivery system of the Young's Drug Store. This business owner had various unusual advertising techniques including mile posts all over central West Virginia that showed how many miles it was to Young's Drug Store, where "The best is none too good for the sick." The driver here is unidentified. (Photo courtesy of UCHS, Sally Young Waddell Collection.)

**Fair Price Gas and Oil Company.** This 1941 photograph shows the unidentified, efficient staff at this Buckhannon service station. H.D. Abbott was the owner of the station located on Island Avenue. (Photo courtesy of UCHS, Bekki Lewis Leigh Collection.)

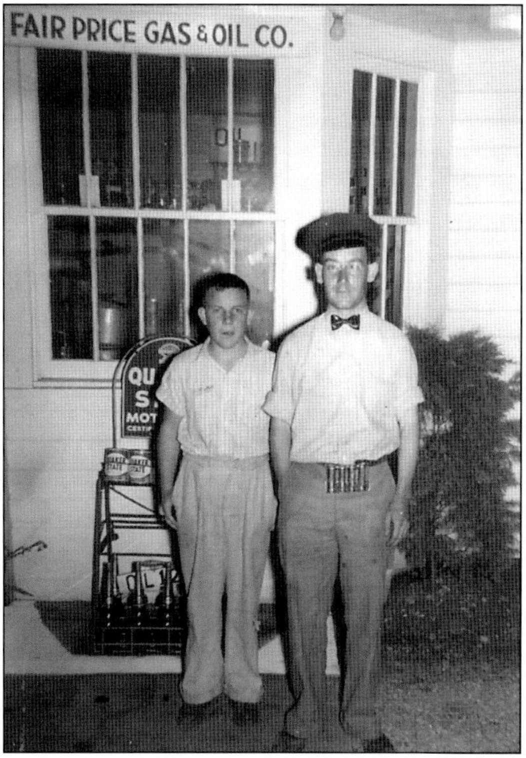


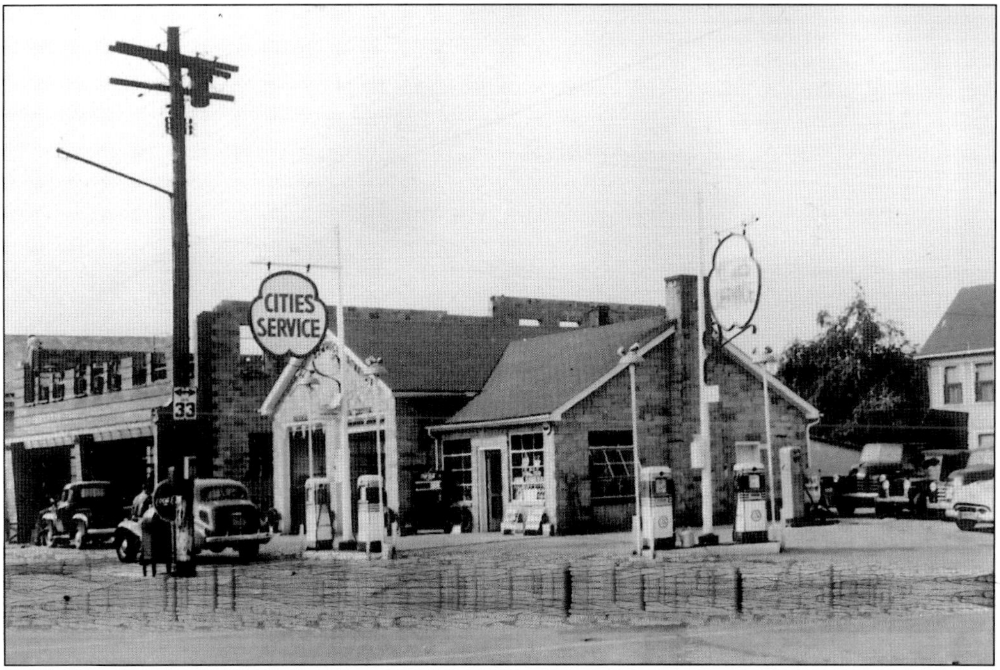


**Corner of Main and Locust Streets.** This *c.* 1949 photograph shows the Cities Service station on the corner across from the courthouse where the Progressive Bank is located today. The Buckhannon Fire Station is under construction to the left. (Photo courtesy of UCHS, Henry Maple Collection.)

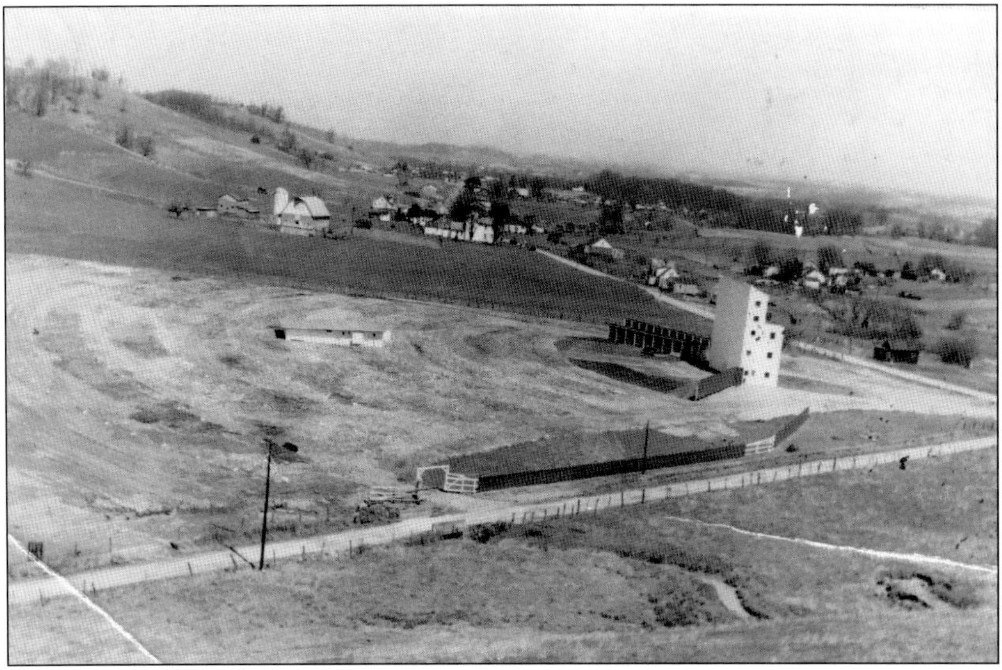

**Garland West Enterprises.** The above photograph was taken in 1949 when Garland West opened his $100,000-outdoor theater in Tennerton. It could host 350 automobiles and boasted a screen size of 40 by 48 feet. The first film to show was *Copacobana*. West also owned the Colonial Theater on East Main Street and the only swimming pool in Buckhannon, pictured below on East Main Street. This property was eventually purchased by the Hinkle family. (Photos courtesy of UCHS, Lota Marie West Wilfong Estate Collection.)

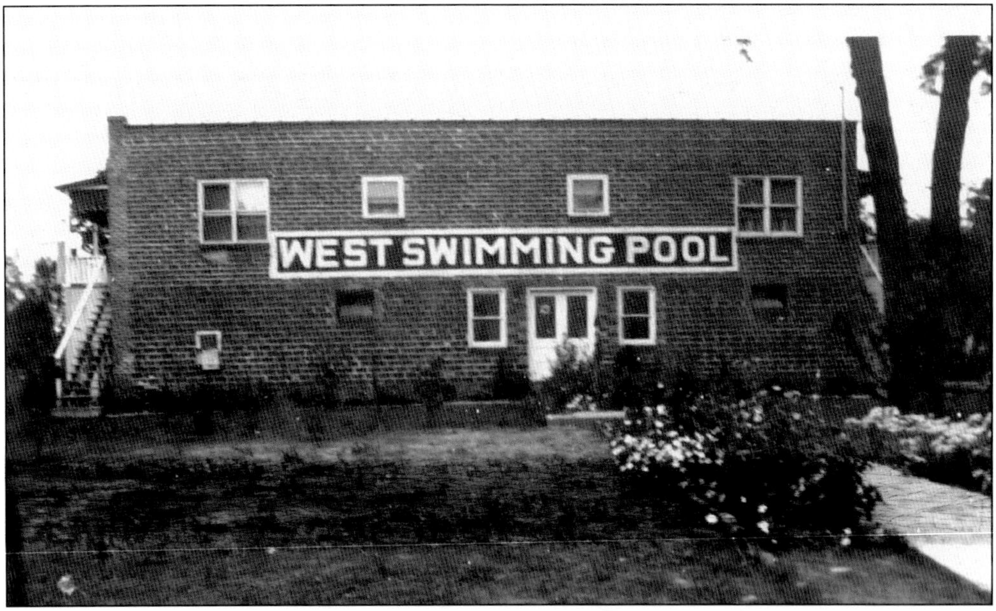

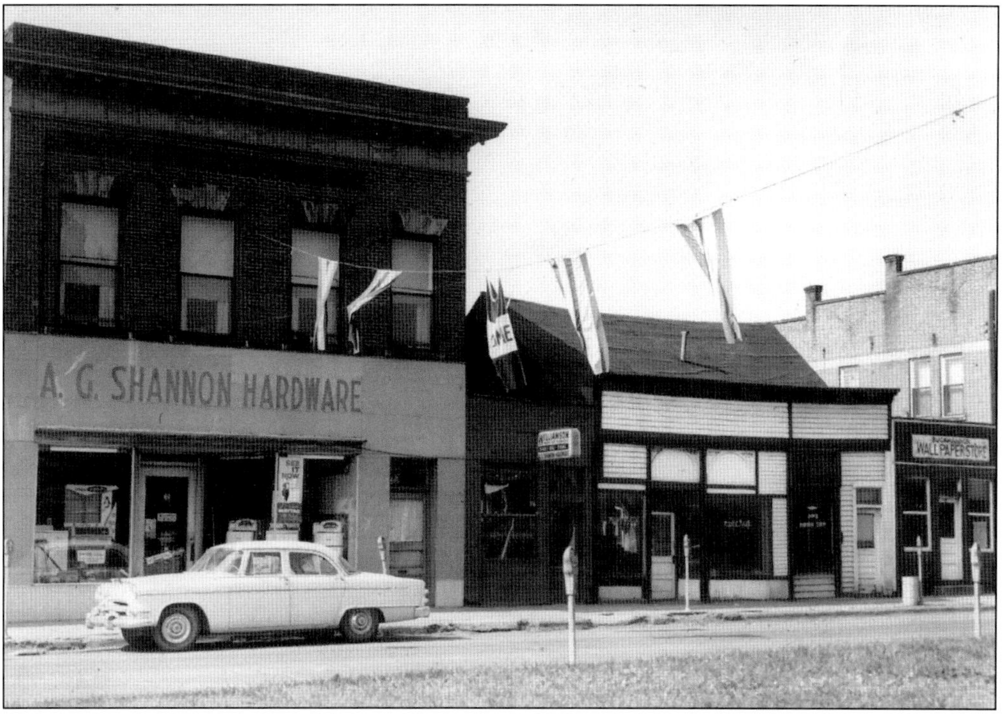


**A.G. Shannon Hardware.** This 1955 photograph shows the south side of East Main Street, near the Florida Street corner, when Shannon's Hardware was the key business along with the Musick Mart, Jim's Barber Shop, and Buckhannon Wallpaper Store. A.G. Shannon began his business in 1922 as Upshur Hardware and changed the name to Shannon's in 1940. (Photo courtesy of UCHS, Raymond Phillips Collection.)

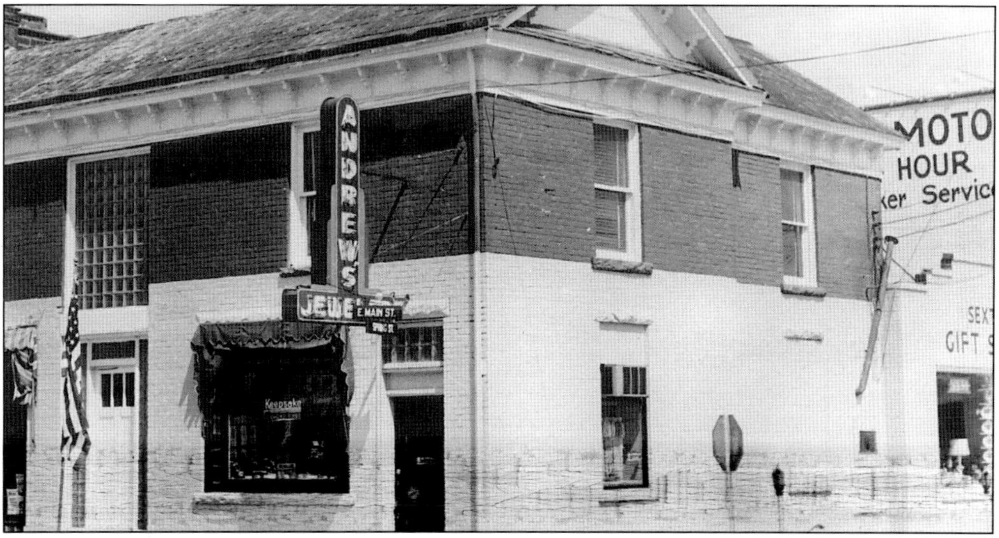


**Corner of Main and Spring Streets.** In this *c.* 1963 photograph, Andrew's Jewelry was located where the Inter-Mountain Newspaper office is today. This building was originally situated further back from the street, and during the Civil War era, Marcia Sumners Phillips wrote in her famous diary from these windows. (Photo courtesy of UCHS, Home Hardware Collection.)

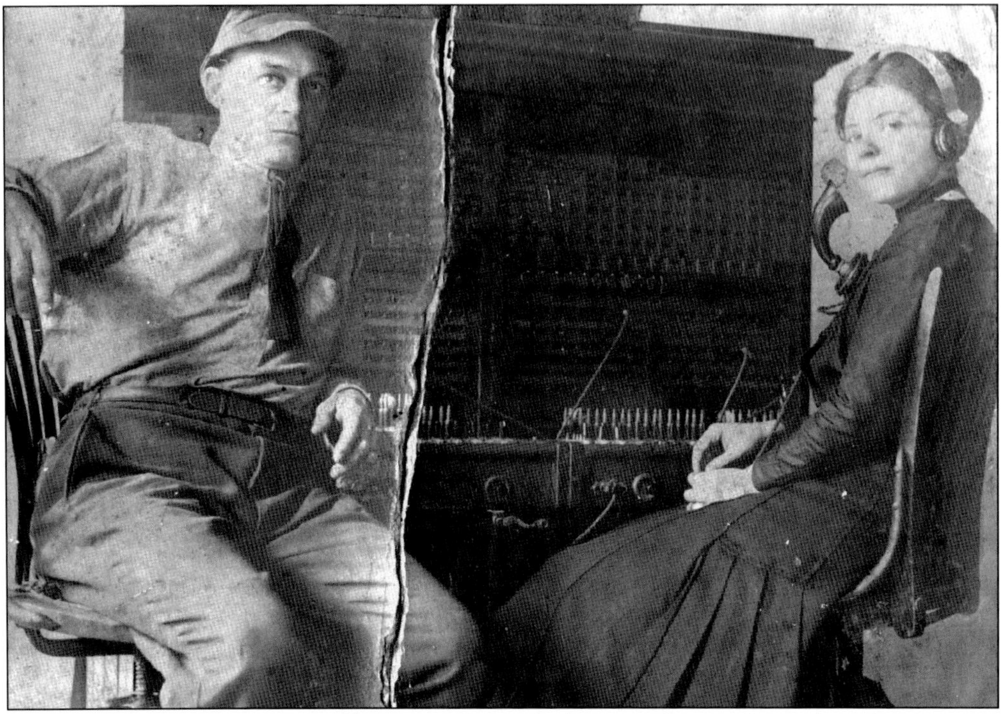

**TELEPHONE SWITCHBOARD.** Buckhannon's first telephone exchange, located in the Simpson Building, was opened for service in 1904. Pictured here at the switchboard is Georgia L. House with an unidentified man. (Photo courtesy of UCHS, Steve Holmes Collection.)

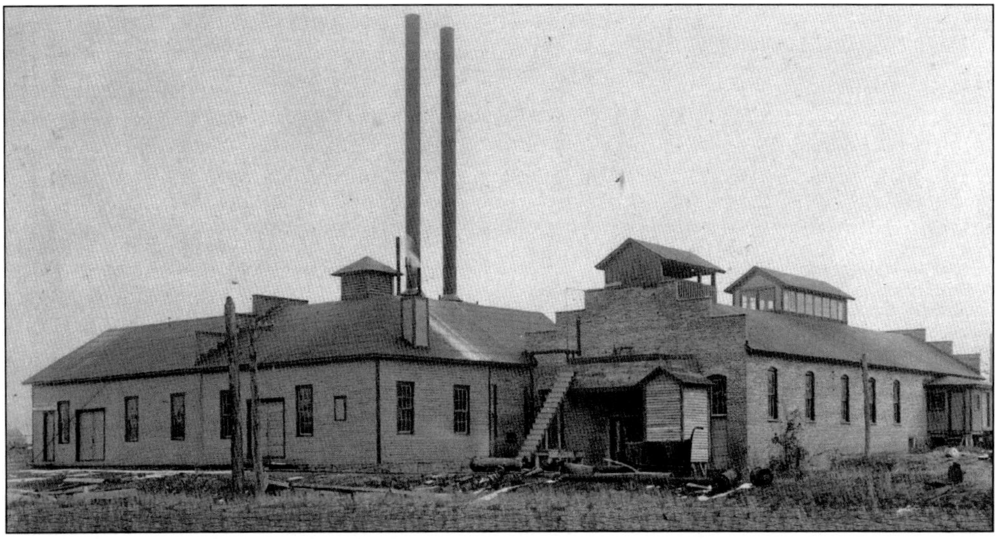

**BUCKHANNON LIGHT & WATER COMPANY.** Privately owned and organized in 1902, Buckhannon Light & Water Company was located on Wood Street in South Buckhannon. They also manufactured "artificial ice" by pumping water from the Buckhannon River to serve city residences. Ice was made from boiled and filtered water, "free from germs or vegetable matter of any description." It was sold locally and shipped to surrounding areas via the B&O Railroad. Part of this building today is occupied by A.F. Wendling. (Photo courtesy of UCHS, Joy Tenney Shingleton Collection.)

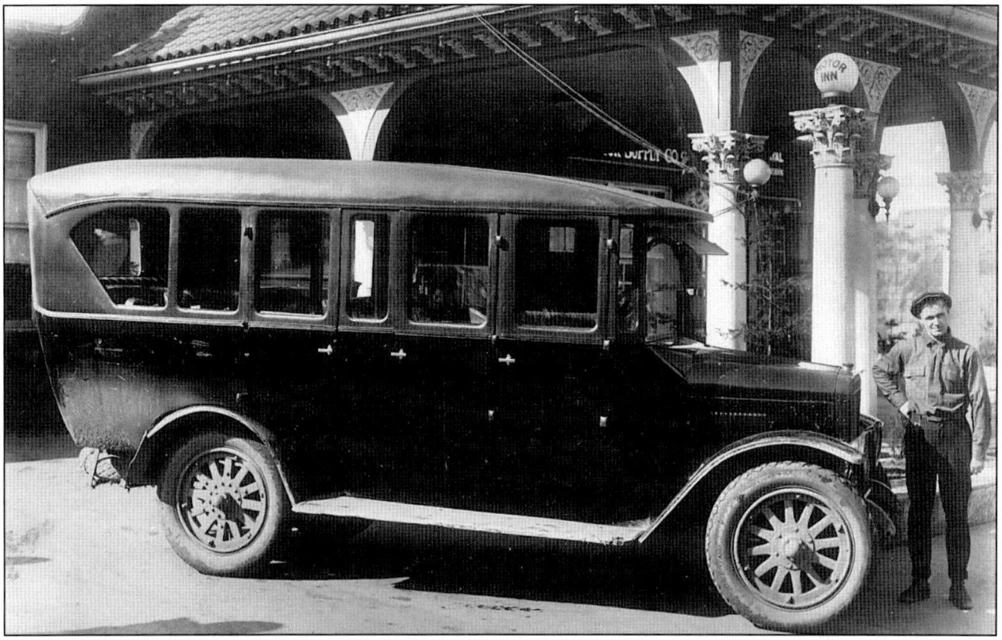

**Early Upshur County Taxi.** Pictured here is Troy T. Vincent of Rock Cave, between 1915 and 1920. Vincent operated one of the first taxies in Upshur County. The non-local location of the "Motor Inn" is unknown. (Photo courtesy of UCHS, Beulah Riffle Collection.)

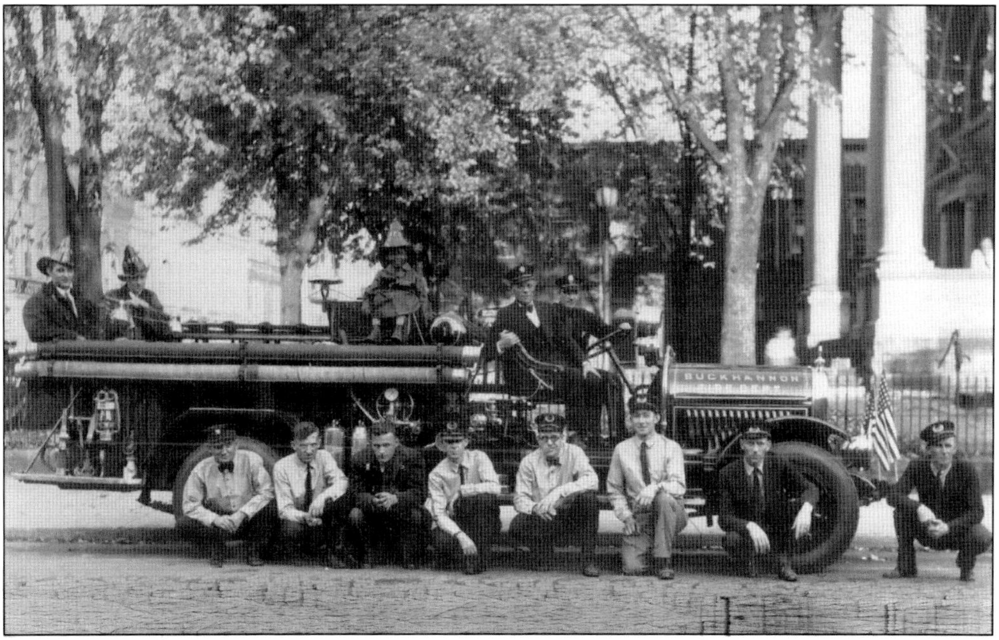


**Buckhannon Fire Department.** This 1929 photograph shows, from left to right, the following: (front row) Bob Travis, Mac McGowan, unidentified, Charlie Post, Garland West, unidentified, Ernie Andrews, and ? Travis; (back row) two unidentified people, ? Carter, ? Curtis, and Charles Madison. As early as the 1870s, calls were made for the formation of a hook and ladder company. Buckhannon Fire Department records begin in 1903 when A.C. Fox became chief with 31 volunteers. (Photo courtesy of UCHS, Benny J. Hibbs Collection.)

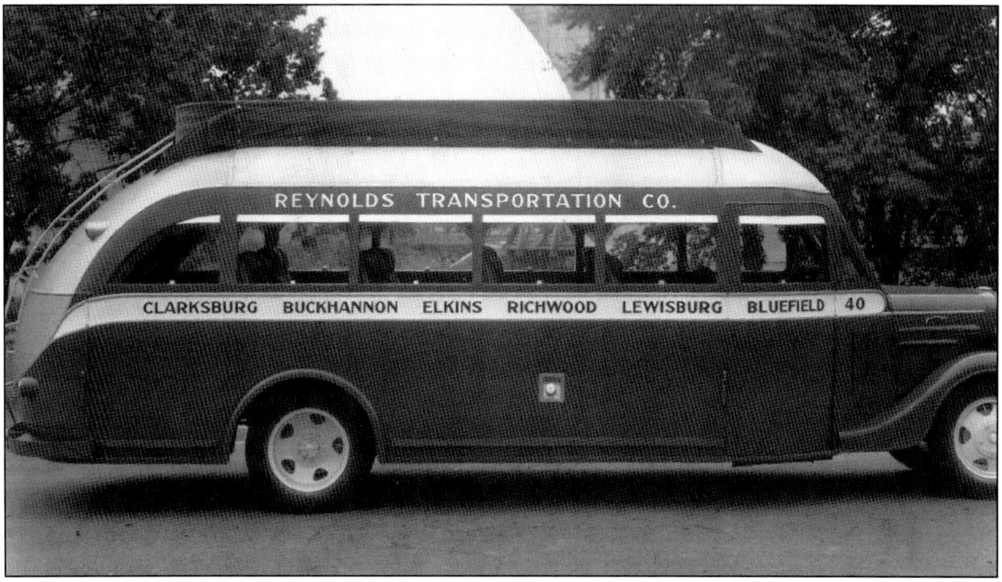


**REYNOLDS TRANSPORTATION CO.** This brand-new bus was purchased in Sidney, Ohio for the Tenney's Reynolds Transportation Company in the early 1940s. M.H. "Monk" Tenney operated both the Reynolds Bus Line and the Tenney Taxi for many years in Buckhannon. (Photo courtesy of UCHS, Joy Tenney Shingleton Collection.)

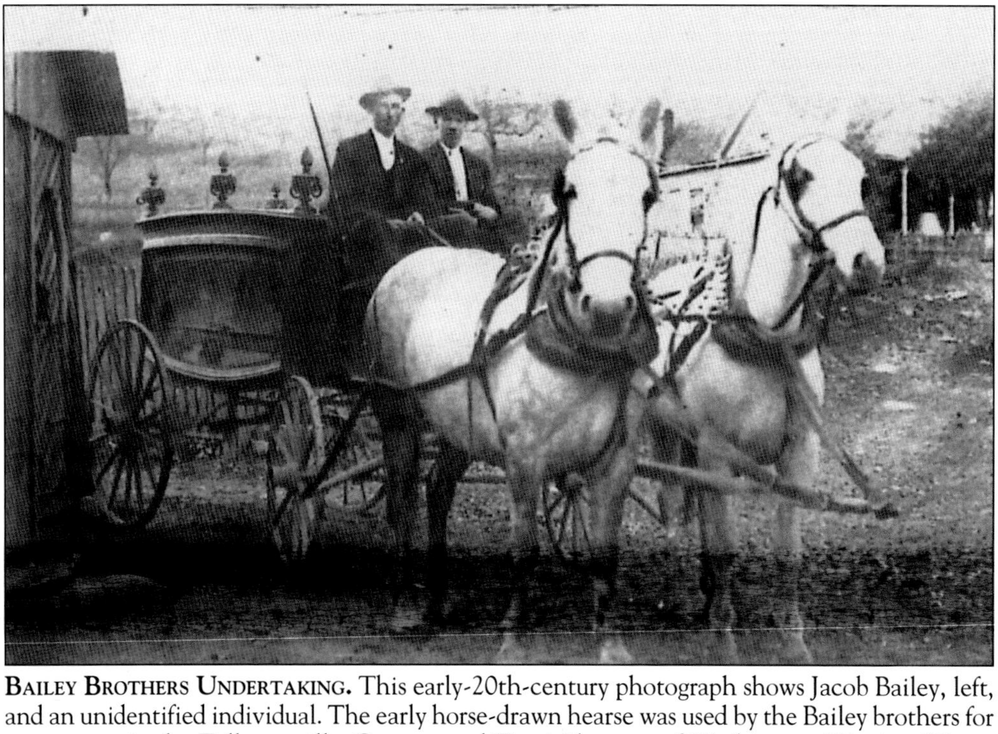

**BAILEY BROTHERS UNDERTAKING.** This early-20th-century photograph shows Jacob Bailey, left, and an unidentified individual. The early horse-drawn hearse was used by the Bailey brothers for many years in the Tallmansville, Queens, and Ten Mile areas of Washington District. (Photo courtesy of UCHS, Tom Bailey Collection.)

# *Seven*

# INDUSTRIES

*Large-scale industry came to Upshur County with the advancement of the railroad. The West Virginia and Pittsburgh Railroad Company first made it to Buckhannon in 1883, and by 1904, the Coal & Coke Railroad had made its crossing of the county. Timbering and sawmills sprung up everywhere, especially in the southern end of the county with Alexander, Stockerts, and Ellamore taking the lead. The commercial mining of coal, first at Lorentz in 1901, soon lead to the bigger operations in Adrian, Hodgesville, and other communities. When natural gas became available, so did glass-making, with Imperial in Meade District furnishing much of the glass sand used. Chemicals were produced at Selbyville and leather was tanned in Buckhannon. The Buckhannon pottery and brick industry flourished for a few years also.*

*Today, coal mining and timbering are the only industries from the past that linger on. They join forces with various modern manufacturing that takes place here.*

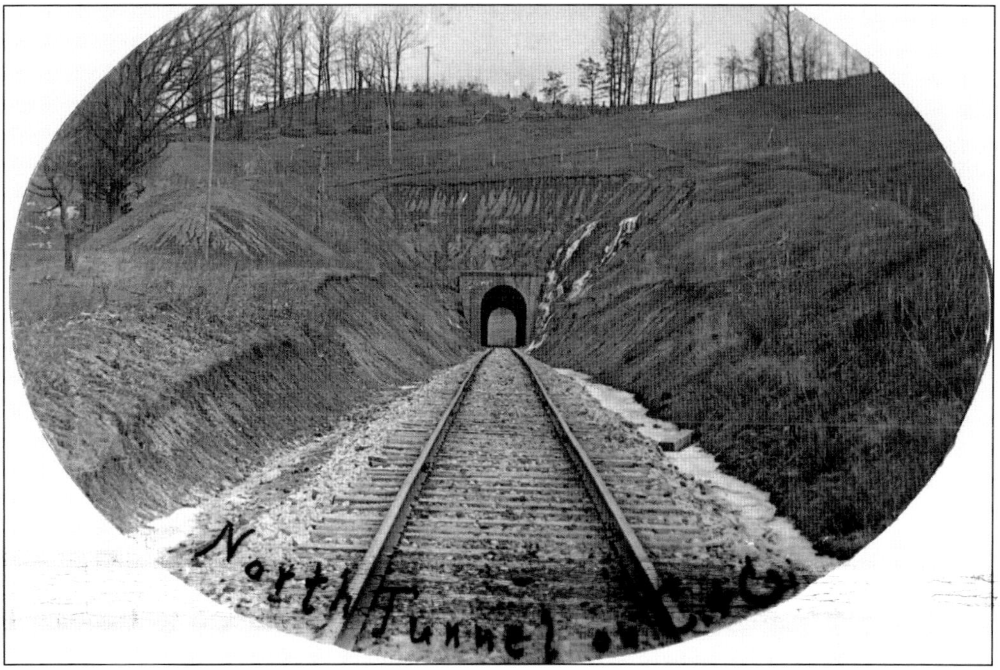


**NORTH TUNNEL ON THE COAL & COKE RAILROAD.** This photograph was take near Abbott in Meade District shortly after it was built in 1904–1905. The Coal & Coke Railroad ran from Elkins to Charleston and passed across Upshur County from Midvale to Frenchton. (Photo courtesy of UCHS, Mary Alice Bragg Collection.)

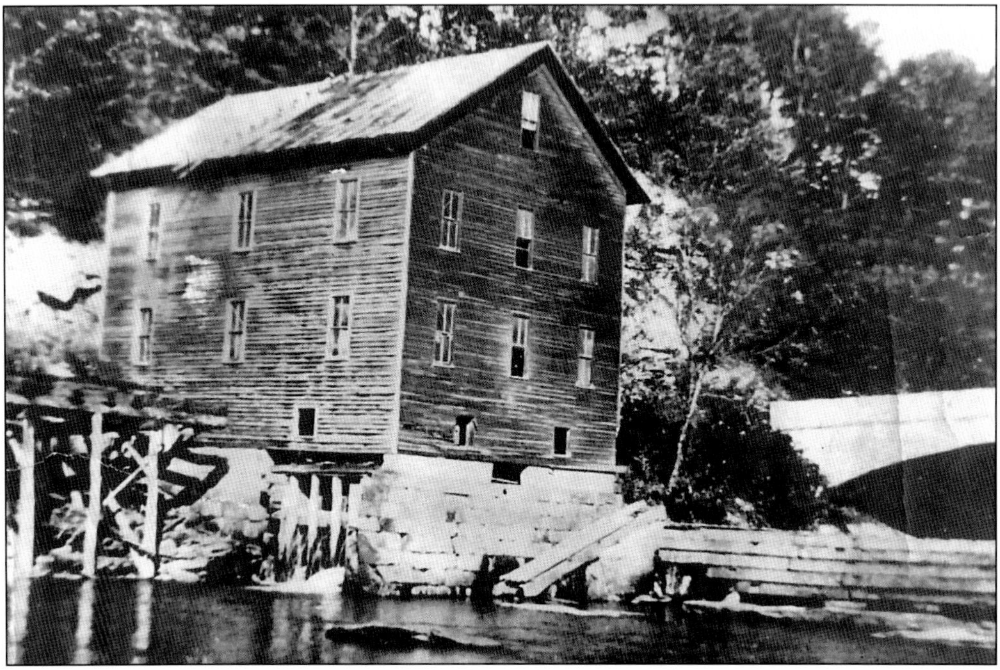

**Ours Mill.** In 1883, Nicholas Ours Jr. built his four-story mill on the Buckhannon River at Nixon near Sago. Located on the east side of the river in Washington District, this mill was the center of commerce for the area. Operated for years by Thaddeus Ours, it was destroyed by fire in 1931. (Photo courtesy of UCHS, Leila Tenney Ours Collection.)

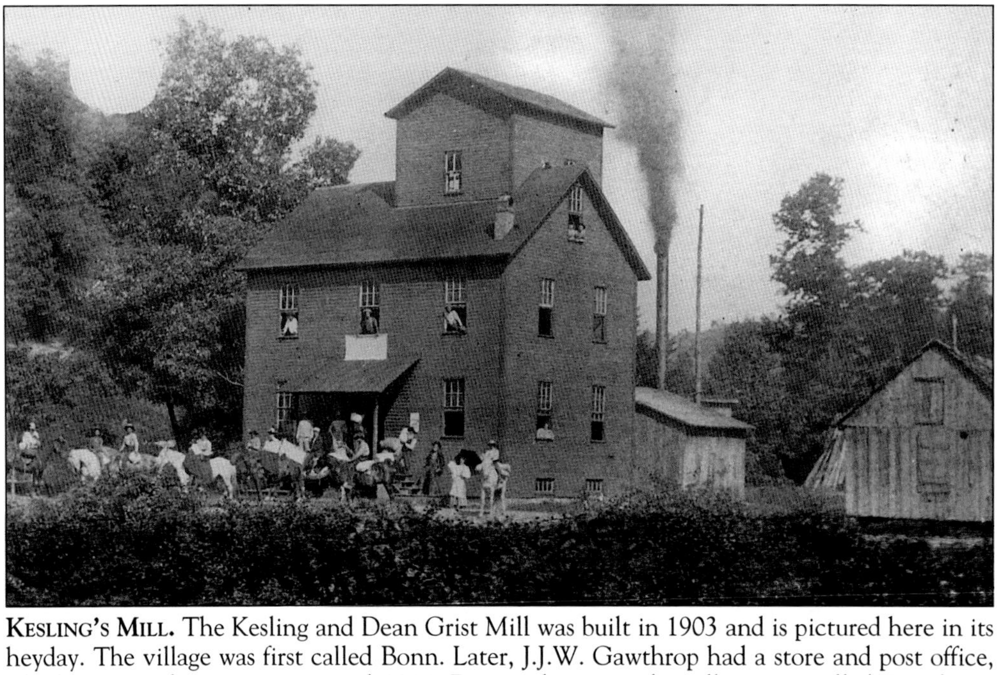

**Kesling's Mill.** The Kesling and Dean Grist Mill was built in 1903 and is pictured here in its heyday. The village was first called Bonn. Later, J.J.W. Gawthrop had a store and post office, which remained in operation until 1914. During that time the village was called Gawthrop. Since 1914, the Union District community has been known as Kesling Mill. (Photo courtesy of UCHS, William Wright Collection.)

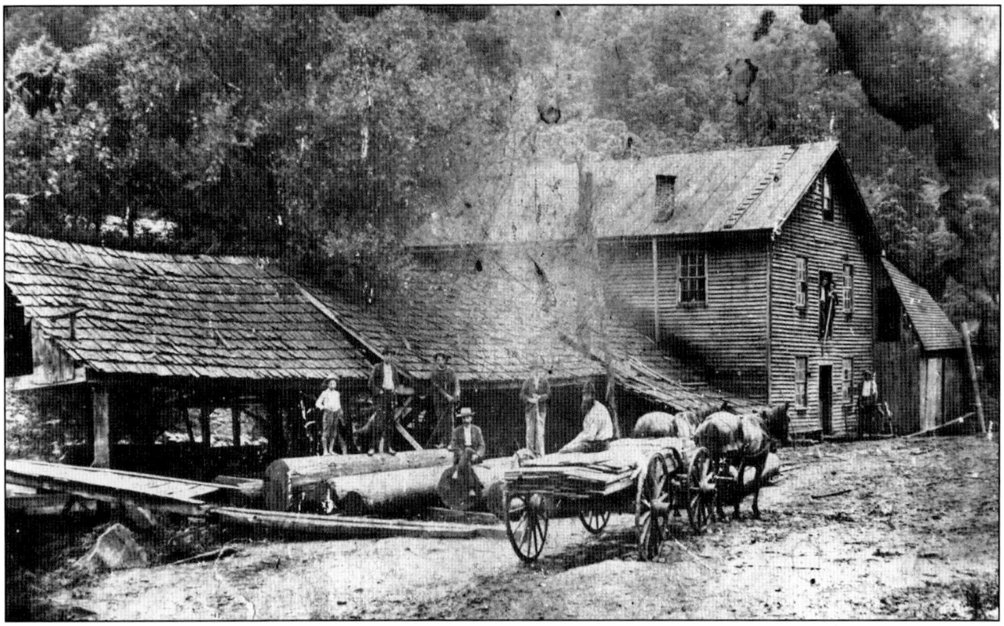

**HOLLEN'S MILL.** This *c.* 1898 picture shows the Hollen's grist and sawmill, which was located on the Middlefork River in Queens, Washington District. Queens was named for Armstead Queen who built his mill in 1845. The post office was established in 1868 and closed in 1963. Early New Englanders settled a bit further south in 1814 but were forced to move away by 1830 because of unclear land titles. (Photo courtesy of UCHS, Tom Stockert Estate Collection.)

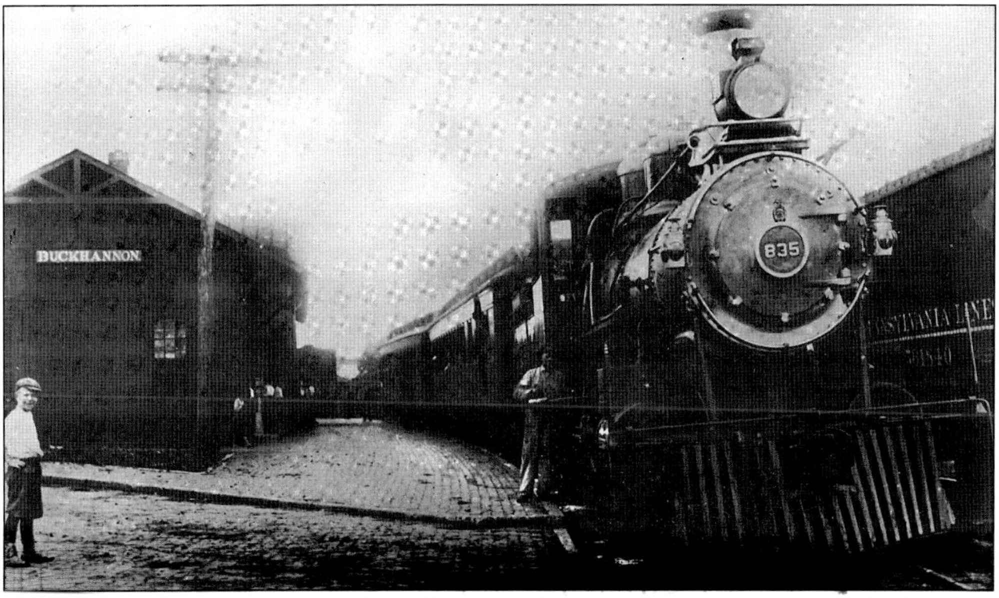


**BUCKHANNON DEPOT.** Engine number 835 of the B&O Railroad pulls into the Buckhannon station in the early 1900s. On June 11, 1883, the first train entered Buckhannon on a passenger run from Weston on the West Virginia and Pittsburgh Railroad Company. The B&O later acquired this company and extended the rail services to Pickens with the first train arriving there on July 4, 1892. The last passenger service on that line ended on October 25, 1958. (Photo courtesy of UCHS, Don Henderson Jr. Collection.)

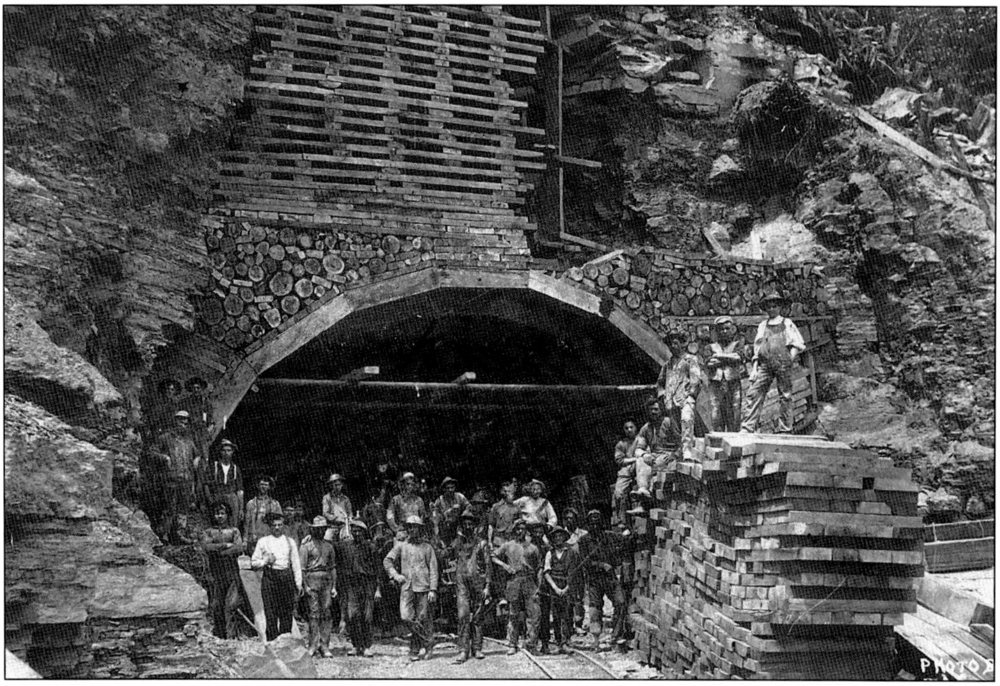

**BUILDING THE SHIPMAN TUNNEL.** The construction of the Shipman Tunnel on the Coal & Coke Railroad is pictured here *c.* 1904. Located in Washington District near Tallmansville, this is one of the many tunnels built along the line primarily by African Americans and Italians for Henry Gassaway Davis of Elkins. (Photo courtesy of UCHS, Billy Bailey Collection.)

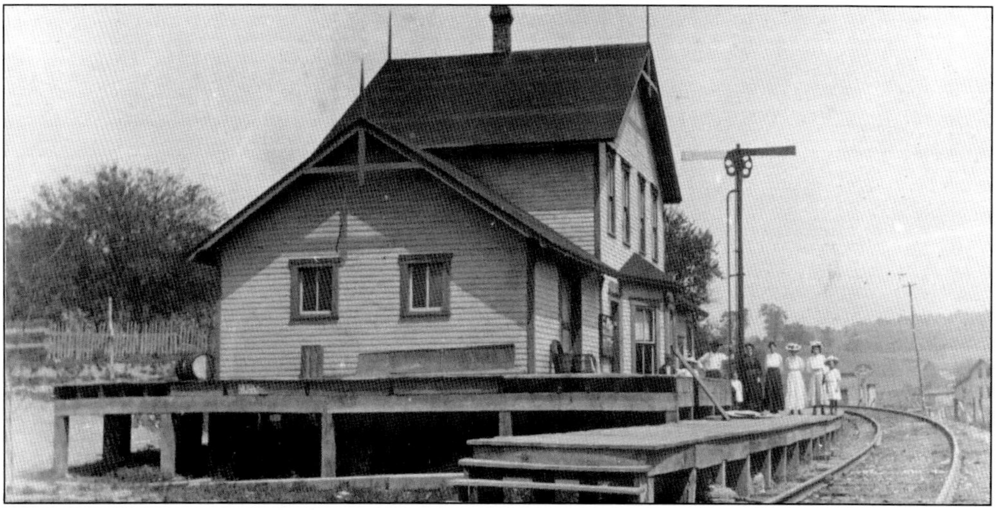

**MIDVALE STATION.** Unidentified people wait for the train at the Midvale Station near Ellamore in Union District in the early 20th century. The Coal & Coke Railroad was a main source of transportation for area travelers and made stops in Upshur County entering from Randolph County at Midvale, Gerwig (near Nays Chapel), Sand Run, Goodwin, Strader (Tallmansville), Nixon (where the Ours Mill was located), Sago (where it crossed the B&O line), Adian, Abbott, and Frenchton, where it entered Lewis County. The last passenger run was made on September 2, 1939, and the tracks were taken up during the 1940s. (Photo courtesy of UCHS, Sheila Tenney Thomason.)

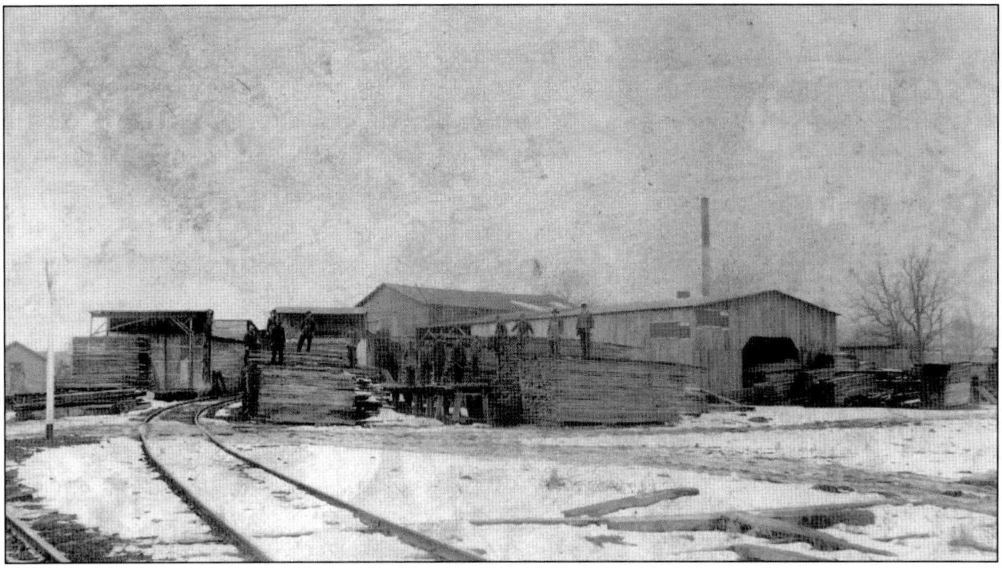

**LUMBER MILL.** Pictured in this *c.* 1912 photograph by Hode Clark is the Upshur Planing Mill Company, located at the end of College Avenue where today's Hinkle's Rail Fence operation is located. The company was organized in 1911 by A.H. Tenney. Other mills in operation at that time in Upshur County included G.F. Stockert & Bailey Lumber Co. of Holly Grove, H.B. Morgan & Son (planing mill), D.G. Watkins & Son (finished lumber), and the Alton Lumber Co. (Photo courtesy of UCHS, Joy Tenney Shingleton Collection.)

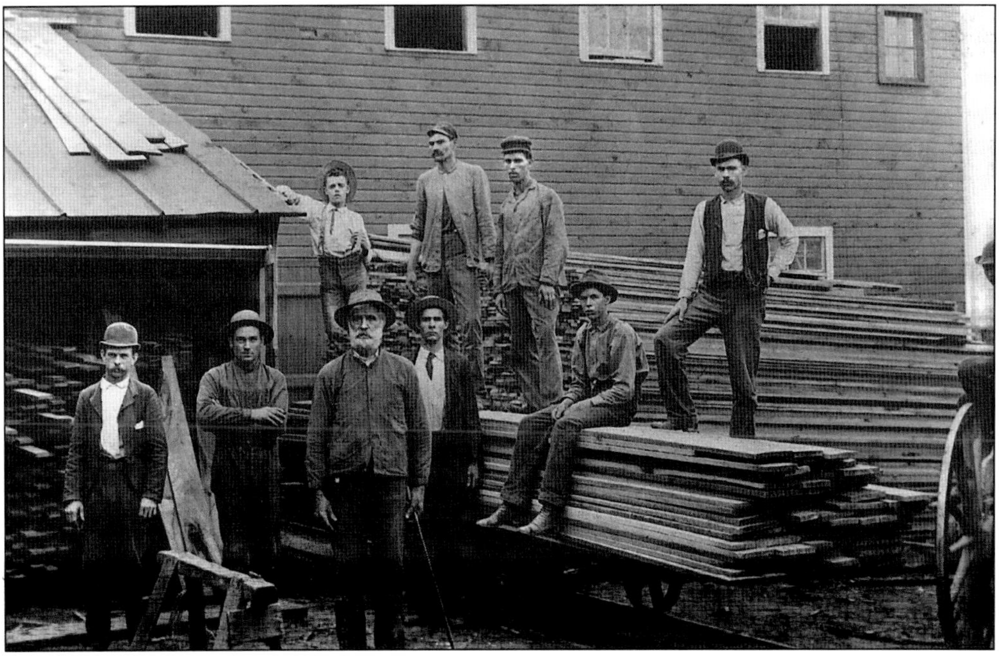

**H.S. STOCKERT LUMBER MILL.** Lumbering was booming in the early 20th century in Upshur County, and this *c.* 1900 photograph depicts the crew at the Stockert Mill. This company was large enough to have a lumber camp in southern Washington District named Stockerts and even boasted a post office from March 22, 1898 until September 15, 1909. (Photo courtesy of UCHS, Tom Stockert Estate Collection.)

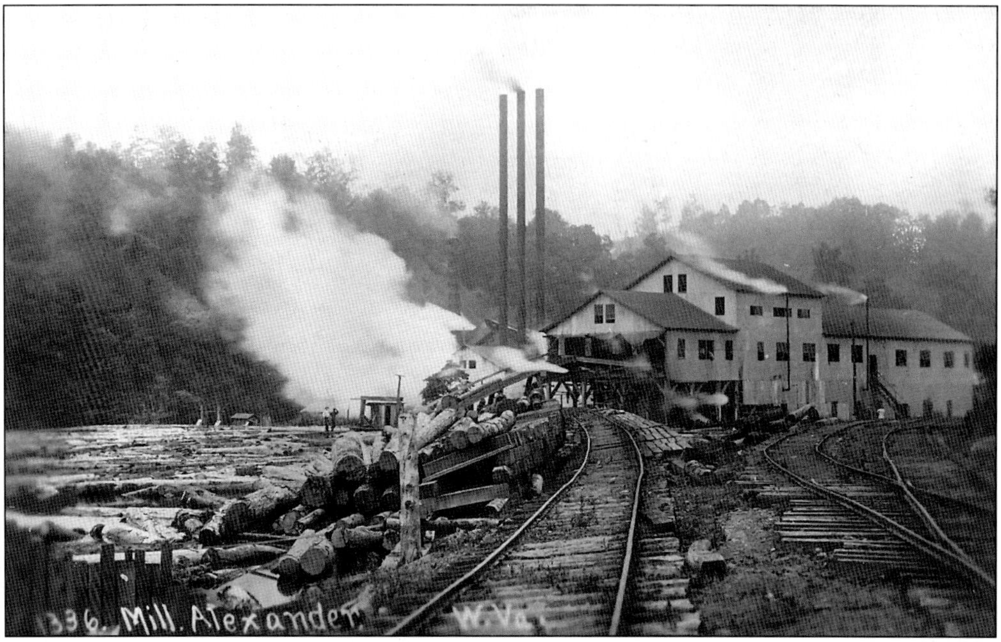


**Lumbering in Alexander.** Located in Banks District, Alexander was a major lumbering center in the early 1900s. This 1920s photograph shows the heyday of one of the village's various lumber plants, which included Alexander Boom and Lumber Company as well as Croft Lumber. Alexander was named for John Alexander, the first postmaster in 1890. (Photo courtesy of UCHS, Boyles Carter Collection.)

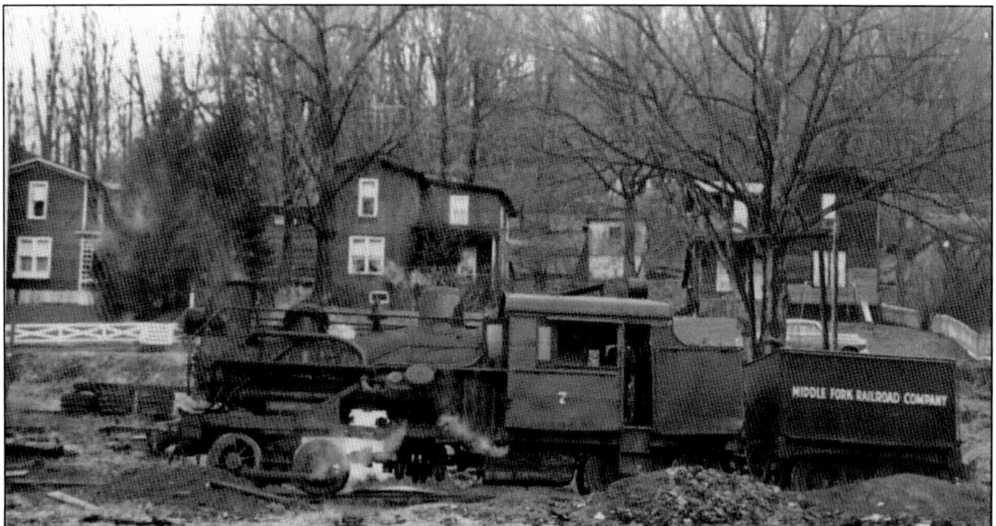


**Middle Fork Railroad Engine at Ellamore.** This 1959 photograph of the Middle Fork RR Heisler #7 engine indicates that the engineers were Paul Buntz, Cecil Brown, and Doc Carlson. The Moore and Kepple Lumber Company was organized at the beginning of the 20th century and was located on both the Upshur and Randolph County sides of the Middle Fork River at Ellamore. The mill closed in 1946, but the company operated this railroad until 1959. The village was named in honor of Ella Moore, mother of J.B. Moore, the mill owner. (Photo courtesy of UCHS, David Armstrong Collection.)

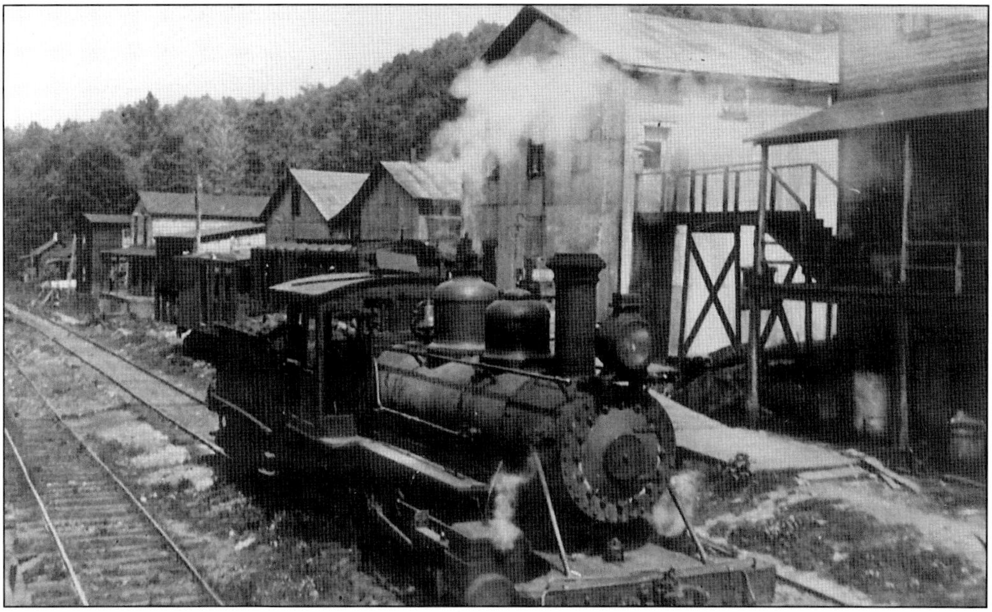

**ENGINE NUMBER 6.** Engine number 6 of the Croft Lumber Company in Alexander, seen in this early 20th-century photograph, remained in use during the company's heyday and until its final operations on the left fork of the Buckhannon River. (Photo courtesy of UCHS, Howard Hiner Collection.)

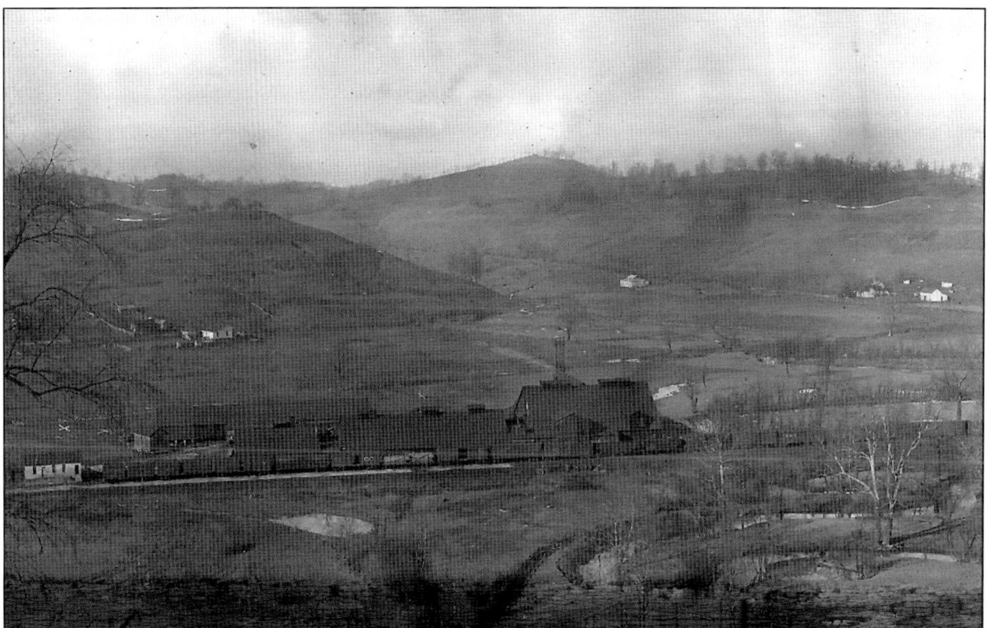

**EQUITABLE WINDOW GLASS PLANT.** Pictured in this early-20th-century Hode Clark photograph is the Buckhannon plant that produced window glass (in sizes from 8 by 10 inches to 62 by 74 inches) using sand from Imperial in Meade District. Established in 1902, the business was located just off the Weston Road in Leggett Addition. The Clarksburg Road can be seen with the buildings in the background. S.A. Moore and the Quertinmont family are names associated with this operation. (Photo courtesy of UCHS, Alan Sturm Collection.)

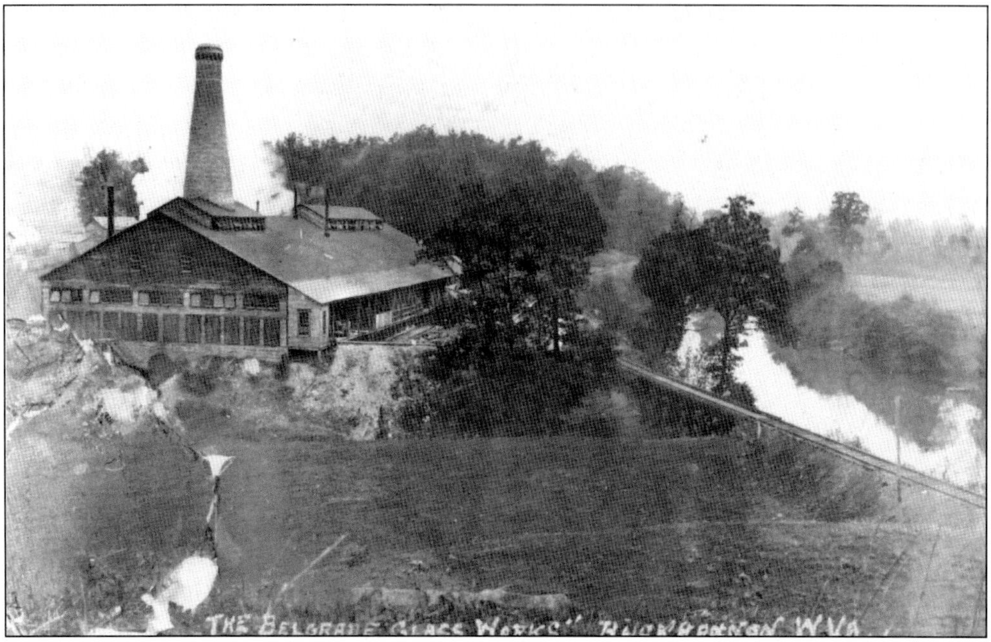


**Belgrade Glass Plant.** Established in 1903 in Tennerton, Belgrade Glass Plant was first known as the Steimer Glass Company and produced the two well-known patterns of tableware "Frosted Star" and "Chicken Wire" until 1906. By 1910 the company became known as Belgrade Glass Company and was in operation when this photograph was made in the 1910s. The operation was destroyed by fire on October 27, 1922. (Photo courtesy of UCHS, Don Henderson Jr. Collection.)

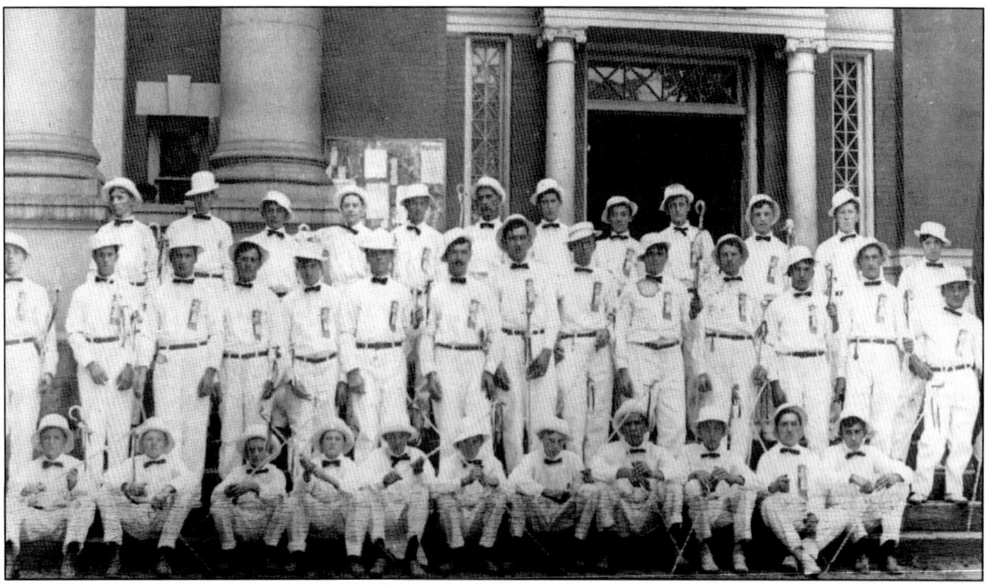

**Belgrade Glass Workers.** Seen here *c.* 1911, workers at the Belgrade Glass Company gather as members of the Glassworkers Local Union No. 97 at the Upshur County Courthouse to commemorate Labor Day. Note their badges that indicate the union number and their glass canes, symbols of the glassworkers' union. (Photo courtesy of UCHS, Malwina Schmidt Snyder Collection.)

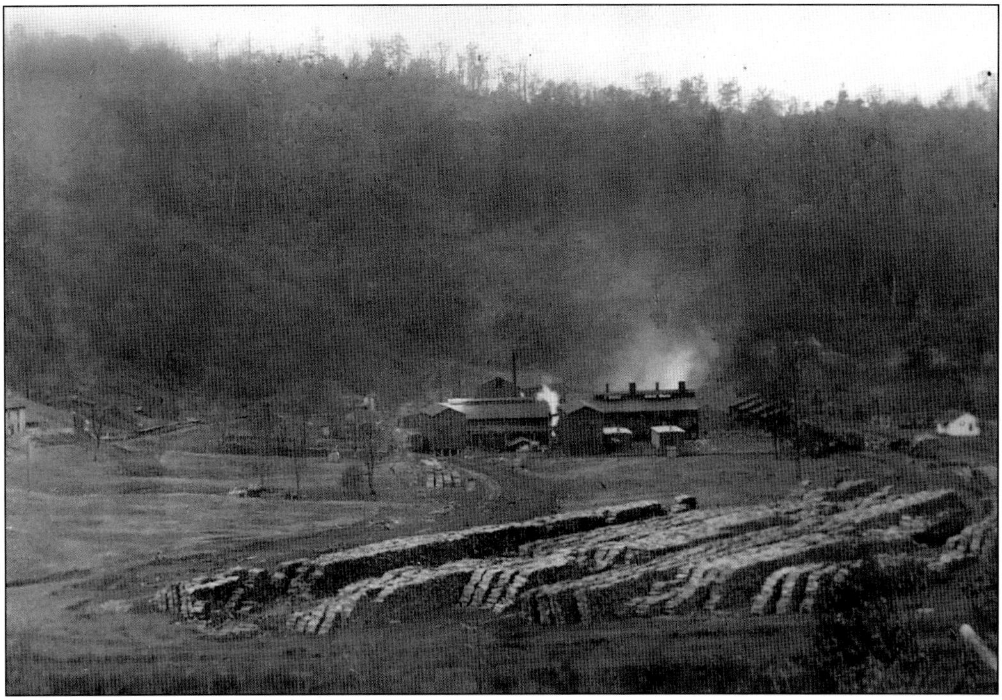

**Buckhannon Chemical Plant.** Pictured is the Buckhannon Chemical Plant located in Selbyville, Banks District. This early-20th-century photograph depicts the thriving business that was established in 1903 and continued until the early 1930s. It produced charcoal, acetate of lime, and wood alcohol. Today, the site is used for the Upshur County Youth Camp and is owned and maintained by the Upshur County Commission. (Photo courtesy of UCHS, Noel W. Tenney Collection.)

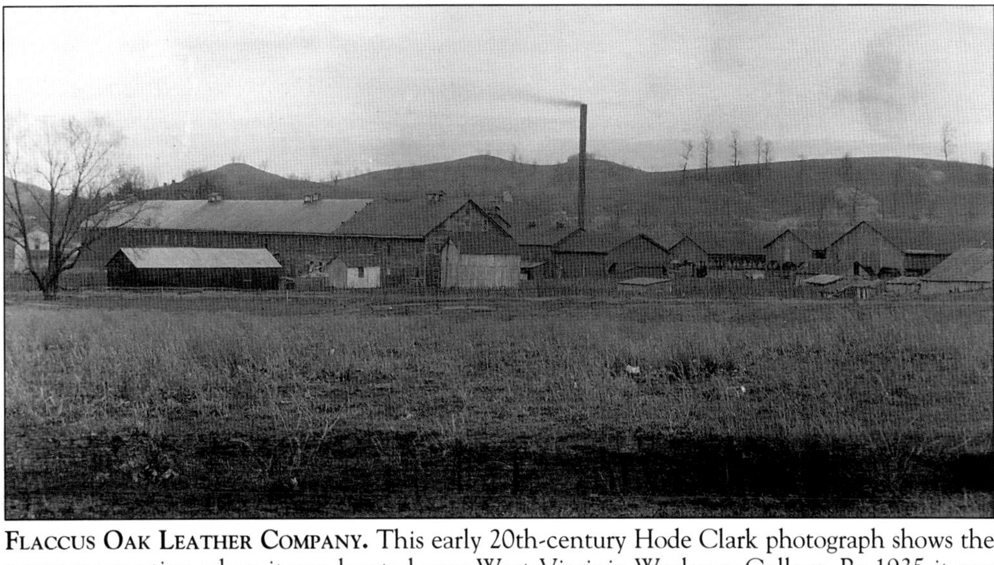

**Flaccus Oak Leather Company.** This early 20th-century Hode Clark photograph shows the tannery operation when it was located near West Virginia Wesleyan College. By 1935 it was considered to be Buckhannon's leading industrial operation. On the evening of September 25, 1935, it was destroyed by a fire so illuminating that it was seen in Weston, 15 miles away. (Photo courtesy of UCHS, Alan Sturm Collection.)

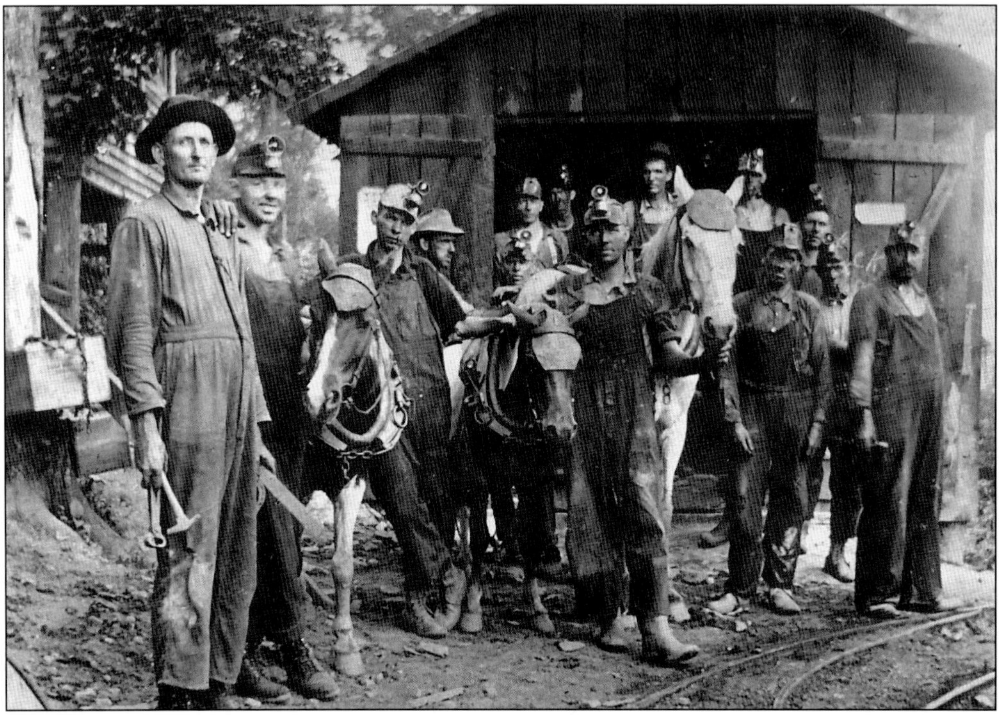

**The Small Coal Operations.** Pictured here is one of the many small coal mining operations that existed in Upshur County in the early 20th century. Nearly every community that had a seam of coal had a small working mine. Shown here is the Freeman Phillips Mine located near Beans Mill, *c.* 1920. The workers are unidentified. (Photo courtesy of UCHS, Reatice Fultz Collection.)

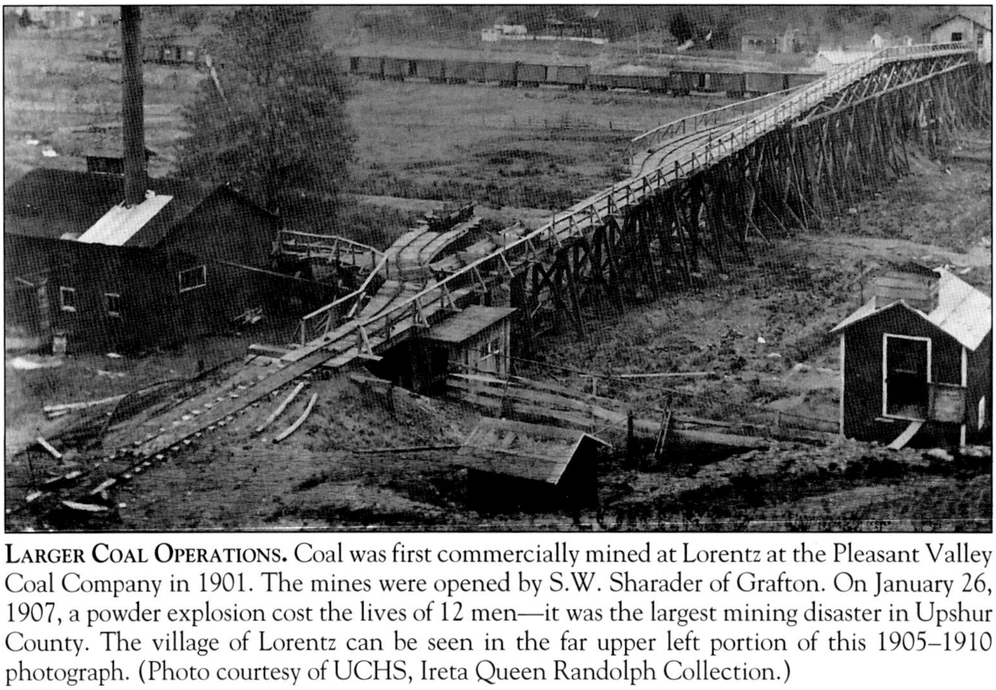

**Larger Coal Operations.** Coal was first commercially mined at Lorentz at the Pleasant Valley Coal Company in 1901. The mines were opened by S.W. Sharader of Grafton. On January 26, 1907, a powder explosion cost the lives of 12 men—it was the largest mining disaster in Upshur County. The village of Lorentz can be seen in the far upper left portion of this 1905–1910 photograph. (Photo courtesy of UCHS, Ireta Queen Randolph Collection.)

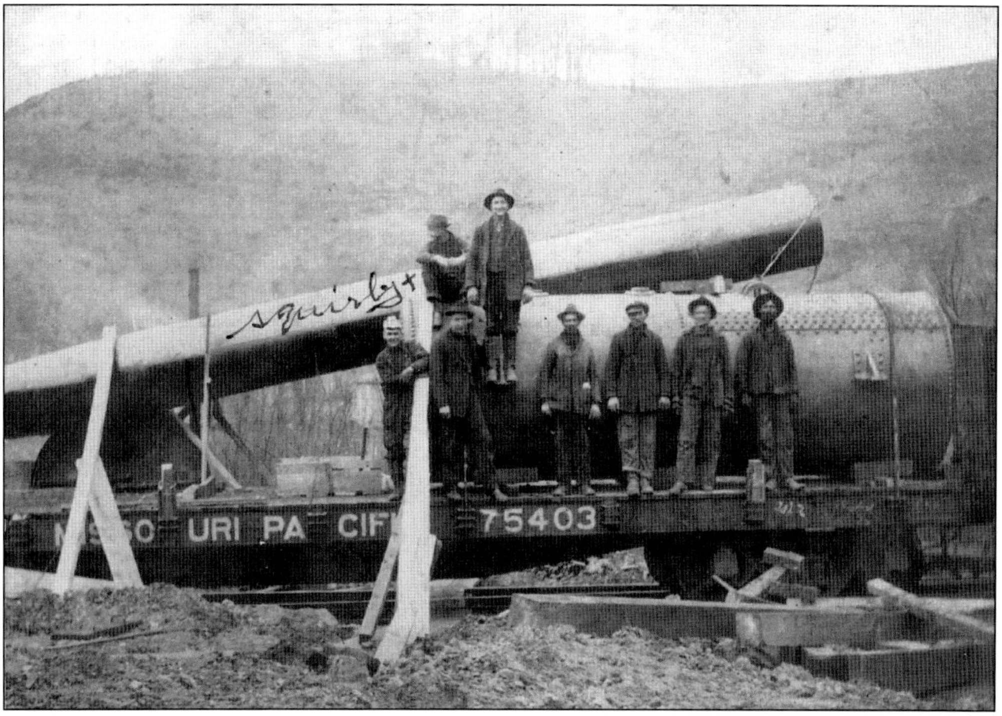


**Buckhannon River Coal Company Boiler.** This 1920 photograph of men unloading a boiler to be constructed for the coal company in Adrian shows, from left to right, (front row) Ray Patterson, Walter Perrine, Marcellus Lane, Johnny Malcolm, Hance Hawkins, and Worthy Lane; (back row) Abe Buckhannon, and Johnny Whitehair. (Photo courtesy of UCHS, Rena Lane Collection.)

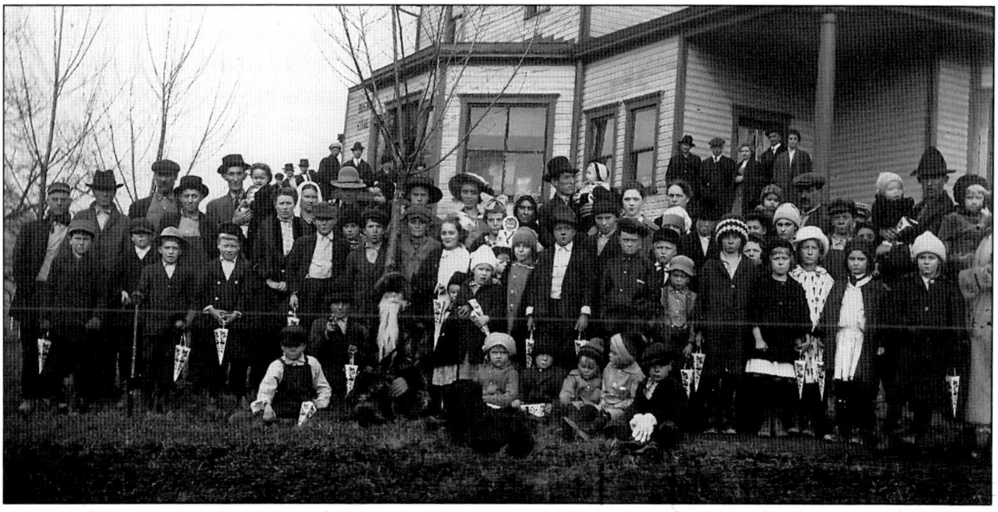

**A Coal Company Christmas Party.** Adrian, in Meade District, was built around coal and the railroad, having several major coal companies operating in the town from about 1904 until the 1940s. The largest of these operations was the Buckhannon River Coal Company, and the children of its workers are pictured here celebrating Christmas. Near the center of the photograph, beside the tree, is Mr. Buckhannon, playing Santa. The children all recognized him by his black dog nearby. (Photo courtesy of UCHS, Fred Brooks Collection.)

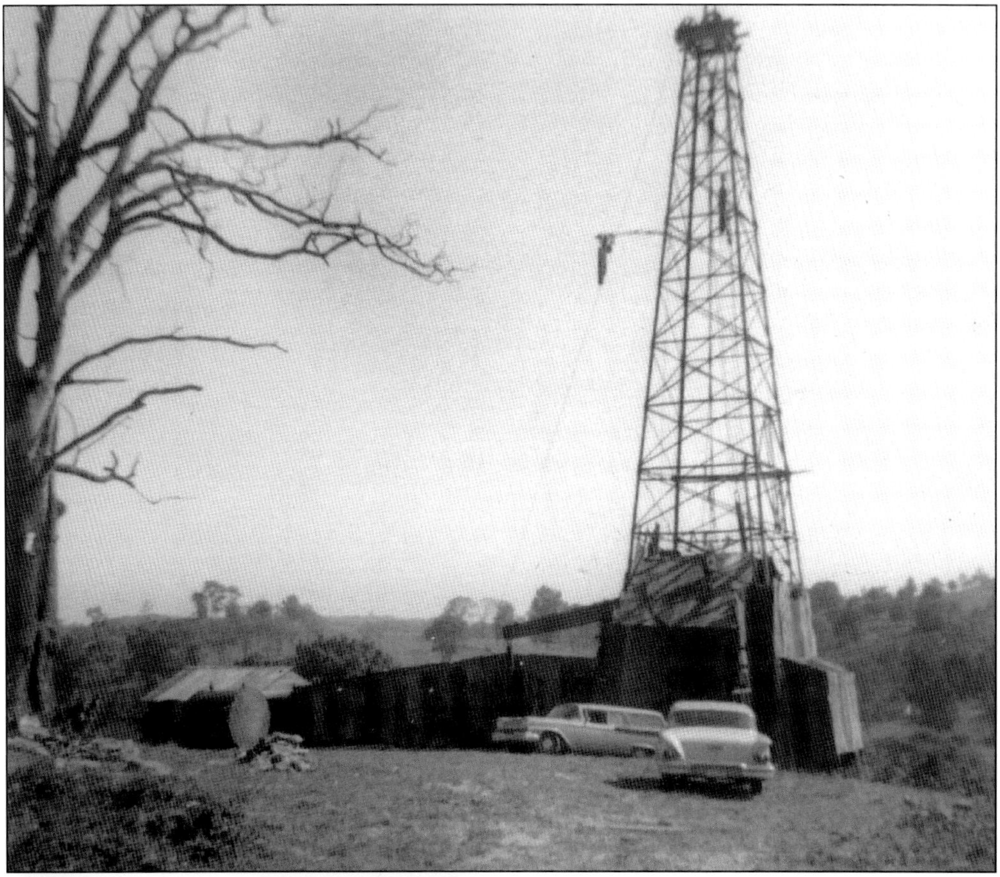

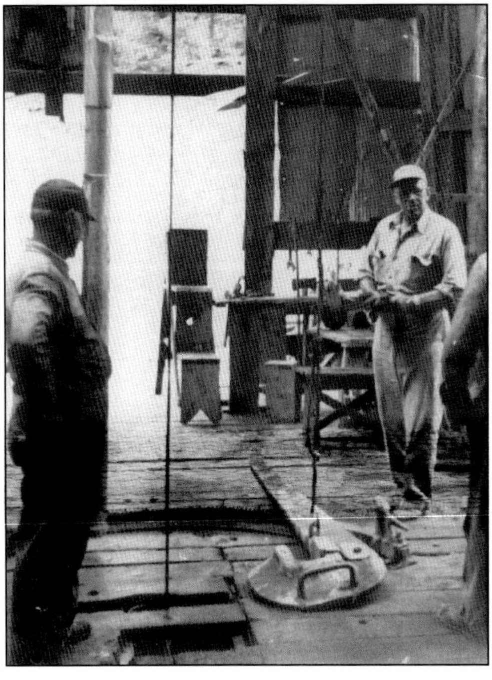

**Oil and Gas in Upshur County.** These photographs show the industry in the 1950s when an oil and gas drilling resurgence began. Pictured in the above photograph is the typical well-drilling rig, while the lower photograph shows Clyde Harper, left, and P. D. Williams, who was one of the original founders of Union Drilling. The first well in Upshur County was drilled prior to 1895 on Turkey Run. Commercially, wells were drilled between 1908 and 1918 by various companies, including Frenchton Oil and Gas Company. Other company names included French Creek, Regal, Bartlett-Hiner, and Buckhannon Relief Oil and Gas Companies; Cumberland and Allegheny were the major distributor. (Photos courtesy of UCHS, Amy Williams Tenney Collection.)

# *Ten*

# Farming and Agriculture

*The first official census for Upshur County was taken in 1860 and showed that the overwhelming majority of its male inhabitants were listed as "farmer." Although the geography of the region does not allow for large-scale farming, there have always been small farms, and many residents of Buckhannon today have gardens behind their homes. Upshur County has always been regarded as a rural area. In 1916, the farmers of the county organized the Farm Bureau. The first "county agent" was employed that year, and in 1919 the first "home demonstration agent" was hired. Through the West Virginia University Cooperative Extension Service and the Methodist Church's "Town and Country" ministry program (under the direction of Rev. A.H. Rapking), a program that became known as the "Country Life Conference" was established by 1922. Communities were scored on community spirit, citizenship, recreation, health, homes, schools, churches, businesses, and farms. Many community histories were written at that time.*

*Because of the greater ease of transportation, many rural residents now come to "town" to work and perhaps even sell their excess produce but return to the country to live.*

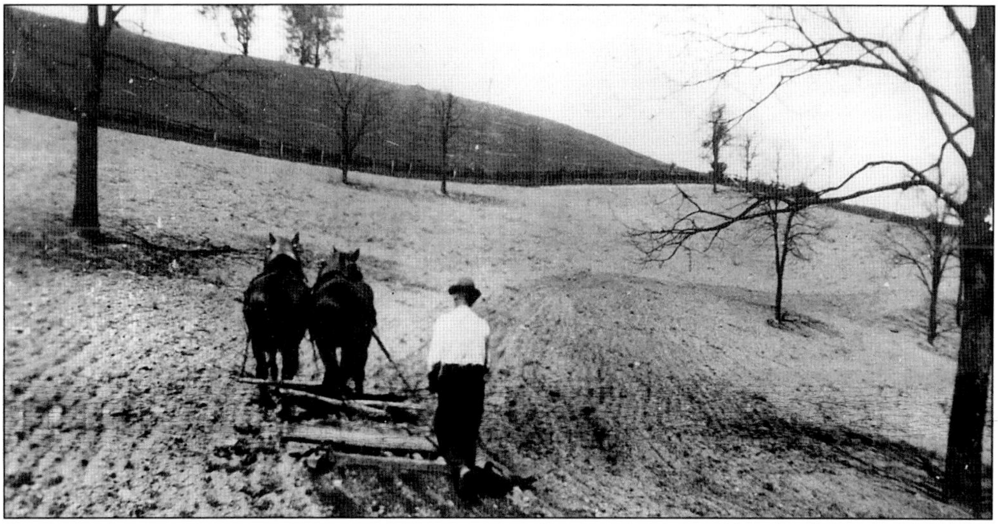

**Bailey Farm, Flat Rock.** This 1945 photograph shows Jacob Bailey harrowing on his farm in Flat Rock, Washington District. Small farmers were nearly able to be self-sufficient during the Great Depression and the war years. (Photo courtesy of UCHS, Tom Bailey Collection.)

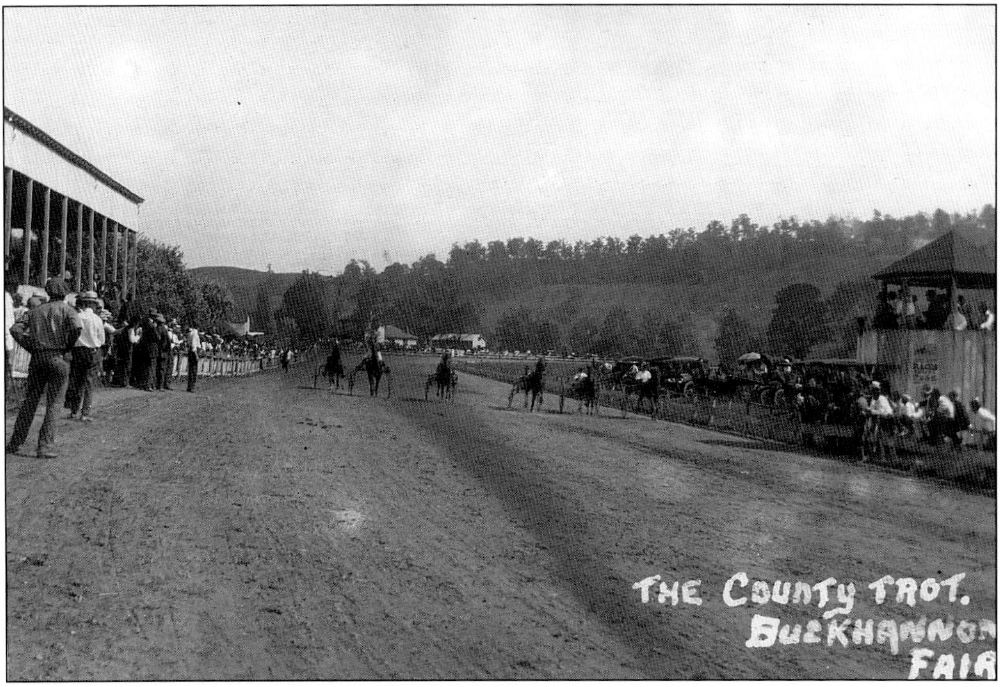


**UPSHUR COUNTY FAIR.** This c. 1915 Hode Clark photograph shows the Upshur County Fair Grounds located on 28.5 acres along the old Weston Road near West Buckhannon. Established in 1904, the fair became central West Virginia's main attraction for horse racing, animal and agricultural exhibits, and a carnival midway. By the late 1930s, the fairgrounds were no longer used, having been purchased in 1938 by the Upshur County Singer's Association for their "Harmony Acres." (Photo courtesy of UCHS, Alan Sturm Collection.)

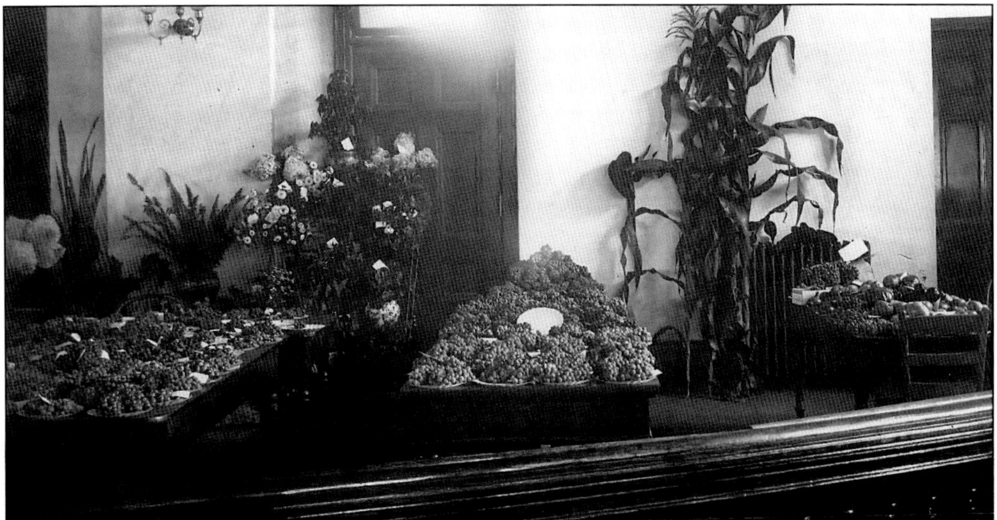

**AGRICULTURAL EXHIBIT.** The role of agriculture and farming in Upshur County has always played a significant part in the general life of the people as pictured in this courthouse display of produce, c. 1904, at the first Upshur County Fair. (Photo courtesy of UCHS, Noel W. Tenney Collection.)

**Fruit Picking Ladder.** This early-20th-century Fred Brooks photograph shows unidentified ladies posing on this unusual agricultural device. In Mrs. H.G. Sturm's "Upshur County, West Virginia: Lifts itself by its own boot straps," in the 1920s, she writes, "the generally thin soil together with the hilly surface and varied climate makes stock-raising, general farming, and orcharding" the chief agricultural pursuits. In that same work, she indicates that there were 2,200 Upshur County farms in 1920 with an average of 87 acres each. (Photo courtesy of UCHS, Fred Brooks Collection.)

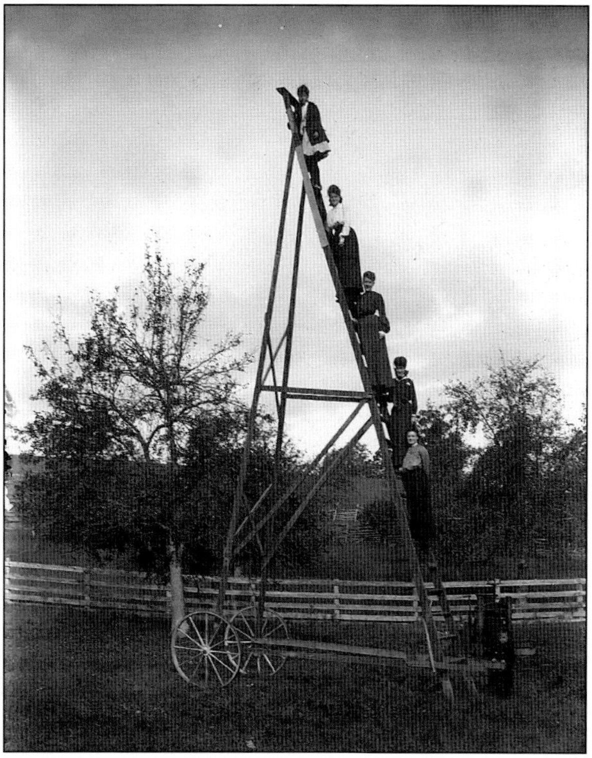

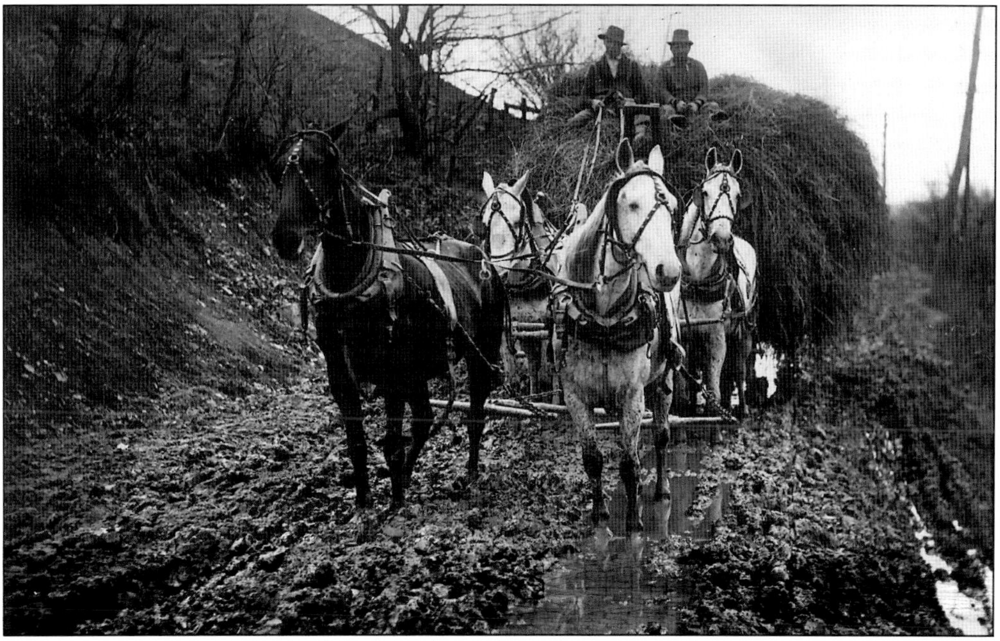

**Hay Wagon.** A wagonload of hay from the early 20th century indicates the type of farm power used and the condition of the county roads. A soil survey of 1917 for Upshur County stated that "a few roads in the northwest corner of Upshur are in good condition during dry season, but otherwise main roads are fair to poor. Practically all secondary roads are very poor." (Photo courtesy of UCHS, Howard Hiner Collection.)

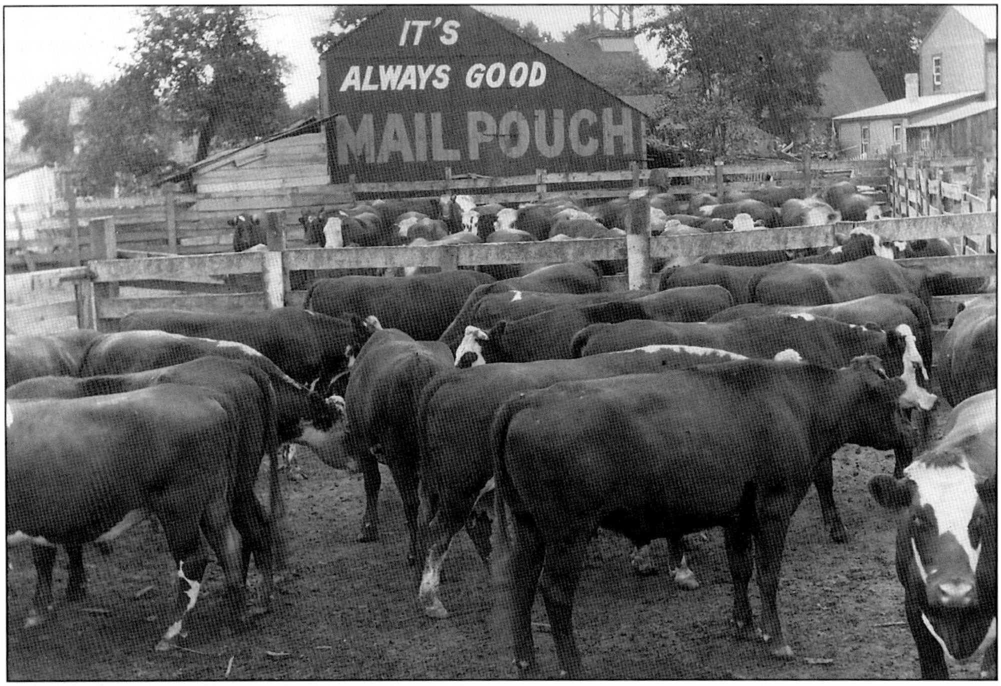


**Buckhannon Stockyards.** The earliest of the stock sale yards is pictured in this early-20th-century Hode Clark photograph. It was located near the railroad tracks on the old Clarksburg road about where today's Davis Health Services is now at 11 North Locust Street. The old Baptist Church building is pictured just above the Mail Pouch barn. From there, the stockyards moved to the south edge of town where Moore Business Forms was situated in 1964, forcing the third location of this agricultural business to its present site on Red Rock Road. (Photo courtesy of UCHS, Alan Sturm Collection.)

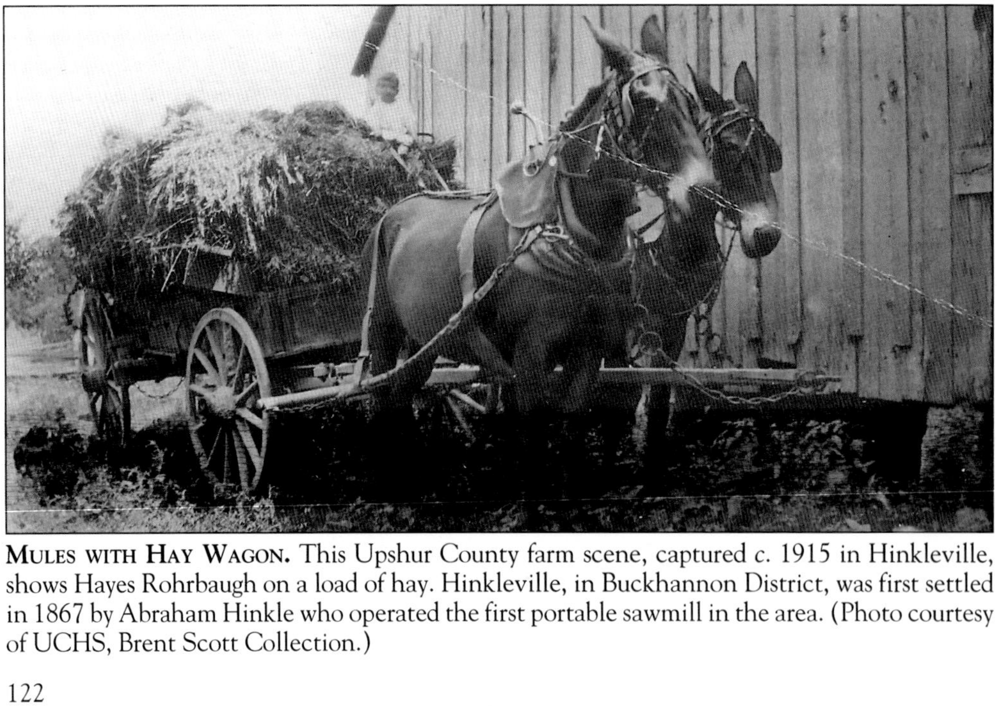

**Mules with Hay Wagon.** This Upshur County farm scene, captured *c.* 1915 in Hinkleville, shows Hayes Rohrbaugh on a load of hay. Hinkleville, in Buckhannon District, was first settled in 1867 by Abraham Hinkle who operated the first portable sawmill in the area. (Photo courtesy of UCHS, Brent Scott Collection.)

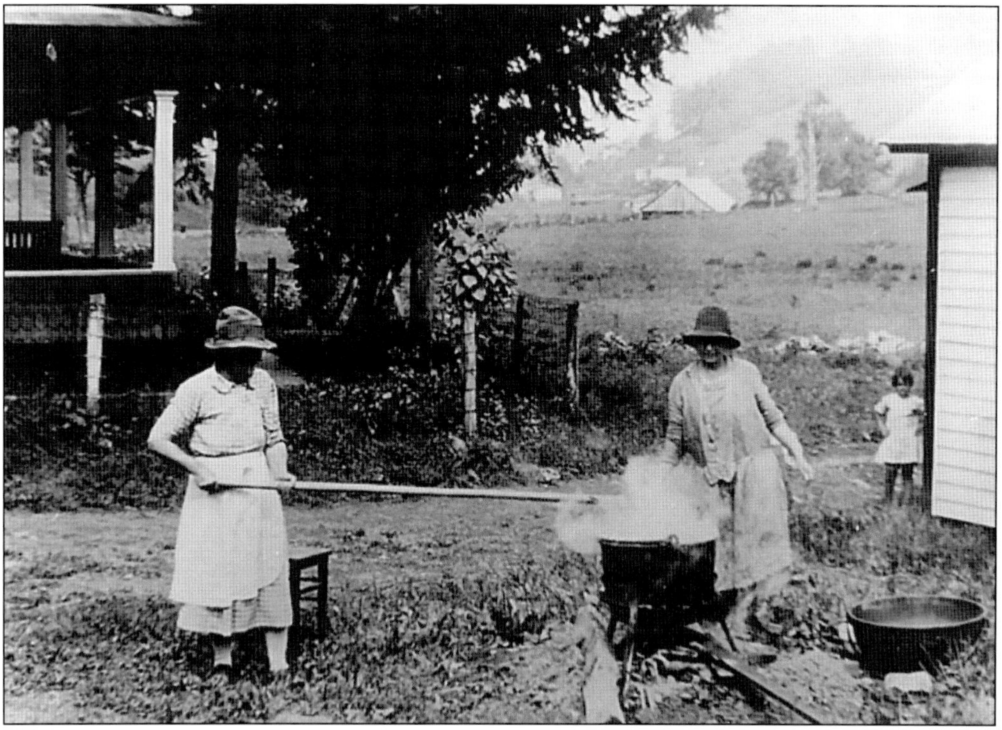

**Applebutter Making in Tallmansville.** This 1929 photograph, taken by Violet Reed, was used in the "Country Life Conference" publication "Strader Mirror" and depicts applebutter being made at the Floyd Reed farm in Washington District. From left to right are Rebecca Foster, Iva Reed, and Marjorie Craven (child). (Photo courtesy of UCHS, Noel W. Tenney Collection)

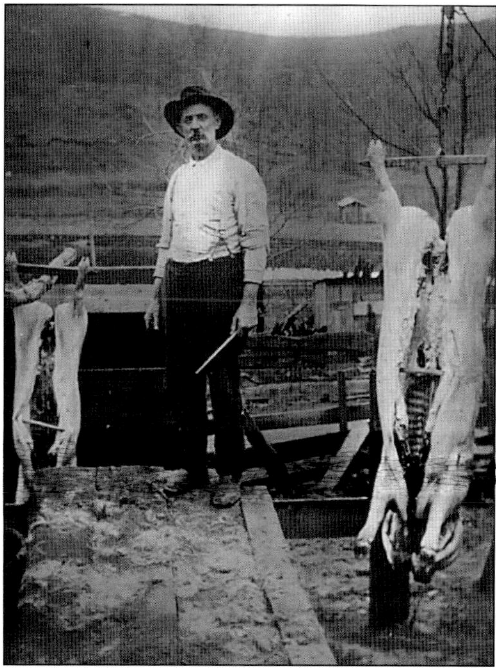

**Hog Butchering in Lorentz.** This early-20th-century photograph depicts a typical autumn activity on the farm of W.B. Miles, pictured here. Farmers were usually able to produce most of the food needed by their families, including both animal and garden products. (Photo courtesy of UCHS, Ralph Miles Collection.)

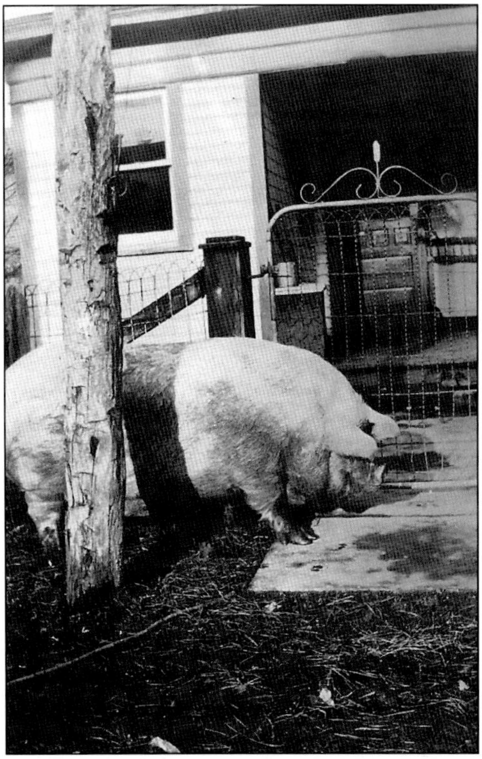

**Backporch Guest.** The Floyd Reed farm in Tallmansville was a model one with many modern "town" conveniences when this 1930s photograph was taken. It had the only community telephone, hot water radiator heat in the house, and a "Delco" battery power system for electricity. Even then, no distinct separation between human and animal territories existed, shown by this barnyard guest appearing at the backdoor of the farmhouse. (Photo courtesy of UCHS, Marjorie Craven Miles Collection.)

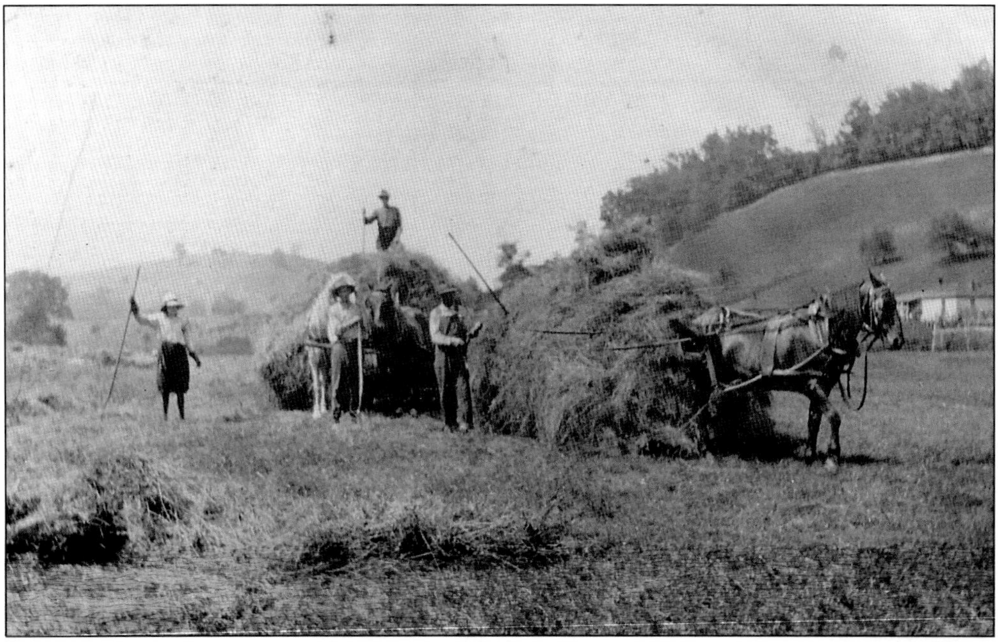

**Haymaking in Tallmansville.** Family members and hired hands at the Floyd Reed farm in Washington District are depicted in this 1930s summer haymaking activity. Hay continues to be the largest cash crop produced in Upshur County's agricultural arena. During the Great Depression hired hands on this farm earned 10¢ a day along with room and board. (Photo courtesy of UCHS, Marjorie Craven Miles Collection.)

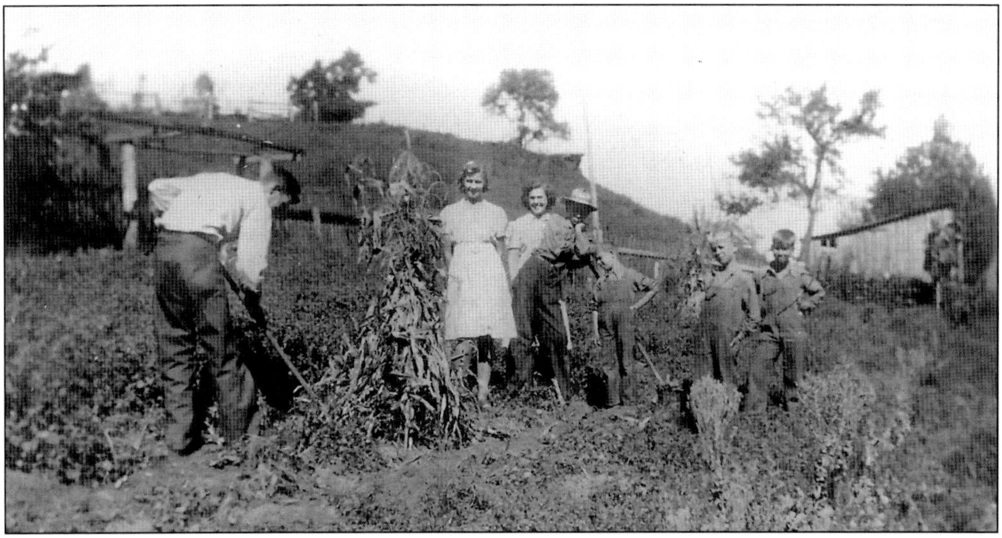

**The Bailey Farm at Flat Rock.** Pictured in these early 1940s farm scenes at the Jacob Bailey farm in Washington District are gardening activities and apiary, or bee keeping. The above photograph shows members of this large family, who won the "Farm Family Award," at their Flat Rock farm. The parents of this family were Jacob and Hazel Foy Bailey and the children were Arthur, Ward (who was killed in WW II), Harry, Ralph, Billy, Tom, Bob, Earl, Carl, Lorraine, Norma, and Keith. The photograph below shows "Jake" Bailey capturing a "bee swarm." (Photos courtesy of UCHS, Tom Bailey Collection.)

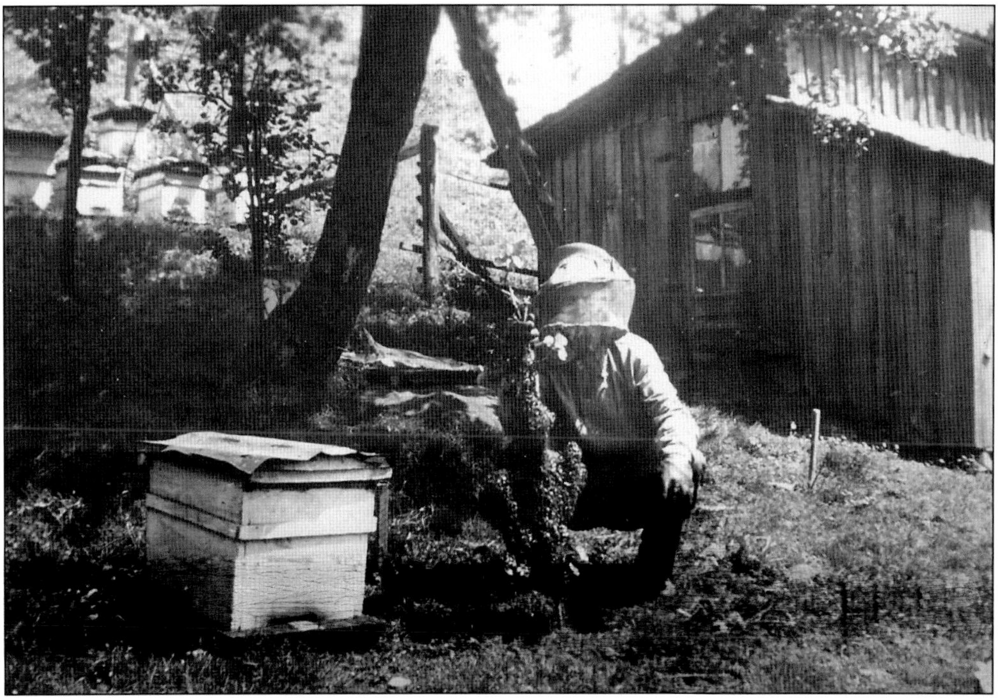

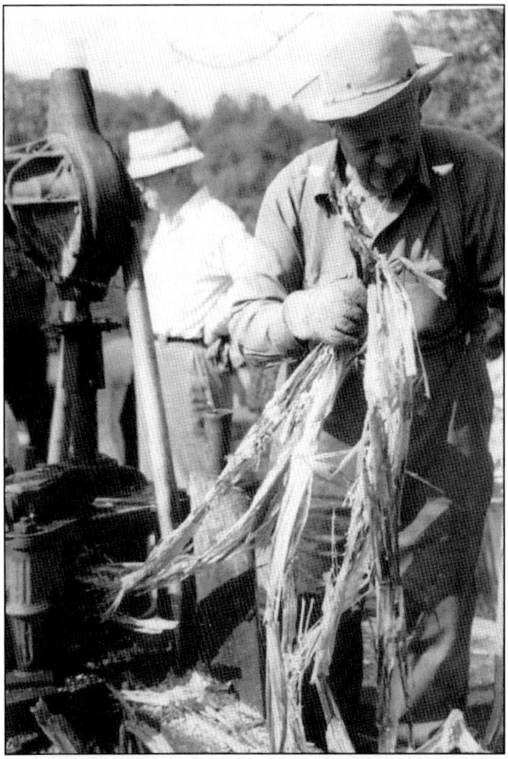

**Molasses Making.** Communal activities have always been a part of rural agricultural life. Pictured in these two photographs is the act of molasses making. The image at left shows Hartsel "Bum" Tallman in charge of the press by which the cane juice is squeezed from the stalk. The man behind him is unidentified, but the activity took place at the Glen Glass farm. The photograph below shows the actual "cane boiling" at the Bobby Joe Tallman farm in Washington District with only Dana Tenney Tallman, upper right, identified. Both photographs are from the 1960s. (Photos courtesy of UCHS, Tom Bailey Collection and *Record Delta* Collection.)

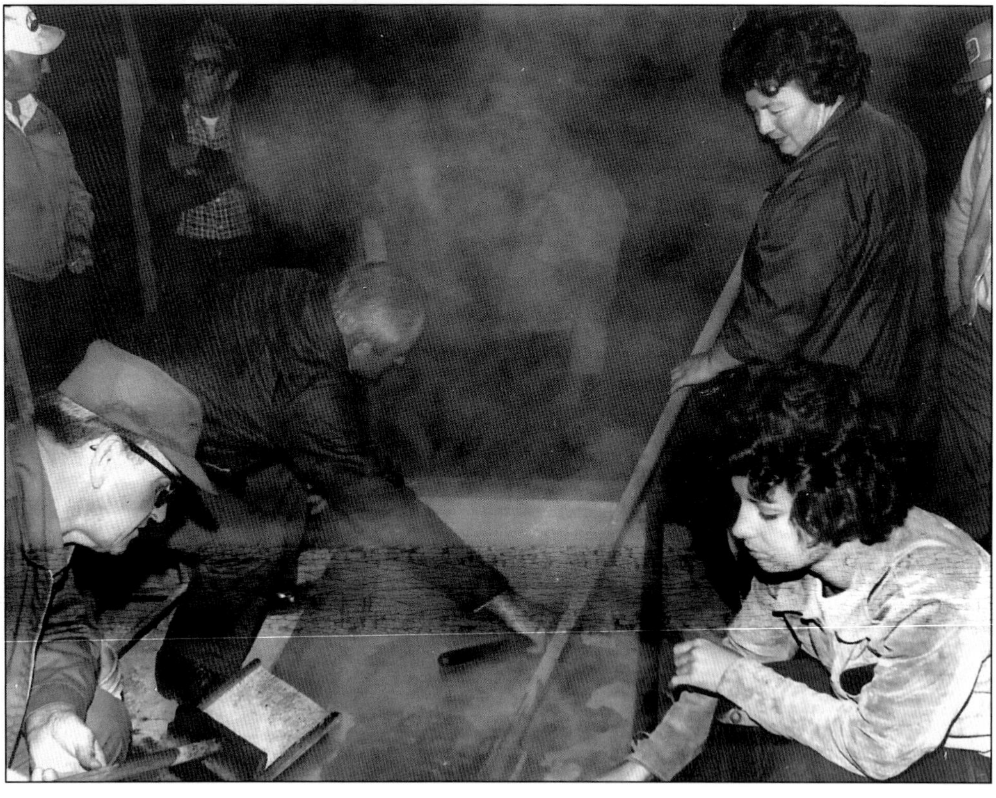

**French Creek Game Farm.** Depicted in these 1930s photographs are scenes from the early days of the State Game Farm or what is now known as the West Virginia Wildlife Center. The top photograph shows Ralph "Boonie" Young with trapped red foxes. His role was also to cultivate native animal species that would then be released into the wild. The photograph below shows unidentified individuals, except for young Willa Young Score (third from left) at the Ralph Young turkey farm in French Creek. The game farm also placed rare or representative native animals on display for the general public to view during the farm's early days. (Photos courtesy of UCHS, Willa Young Score Collection.)

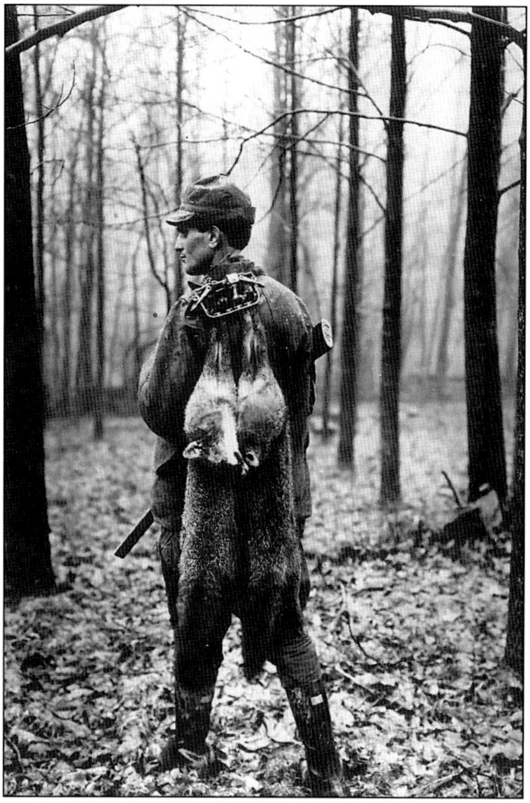

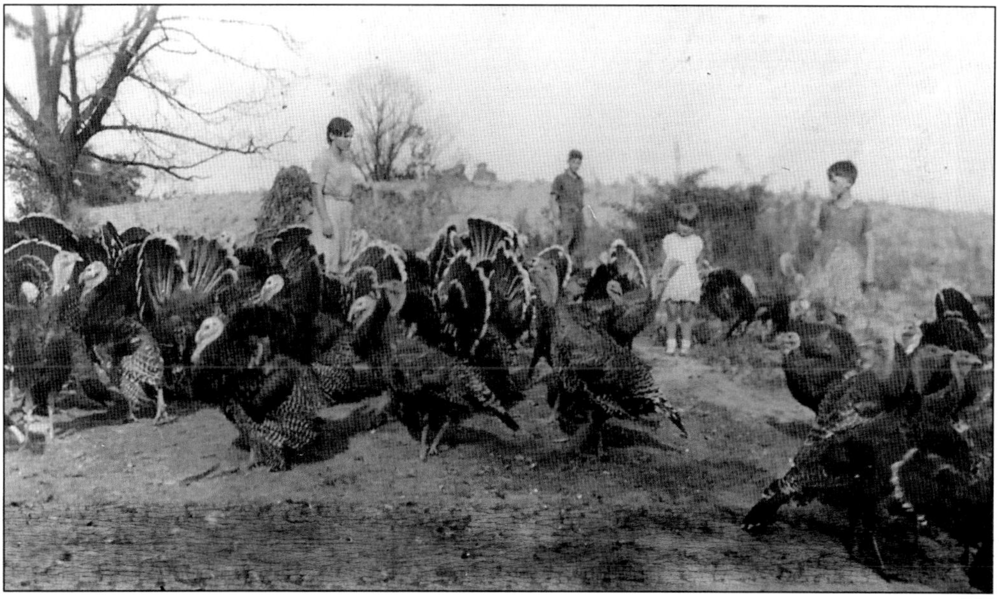

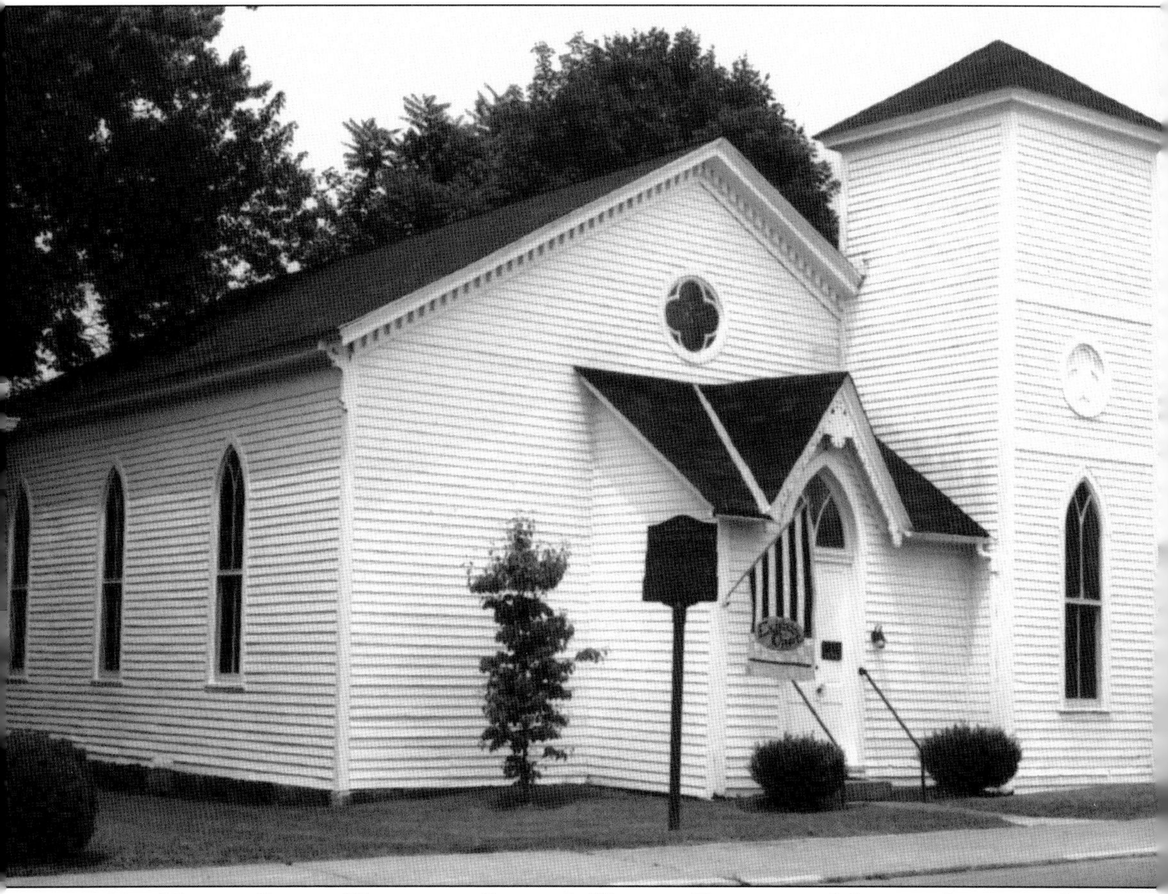

THE UPSHUR COUNTY HISTORICAL SOCIETY'S HISTORY CENTER AND MUSEUM. Constructed in 1856 by the Methodist Episcopal Church South (Southern Methodist) as a simple wooden structure in the Greek Revival style, this building saw action during the Civil War when it was commandeered by the federal government as a food commissary. On August 30, 1862, following the battle of Watertank Hill, 20 to 30 prisoners who were captured there were marched first to the courthouse and "after their weapons had been destroyed, the prisoners were taken to the Southern Methodist Church on West Main Street. The building contained thousands of bushels of oats and corn, all of which were taken into the street and burned by the prisoners. The hundreds of sacks of green coffee at one time were shoe deep in the street." A mini-mural designed and painted by Noel W. Tenney depicting this night hangs in the building's interior.

In 1889, the Protestant Episcopal Church purchased the building and installed the colored glass windows, vaulted the ceiling, and added the bell tower and foyer. In 1968, the building was purchased by the Church of Christ Christian, and in 1986 it became the property of the Upshur County Historical Society. It was listed in the National Register of Historic Places in 1992. Today this historic building serves as the History Center and Museum for the Upshur County Historical Society and annually produces a changing major exhibit along with permanent displays. (Photo courtesy of UCHS, permanent collection.)